# IN ARDEN:

# EDITING

# SHAKESPEARE

## ESSAYS IN HONOUR OF

## RICHARD PROUDFOOT

*Edited by*
*Ann Thompson and Gordon McMullan*

The Arden website is at
http://www.ardenshakespeare.com

The general editors of the Arden Shakespeare have been W. J. Craig and
R. H. Case (first series 1899–1944) Una Ellis-Fermor, Harold F. Brooks,
Harold Jenkins and Brian Morris (second series 1946–82)

Present general editors (third series)
Richard Proudfoot, Ann Thompson and David Scott Kastan

This edition of *In Arden: Editing Shakespeare*
first published 2003 by The Arden Shakespeare

© 2003 Thomson Learning

Arden Shakespeare is an imprint of Thomson Learning

Thomson
High Holborn House
50–51 Bedford Row
London WC1R 4LR

Typeset by LaserScript, Mitcham, Surrey

Printed in Croatia by Zrinski

*British Library Cataloguing in Publication Data*
A catalogue record for this book is available from the British Library

*Library of Congress Cataloguing in Publication Data*
A catalogue record has been requested

ISBN 1-904271-31-6

NPN 9 8 7 6 5 4 3 2 1

# IN ARDEN:

# EDITING

# SHAKESPEARE

# THE ARDEN SHAKESPEARE

*Second series

# CONTENTS

# CONTRIBUTORS

**A.R. Braunmuller** is Professor of English and Comparative Literature at the University of California, Los Angeles. He is editing *Measure for Measure* for Arden 3.

**John Russell Brown** is Professor of Theatre at Middlesex University; he edited *The Merchant of Venice* for Arden 2.

**Anthony B. Dawson** is Professor of English at the University of British Columbia. He is editing *Timon of Athens* for Arden 3.

**Juliet Dusinberre** is a Fellow of Girton College, Cambridge, and is currently editing *As You Like It* for Arden 3.

**R.A. Foakes**, Professor Emeritus at the University of California, Los Angeles, edited *Henry VIII* and *The Comedy of Errors* for Arden 2 and, more recently, *King Lear* for Arden 3.

**Suzanne Gossett**, Professor of English at Loyola University Chicago, is currently completing an edition of *Pericles* for Arden 3 and is a general editor of Arden Early Modern Drama.

**Barbara Hodgdon** is Professor of English at the University of Michigan. She is editing *The Taming of the Shrew* for Arden 3.

**E.A.J. Honigmann** was Joseph Cowen Professor of English Literature at the University of Newcastle upon Tyne from 1970 to 1989. He is the editor of *King John* for Arden 2 and *Othello* for

Arden 3, as well as of Harold Jenkins's *Structural Problems in Shakespeare* (Arden, 2001).

**G.K. Hunter** is Professor Emeritus at Yale University. He edited *All's Well That Ends Well* for Arden 2.

**Lynette Hunter** is Professor of Rhetoric at the University of Leeds. She is co-editing *Romeo and Juliet* for Arden 3 with Peter Lichtenfels.

**Peter Lichtenfels** is Director of the Acting School at Manchester Metropolitan University. He is co-editing *Romeo and Juliet* for Arden 3 with Lynette Hunter.

**Gordon McMullan** is Reader in English at King's College London. He edited *Henry VIII* for Arden 3 and is a general editor of Arden Early Modern Drama.

**Giorgio Melchiori**, CBE, FBA, is Professor Emeritus, University RomaTre. He edited *The Merry Wives of Windsor* for Arden 3.

**John Pitcher** is a Fellow of St John's College, Oxford. He is completing an edition of *The Winter's Tale* for Arden 3.

**Lois Potter** is Professor of English at the University of Delaware. She edited the *Two Noble Kinsmen* for Arden 3.

**Eric Rasmussen** is Professor of English at the University of Nevada, Reno. He co-edited *Henry VI, Part 3* with John D. Cox for Arden 3.

**Ann Thompson** is Professor of English Language and Literature at King's College London. She is a general editor of Arden 3 and is co-editing *Hamlet* with Neil Taylor.

**John J.M. Tobin** is a Professor of English at the University of Massachusetts-Boston. He is editing *King John* for Arden 3.

**Helen Wilcox** is Professor of English Literature at the University of Groningen, The Netherlands; she is editing *All's Well That Ends Well* for Arden 3.

**George Walton Williams** is Professor of English Emeritus at Duke University. He is associate general editor of Arden 3, with particular responsibility for the Histories.

**H.R. Woudhuysen** is Professor of English at University College London. He edited *Love's Labour's Lost* for Arden 3 and is co-editing the *Poems* with Katherine Duncan-Jones.

Richard Proudfoot.

© *Nicola Bennett*

# INTRODUCTION

## Ann Thompson and Gordon McMullan

### I

'My gratitude to Richard Proudfoot has remained constant (or rather, has grown with the years). He chose the editor, he read through my drafts and always commented encouragingly (and, to my great advantage, critically). On almost every page I am indebted to him, and I gladly acknowledge this.'

(E.A.J. Honigmann, preface to Arden 3 *Othello*, 1997, p. xv)

'Richard Proudfoot's role as supervising editor has taught me more than I can easily acknowledge. His pragmatic contributions are to be found everywhere in this edition; the language is his on numerous occasions. I do a fair amount of supervisory editing myself, and can only say that Richard has given me a wholly new perspective on how rigorously the assignment must be pursued.'

(David Bevington, preface to Arden 3 *Troilus and Cressida*, 1998, p. xx)

'By far my greatest debt is to my old friend Richard Proudfoot, who helped and taught me so much, long before he became the general editor of the Arden Third Series. The time and patience he devoted to this volume, his many suggestions as well as much-needed corrections, make of this edition a collaborative work.'

(Giorgio Melchiori, preface to Arden 3 *The Merry Wives of Windsor*, 2000, pp. xvii–iii)

'My greatest debt is to Richard, the true editors' editor, whose generosity with his knowledge, time and energy is hugely appreciated by those of us who have been fortunate enough to have our work supervised by him.'

(Gordon McMullan, preface to Arden 3 *Henry VIII*, 2000, p. xx)

'Richard Proudfoot, arguably the world's most conscientious general editor, reviewed multiple drafts of the text with extraordinary acumen and rigour, challenged every assumption and suggested inspired emendations.'

(Eric Rasmussen, preface to Arden 3 *King Henry VI, Part 3*, 2001, p. xvii)

'My greatest debt is to Richard Proudfoot, a general editor of tirelessness, enthusiasm and exemplary tact, who curbed my more flagrant excesses with the irony they merited, made valuable points that had escaped my notice, and guided me with learning, forbearance and sharp critical intelligence through the shoals and turbulences of the long passage from first draft to final copy.'

(Charles R. Forker, preface to Arden 3 *Richard II*, 2002, p. xviii)

This is no flattery, but a typical selection of sincere tributes from editors of recent volumes in the Arden Shakespeare Third Series; similar expressions can be found in every volume. Less experienced editors marvel at the time and care Richard has devoted to their work; more experienced editors are generous with their acknowledgements of how much they have learnt from the experience. The word 'inspired' occurs as frequently as the word 'rigorous'; phrases such as 'the true editors' editor' and 'the world's most conscientious editor' are common, and Giorgio Melchiori speaks for us all when he says that his edition became a collaborative work. In all fairness, the name of Richard Proudfoot should be on the cover of every volume, not just as general editor but as, in effect, co-editor. The relatively short list of works published under his own name not only belies the true scale of his contribution to scholarship but testifies to his pursuit of a career which has been and continues to be generous and self-effacing to an extent younger scholars find difficult to credit.

Richard's scrupulous attention to an edition, 'from first draft to final copy', can be daunting at first: if you have reached the stage in your career when you are accustomed to being commissioned to produce a book or an essay and to having what you produce accepted with only minor modifications, it can be a shock to get your typescript back covered with detailed suggestions and corrections and accompanied by at least twice its own length of additional notes and comments. When you have recovered your self-confidence sufficiently to work through Richard's responses, you discover, perhaps grudgingly to begin with, but delightedly as you persist, that you have encountered the most thoroughly engaged reader imaginable who will indeed interrogate your every assumption, respond to your every suggestion, add depth and breadth to your scholarship, and save you from a world of errors that would otherwise have been seized upon by reviewers.

With hindsight it seems obvious that Richard's academic destiny was indeed to become general editor of the Arden Shakespeare, after quite a lengthy apprenticeship with the Malone Society (see Biographical Note, pp. 269–70). His retirement three years ago has enabled him to devote even more time to the editions and we anticipate that he will be the first general editor to see an entire Arden series through from conception to completion. With sixteen volumes published and two in press, we are about half way through, and we are anticipating an increased rate of production as more volumes approach completion. In addition, a new Arden series has recently been initiated, entitled Arden Early Modern Drama, which will provide modernised editions of non-Shakespearean plays and thus extend the Arden name beyond the Shakespeare canon. It thus seemed an appropriate point at which to invite members of the 'Arden community' – editors of volumes published in both Arden 2 and Arden 3, and those still working on their Arden 3 volumes – to contribute to a collection of essays on editing Shakespeare to be published in honour of Richard. They bring experience of editing from a range of Shakespeare series – New Cambridge, Oxford, Penguin and Variorum, among others – and from series of other dramatic and non-dramatic authors, such as the Malone Society, Revels and Longmans Annotated Poets. The result is inevitably eclectic, but we hope the volume functions as a kind of snapshot both of the current condition of editing and of Richard's significance in the field.

## II

It is appropriate that several contributors to this collection have chosen to focus on the relation between editing and stage practice, since Richard has always had a strong interest in theatre, not only as a tireless playgoer but also as a practitioner – an actor in and director of numerous student productions of Shakespeare and other dramatists (see p. 270). While editors of volumes in the second Arden series could and often did choose to ignore the stage history of their plays, editors in the third series are urged, indeed required by the Editorial Guidelines, to present their plays as texts for performance, making appropriate reference to stage, film and television versions in their commentaries as well as in their introductions. This emphasis on the practical stage – and Richard's lifelong determination to treat plays as texts for performance, not as glorified poems – is reflected in the present volume.

Yet the injunction to treat the plays as theatrical, rather than poetic, texts is by no means a straightforward one, as several of the essays make clear. For Tony Dawson, while 'editing any Shakespeare text these days means confronting performance' (p. 33), this development should not be the basis for unhelpful claims of 'authenticity': 'far from tapping in to the authentic Shakespeare,' he argues, 'performance (necessarily contingent, transitory, evanescent and collaborative) contributes instead to "Shakespeare's" inauthenticity, or at least to his (its?) constantly changing, inessential "nature"' (p. 39). In this context, the most radical engagement with both practical theatre and the process of editing represented here is outlined by Peter Lichtenfels and Lynette Hunter in an essay which serves as a manifesto for their forthcoming Arden 3 *Romeo and Juliet*. Lichtenfels is a theatre director, not an editor, and thus approaches the task very differently from someone with bibliographical training. As Arden editors, Hunter and Lichtenfels are 'interested in the extent to which theatre practice contributes to and interrelates with editorial practices' (p. 138), and they outline their plan to create 'a reconstructed text close to what was available to a sixteenth or early seventeenth century actor or reader, yet readable in the twenty-first century, and with which actors, directors, readers and critics may engage, adapt, cut and analyse for contemporary purpose' (p. 139) – a contentious process which aims, for instance, to retain much early (and, of course, non-authorial) punctuation because in performance it was found to be 'exceptionally helpful in understanding the dynamics of a scene' (p. 145).

Most editors are chary of such wholesale engagement with the specifics of a particular performance, but there is no doubt that performance has become a key, if not the key, factor in differentiating the current series of Shakespeare editions from those of the mid-twentieth century. George Williams notes that where Arden 2 'placed academic scholarship first, Arden 3 is giving equal attention to the theatrical presentation on stage' (p. 111). John Russell Brown echoes this. 'The contrast between a play read and a play experienced,' he observes

> has increasingly occupied critics and scholars so that editors of a Shakespeare text will today take as much care with stage directions as with dialogue and, in annotation, will often indicate what particular performers have contributed or what performances seem to be required by the text (p. 157).

This development has entailed much closer editorial attention to the non-verbal aspects of performance. Brown, for instance, offers a sustained examination of the function of silences in *Hamlet*, especially those of Ophelia and Gertrude, focussing on both the impossibility and the necessity of adequately annotating such performative elements. Williams insists – with characteristic force – that editors should not be afraid to edit with performance in mind: 'I argue,' he writes

> that every editor should be a director, whose page is his stage. Some editors are reluctant to accept that responsibility; they are fearful of infringing the domain of the director. They should not be. Directors are constantly infringing the domain of the editor. Directors always edit (p. 112).

Such domain-infringements have been both the impetus for much of the best recent editorial work and the source of hard-fought critical battles.

Stage directions, the focus of both Williams's essay and that of R.A. Foakes, tend in particular to invoke issues of judgement: 'where the original direction is wrong, the editor should emend so that the printed text presents what is theatrically right, while what is wrong is preserved in the footnote,' argues Williams (p. 113). Foakes, by contrast, is uncomfortable with such assertions of right and wrong, thinking 'that the matter is more complicated' (p. 125) and looking at early evidence to expand on these complications. What is clear, even if opinions are divided on the rights and wrongs, is that editors, like directors, have sooner or later to make decisions, and that those decisions will almost certainly have larger ramifications for the reading or performance of the play than is apparent in the immediate locale of the decision. The question of editorial certainty and/or humility thus lies behind much of the discussion. And several of the essays make it clear that the question of editorial intervention – either the fact or the extent of intervention – is currently in flux. Some contributors (Gossett, Hodgdon, Potter) analyse the ways in which editorial tradition has intervened to close down or evade certain possibilities offered by the early texts; others (Williams, Foakes) encourage informed and experienced editors to give readers more assistance than is customary. While, by definition, none of the contributors to this collection subscribes to the 'unediting' argument, it is clear that the debates it has provoked have been of considerable value, as well as of unease, to editorial practitioners.

## III

The focus on performance is simply one strand in the remarkable range of developments that have taken place in the field of editing over the last few years. When Richard took over as general editor of the Arden Shakespeare, he could hardly have predicted the recent explosion of work in the field in editing and textual criticism – a field which has moved back from the periphery of English studies to the much-debated centre – nor could he have foreseen the engagement of theorists with editing and editors with theory that is now characteristic of the best editions. For far too long, English departments were divided, counterproductively, between those who edited and those who didn't, between 'theorists' (characterized as challengers of an establishment embodied most clearly in their editing colleagues) and 'editors' (characterized as defenders of 'scholarship' against the fragment-ing, politicising impetus of theory), a division and a set of characterizations which did scant justice to the best work in either camp. This division has modulated recently into a distinction between the old New Bibliography and the new New Philology, between editing a text imagined either as authorial or as collaborative and socialized. As Giorgio Melchiori and Tony Dawson – from very different critical standpoints – make clear, this distinction breaks down remarkably rapidly once you begin to examine the practice of the best and least dogmatic of the New Bibliographers and once you assess the dependence of recent assertions about the nature of the text on discoveries achieved through New Bibliographical methodologies.

Melchiori, in particular, insists on the achievements of the New Bibliography, vehemently resisting recent attacks and pointing out that performance-oriented criticism of the New Bibliography has failed to notice how performance-aware the New Bibliographers in fact were. Dawson, too, notes that New Philologist attacks on their predecessors sometimes seem 'to be holding them to standards which they would not apply to their own work, demanding veridical [evidence] when they are content with circumstantial' (p. 40). 'They are engaged,' he argues, 'in a forensic historical inquiry that aims at plausible, even likely, explanations,' suggesting that, 'most of the time, that is what "truth" is' (p. 40). He notes that the New Philologists are 'as invested in their ideas of discontinuity and rupture as the earlier textual scholars were in continuity and correctness' (p. 41), finding from his own work on *Troilus and Cressida* that without some narrative that includes an idea of a *non-material* 'work' behind the manifest physical evidence contained in the actually existing versions, there is no coherent way to establish actual historical relations. One has to imagine a 'work' that is not simply equivalent to those two material objects Q and F.

To put all this another way, *Troilus and Cressida* is both the material texts in which it has survived ('poems' in McGann's sense) and the conceptual object that emerged from Shakespeare's brain ('the work' in Tanselle's sense) and was transmitted by his hand to the paper on which it first found material expression (p. 41).

The difference between Melchiori and Dawson, then, despite the apparent gulf between their theoretical positions, is in the end not all that great: both believe in something Shakespeare wrote, arguing that 'the text is born in the brain of its comically talented author, but when it grows up it becomes a book' (p. 42). What has yet to be achieved, it seems, is a convincing engagement of this position with the question of the 'sociology of the text,' the collaborative process seen by many critics as a more accurate model of textual production than one based on individual agency. While it is true that much of the work of the New Philologists is paradoxically dependent on that of the New Bibliographers, to say so is often to elide certain fundamental differences between their positions, and debate on this issue will undoubtedly continue to flourish for the foreseeable future.

# IV

As several of the essays in this collection make clear, the juxtaposition of feminism and editing has been enormously productive in recent years as – after decades in which editing was a largely male preserve – women began to edit Shakespearean and other texts and to examine editing practice in the light of feminist theory and consciousness. Suzanne Gossett notes the 'essential problem of editing' (p. 76), namely that 'all our commitments, including our sexual politics, may have textual consequences' (pp. 76–7), and she uses the term 'feminist-inflected editing' to describe her own work on *Pericles*, providing a series of instances of the ways in which feminism enables an editor to see beyond the questionable assumptions underlying certain persistent editorial emendations – such as the notion implicit in the insertion of a stage direction at one point in *Pericles* because it has been assumed that 'a man cannot emote with a baby in his arms' (p. 68). Lois Potter, in a similar way, sets out to uncover the problems editors have had with the 'embarrassment' of the sensuous Desdemona who is rather more apparent in the Folio *Othello* of 1623 than in the Quarto of a year earlier. 'The textual evidence, in all its contradictoriness,' she argues, 'suggests that someone – probably the author, but possibly not only him – was uncertain about how to achieve a balance between Desdemona's sexuality and her innocence' (p. 92). For Potter, what matters is the fact that the authorial/editorial activity that created the differences between the two texts 'works in both directions – making Desdemona sometimes more sensual and sometimes less so' (p. 92), undermining the editorial tendency to insist upon polarized characterization.

Barbara Hodgdon provides a practical exemplification of the interaction of performance studies with feminism in her demonstration of the way in which 'protocols of editorial literacy' have 'suppressed [the] theatrical literacy' of *The Taming of the Shrew* (p. 95). In a spirited defence of the performative sinuousness of the play, she notes – in the context of an editorial tradition which, for instance, emends F to enable Katherina and Petruchio to exit together two lines before the end of the play, even though Petruchio in fact exits alone in that text – that 'the *Shrew* we have been reading (and in most cases, seeing) all these years is a selective editorial collaboration' with historical performances of the play from the seventeenth century to the present (p. 105). She thus shows how editors have, over the centuries, 'substituted one performative literacy for another' by 'importing other perfor-mances, other printed texts,' into the received text until 'modern editions reveal a Petruchio who owes his stage life less to "Shakespeare" than to Rowe' (p. 101). 'What are the implications of editorial re-performances,' she asks

> figured in older bibliographical traditions as 'theatrical contagion' –
> which work to create normative fantasies of Petruchio as brutal
> servant-beater and, with a causally related reading, to mark him as
> one who displaces onto his servants the physical abuse he 'intended'
> for Kate? (p. 102)

She thus argues that 'it is Rowe and modern editions, as much as
if not more than "Shakespeare", who are responsible for the play's
"hard opinions", for its problematic theatrical reputation' (p. 102).

## V

One notable effect of the convergence of textual editing and
critical theory in recent years has been increased and on-going
reflection on the shape and nature of the edition itself, on the
organization of the introduction (of which the new emphasis
on performance is a major, though not the only, aspect), the
function of the commentary, and the value of textual notes. The
question of annotation produces a remarkable range of responses:
the extensive market research conducted prior to the launch of
Arden 3 suggested that what readers most and least liked about
Arden editions was the extent of their annotations (though
whether this is a comment on annotation or on market research
remains unclear). Certainly, textual/collational notes in particular
provoke a varied set of metaphors – and not entirely
complimentary ones – from the 'nest, grave, or carpet of variants'
(p. 4) quoted by A.R. Braunmuller to the 'band of terror', 'barbed
wire' between text and commentary, or 'filling of the sandwich'
(p. 211) cited by Eric Rasmussen. The latter two images have been
made redundant by the Arden 3 decision to locate the textual
collation at the foot of the page, below the commentary, but this
decision itself is an issue for debate. Rasmussen resists what he
sees as the current trend against textual notes, offering a potted
history of collations – via Pope, Theobald, Jennens and Malone –
and arguing that the recent tendency to minimize a given
edition's collation provides unnecessary limits on the reader's
engagement with the text and obscures the ideological processes

apparent in the choices made both in early printed texts and in later annotated editions.

According to G.K. Hunter, annotation has, in the most straightforward sense, 'the function of explaining obscure references inside works whose general import is clear enough', but

> At a more sophisticated level, as a response to some general ambiguity, it is concerned with questions more than answers, and operates as the interrogator of texts rather than the explainer. In this function it is concerned to create a space for new modes of understanding, allowing for differences between intention and effect or between one type of reception and another, so that alternative emphases and understandings can co-exist and illuminate one another (p. 177).

For Hunter, the annotator acts 'as a necessary interpreter between one angle of vision and another, one culture and another' (p. 177). It is clear, though, that editors have not always been aware of this cultural function. Helen Wilcox sets out to list the different varieties of footnote – textual, etymological, inter-textual, contextual, dramatic (or theatrical) and critical – and provides an exemplification of the accretion of all these varieties in annotating a particular scene in *All's Well*. Asking what continuities there have been in these types of footnote across the centuries of editing, she suggests, mischievously, that 'there is a measure of continuity . . . in the desire for the footnote to appear factual in its approach, soundly based on painstaking research supplying reliable evidence, even while the materials assembled actually reflect the sympathies, the learning and the priorities of the individual editor' (p. 204).

Editors of course work very consciously within and against a professional tradition. A.R. Braunmuller, like Rasmussen and Wilcox, provides a history of the annotated edition as we know it, asking 'Where . . . do the third series Arden Shakespeare and the New Variorum Shakespeare . . . come from and why and where and how do they include what they do?' (p. 5), showing how late and erratically, for instance, the notion of continuous line-numbering was introduced to Shakespeare editions, and noting that it was not until the late 1850s that the 'three-layer system' (text/ collation/commentary) was acquired from an eighteenth-century edition of Horace which was itself the vehicle for the mockery of scholarly form in Pope's *Dunciad Variorum*. Hunter, too, sets out an editorial history, noting the ideological impetus behind the accretion of commentary. 'The first systematic annotations of Shakespeare's texts,' he observes,

> appear at the point when the claim that these were masterpieces was being argued in terms that the new society thought central to the idea of excellence – and these were the terms not of theatrical effectiveness but of neoclassical literature. ... Shakespeare and his works had to be understood in terms that cut him off from the standards of his own profession and his own time – a time now generally agreed to have been without any proper understanding of classical social or literary values. But it was not enough just to claim that Shakespeare transcended the values of his own age; he had to be seen as embodying ... the values of the age he had arrived in (p. 182).

It was, Hunter notes, the business of a particular generation of scholars – Isaac Reed, George Steevens, Alexander Pope, Lewis Theobald, William Warburton, Samuel Johnson, Edward Capell, Edmond Malone and James Boswell – to establish and celebrate Shakespeare's status as an embodiment of values which the playwright himself would have found alien. Hunter's uncomfortable conclusion is that this enlightenment project is the basis of the work editors continue to do, whether they like it or not.

# VI

Several of the essays stand as demonstrations of the kind of tightly-focussed textual and critical work performed by contemporary editors, from Ernst Honigmann's crisp note on the Ciceronian origins of the 'to be or not to be' speech – which shows that even the most heavily-debated lines in the canon can still produce fresh responses – to Henry Woudhuysen's argument that the presence of blank pages in early modern printed plays, despite the evidence of the printers' need to be sparing with paper because of its expense, suggests that 'printed plays were not always considered to be entirely ephemeral items' (p. 59), an essay which is a fine instance of the kind of study that New Bibliography encouraged and facilitated and which offers possible evidence for debates in which the New Philologists are engaged. Juliet Dusinberre and John Pitcher, for their part, capitalize on the editor's obligation to examine *all* aspects of the play he or she is editing (and not just the personally or culturally appealing ones) in order to overturn conventional thinking about two characters – Sir Oliver Mar-text in *As You Like It* and Autolycus in *The Winter's Tale* – with whom editorial and theatrical tradition has been generally uncomfortable. Dusinberre argues that Mar-text was played not by Robert Armin, as has been assumed, but by his Lord Chamberlain's company predecessor, Will Kemp, since 'Kemp's reputation as an anti-Martinist who had many times brought the house down at the Curtain jesting against the Marprelate Puritans would have created instant recognition and mirth in his audience' (p. 240). Pitcher, in turn, claims that Autolycus, inserted into a play based on material from Robert Greene's *Pandosto*, 'is an objectification of the thief that Shakespeare was accused of being' years before by the Greene persona of the *Groatsworth of Wit* (p. 255). Arguing in this way from his knowledge of *The Winter's Tale* that there was a certain amount of Autolycus in Shakespeare – that 'at least part of him *was* a thief' (p. 265) – provides an exemplification of the editor's function in unearthing the complex intentionalities and intertextualities that inform dramatic characterization in the awareness that authors (as much as actors) create, sustain and shed roles throughout their writing lives.

## VII

The editors are grateful to Jessica Hodge, who was a committed promoter of this collection from the moment of inception and who is very sorely missed at Arden – not least by Richard who, in an e-mail to Arden editors at the time of her departure to another publishing post, noted that 'for all of us who work for the Arden series, Jessica's presence in the office has been a source of reassurance, just as her cheerful words and congenial hosting of our meetings in London, in Valencia and at the annual gatherings of the Shakespeare Association of America have helped to add a lively social pleasure to our participation in the series. We owe her much gratitude and the warmest thanks for her sustained record of achievement as a publisher and for the many ways in which she has supported the project in general and each one of us in our dealings with it.' The editors are grateful too to Nicola Bennett for extracting biographical information – and the photographs – out of Richard's unique filing system (though we imagine the groundwork was laid by the team of archaeologists who spent several weeks excavating Richard's office when he retired from King's).

# PART I

---

# BIBLIOGRAPHY/
# THEORY OF EDITING

# 1

## SHAKESPEARES VARIOUS

### A.R. Braunmuller

*Let me however do them justice.*[1]

Upon first looking into a full-dress, early twentieth-century edition of Shakespeare, E.M.W. Tillyard did not travel in realms of gold:

> I remember discussing with [Aubrey] Attwater what annotated edition of Shakespeare the undergraduates had better use for their set plays. He favoured the Arden, because the textual notes came not at the end but in great prominence immediately under the text. ... I have not forgotten the unchallengeable earnestness of his expression as he pointed to the thick little nest of variant readings and conjectures below the text. ... To work myself up into any comparable state of earnestness was beyond me; all too plainly I lacked the necessary emotional equipment. ... But I no more dared question his reverence in front of the textual variants than if he had taken me for a silent walk through a cemetery, suddenly stopped, and then, pointing to a monument, remarked, 'There, that's my mother's grave.'[2]

Thus Tillyard (1889–1962), upon looking back four decades to his early days as a don, a don who could never be accused of cherishing textual variants: he doubtless did regard 'the thick little nest' as a grave.

If early Ardens dismayed some, consider this description of their massive predecessor,

> that great monument of Lit, its Bible, Furness's *Variorum* edition of Shakespeare. Every Lit man is familiar with these volumes, once light cocoa, now faded, most of them, to museum khaki, but with the

binding, in buckram rough as the ox-tongue leaf, as strong a fortification as ever. ... [I]ts leaves are a printer's triumph. Lippincott's [the publisher] had to fit into every page about an inch and a half – often much less [even none!] – of text, plus an average of three quarters of an inch of textual variants, plus seven inches of double-columned notes; all three, of course, in sharply contrasted type. It is pleasurable. Resting on the carpet of the variants, strongly foundationed by the columned notes ... the text itself, spaciously leaded, really does glow, really does look pearly in its oyster.[3]

So wrote Stephen Potter, who later chronicled one up-manship. Tillyard's thick nest is here a carpet, the twin-columned commentary notes a foundation, the text a pearl rather than an interred corpse.

Like many other authors, editors, and publishers – John Dryden and Jacob Tonson, for example – Horace Howard Furness had too complicated a relation with Joshua Lippincott to be quite so complimentary as Potter, but Furness confirms Potter's remark on the intricacies printing a variorum edition present. Describing his first variorum edition, *Romeo and Juliet* (1870–71), Furness wrote, 'Eight times did I remodel the first twenty pages of that volume. As it now stands it seems a task of no special difficulty, but no-one who has not tried it, can imagine what entanglements impeded me at every step, and how appalling the mass of my materials loomed up before me.'[4] And of course that 'mass' along with the nest, grave or carpet of variants is a controversial feature of a variorum edition and, to a lesser extent, of the current Arden, Oxford and New Cambridge editions modelled on it.[5] Controversial the 'mass' was from the beginning, and reviewers complained about Furness's undiscriminating collection of others' views.[6] Richard Grant White, Furness's near-contemporary, had a view more like recent editorial practice: 'the readings of every editor and notes of every commentator have been carefully examined, adopted when they appeared admissible, and recorded when they were deemed worthy of preservation.'[7]

Although Samuel Johnson rejected some earlier editors' notes, he is the first to discuss compiling temporarily persuasive

commentary as a trial-and-error process: 'The compleat explanation of an authour not systematick and consequential, but
desultory and vagrant, abounding in casual and light hints, is not
to be expected from any single scholiast.'[8] Johnson's edition gave
rise to a family of 'variorum' descendants, ending almost sixty
years later with the twenty-one volume edition overseen by James
Boswell the younger, who felt the burden of inclusiveness:

> According to the plan laid down by Mr. [Edmond] Malone, I have
> inserted all the notes of his predecessors, although ... some of them
> might well have been spared. ... I ... acknowledge with Mr. Steevens
> ... that among the defects of later editions of Shakspeare [*sic*], may be
> reckoned an exuberance of comment. ...[9]

Tracing the shapes of serious editions of Shakespeare, their
controversies and their contemporary avatars, I have moved from
Tillyard and Potter in the twentieth century to Boswell, White
and Furness in the nineteenth to Johnson in the eighteenth.
I must now go further back in the history of editing and
scholarship. Where, when and why does the form of present
scholarly editions of Shakespeare arise? More generally and not
just formally, where, for instance, do the third series Arden
Shakespeare and the New Variorum Shakespeare, successor to
Furness, come from and why and where and how do they include
what they do? There are yet more specific questions: what
preceded the Arden editions and, earlier, the variorum editions of
the eighteenth- to the twenty-first centuries, and why is an
edition called 'variorum'? Scholars have approached these
questions, but they have not precisely faced the issues historically,
formally, nor entirely in disciplinary-professional terms.[10]

Begin with *variorum*, a Latin masculine and neuter plural
genitive. Lexicographers trace the usage to title-page phrases such
as this one, from a luxurious folio edition of Catullus, Tibullus
and Propertius (Paris, 1604): 'Cum variorum doctorum vivorum
commentariis, notis, observationibus, emendationibus & para-
phrasibus ...' (BL 72L4).[11] A Leiden Petronius of 1587 is shorter:
'Cum notis doctorum vivorum' (BL 685d7).[12] Numerous late
sixteenth-century Dutch and early seventeenth-century French

editions of classical texts make similar claims. By the last quarter of the seventeenth century, Robert Clavell's irregular annual catalogues of books 'printed in England' (many are Continental) and available for sale in London have sections with such headings as 'Catalogus librorum notis variorum', 'Titles of All the *Classic* Authors *cum notis variorum*' and 'Authores cum Notis Variorum.'[13]

So, in the late humanist period and after, editions of Latin and Greek texts appear with an ever-increasing quantity of notes by various learned men; at first, the *notae* were mostly short essays, biographical, lexical or interpretive. As in the much later 'variorum' editions of Shakespeare, successive editors first simply reprinted their predecessors' contributions entire and added their own, though space limitations soon led to selection and compression.[14] The next question to be asked is *where* these learned men's 'notes' appear. So long as the commentary is general rather than exegetical, it tends to cluster at the front or (later) at the back of the edited text, rather as a modern edition places the introduction first and appendices last. If the learned commentary is more detailed, however, a second problem arises. How to attach commentary to word, line or passage?

The two questions intertwine: where to put the commentary and how to direct the reader to it. One solution was to adopt the *modus modernus* from manuscript and, later, printed texts of the biblical *glossa ordinaria* and of legal texts such as the Code of Justinian: surround the text with the commentary.[15] A Venetian Virgil of January 1475 has the text in large type centred on the page and boxed by Servius's commentary in smaller type; this edition has been called 'possibly the earliest instance of such an arrangement applied to a literary text.'[16] An edition of Terence (Strassburg, 1496: BL C3c16) is more complex: the play-text appears in roman letters; imitating handwriting, interlinear black-letter Latin glosses (some of one line, some of two, all hovering above the glossed text) and black-letter note-markers (a–z, and then repeating) are interspersed in the text and are keyed to smaller roman-letter commentary that surrounds the text on two (top and outer or outer and inner) or three (top, outer, bottom) sides of Terence's text.

Extensive commentary would, however, defeat the *modus modernus* even in advanced Terentian form.[17] Other reference systems appear: capital letters in a central column dividing the numbered columns of text into numbered-lettered horizontal blocks;[18] numbered chapters and verses (the latter arrived very late for the Bible[19]); otherwise undifferentiated snippets of text followed by learned commentary and clustered after the entire work or sub-sections of it (this system persists as late as Alexander Pope's translation of Homer and beyond to modern works where reference symbols are thought to disfigure the page or distract the reader); letters or printer's ornaments such as asterisks, obelisks and pointing hands; footnotes or endnotes, numbered sometimes consecutively but more usually in a sequence from 1 to 9 that then repeats as needed; lines numbered by 5s or 10s in sequences that recommence with each successive leaf. What now seems so common and normative as to be invisible, continuous numbering of lines through a text or some subsection of it, is a late and long a sporadically adopted method. According to E.J. Kenney, 'continuous numeration of [classical] verse texts does not begin to make its appearance until the last quarter of the sixteenth century in the editions of ... Plantin' and 'first became normal ... in the late seventeenth century.'[20]

'Continuous numeration of verse texts' appears in English translations of classical poems[21] and some English poems (see p. 9) in the later seventeenth century, but took longer to reach editions of Shakespeare. None of the 'variorum' editions of Shakespeare to 1821 has line numbers, for instance, and the standard form in many cases thereafter hardly varies from Samuel Johnson's 1765 edition: footnote numbers (sometimes superscript; sometimes on the line; sometimes in parentheses; sometimes before, sometimes after, the phrase commented on) in the text; collation and commentary intermeddled at the foot of the page; no line numbers within numbered acts and scenes.[22] The editors of the influential 'Cambridge Shakespeare' (1863–66) specially note their line-numbering (by 5s) within each scene, and their edition may have been the first one of Shakespeare so to do.[23]

What about the closely related issue of where to place the commentary and collation in relation to the text proper? For editions of Shakespeare, the answer is uncertain. So far as I have learned, the distinguished chess player Howard Staunton first introduced a rudimentary form of the now-common three-layer system (text/collation/commentary) in the late 1850s and early 1860s.[24]

Shakespeare's editors discovered this page layout, it seems, in Richard Bentley's editions of Horace. *Q. Horatius Flaccus ex recensione ... Richardi Bentleii* (Cambridge, 1711: BL 655b9), lineated by 5s within each poem, includes emended readings in the text and has a single line of rejected readings beneath the text and 'Notae' at the volume's end, keyed by line numbers. The *editio altera* (Amsterdam, 1713: BL 684h4) prints the emended text, similarly lineated, then a line containing the rejected reading and, at the bottom of the page, Bentley's twin-columned commentary and justification of his readings. Both collation and commentary are keyed by line number, and the three layers of text have each a distinct type.[25]

More than a century and a half later, Furness uses this layout complete with different types for text, collation and commentary (recall Stephen Potter's praise, p. 4), but Bentley influenced editions of Shakespeare much earlier. Lewis Theobald and his contemporaries regarded Shakespeare's plays as classics and thus as deserving the editorial treatment Greek and Latin texts received.[26] In 1731, Theobald declared, 'I mean to follow the form of Bentley's Amsterdam Horace, in subjoining the notes to the place controverted.'[27] And so Theobald's first edition (1733) of Shakespeare partly does. Thus, too, most scholarly editions of Shakespeare thereafter, though more than a century would pass before those editions imitated Bentley's separating of collation from commentary.

Shakespeare's was not the first English text given 'variorum' treatment. Dedicating his edition of *Paradise Lost* to the Earl of Bath, Thomas Newton writes, 'You considered him always a classic author in English, and were desirous to have him published as such. ...' (A2v–3r); 'My design in the present edition is to publish the [*sic*, a classicizing touch] Paradise Lost, as the work of a classic author cum notis variorum.'[28] 'The' *Paradise Lost* had already anticipated many relevant editorial innovations. In its ten-book form (1667), it is, I believe, the first original English poem to be printed with line numbers,[29] and later was perhaps the first English poem to be annotated by someone other than its author in Patrick Hume's edition, *The Poetical Works of Mr John Milton* ... together with explanatory notes on each book of the [*sic*, again] Paradise Lost (1695).[30] Earlier, George Gascoigne annotated 'a maske for ... Viscount Montacute' (*A Hundreth Sundrie Flowres*, 1573), and he and/or another more elaborately annotates various writings in *The Poesies of George Gascoigne Esquire* (1575).[31] 'E.K.', perhaps Spenser himself, annotated *The Shepheardes Calender* (1579 and often reprinted); George Chapman had lightly annotated some original poems and more heavily his Homeric translations, but they have no line numbers; Ben Jonson occasionally annotated his plays (e.g., the 1605 quarto of *Sejanus*) and, more often, his masques. Margaret Cavendish's *Poems and Phancies* ... The Second Impression (1664: BL 11624h1) has (presumably) the author's glosses and annotations keyed by superscript italic letters, and in 1667, the year of the lineated ten-book *Paradise Lost*, John Dryden's *Annus Mirabilis* appeared without line numbers, though stanzas are numbered and there are tiny italic citations of parallel or imitated passages from the classics and similarly tiny subheadings for sections of the poem. Alexander Pope's *Dunciad* had line numbers from the start (1728) and light footnoting; his self-annotating of the three-book *Dunciad Variorum* (1729) make him, it is said, 'the first English poet to be annotated in this way'.[32] The claim seems hard to sustain without 'in this way' being further defined.

The year after Newton's 1749 Milton 'with notes of various authors', there appeared a similarly titled Tonson venture, *The Works of Mr. Francis Beaumont and Mr. John Fletcher* ... Collated with all the former editions, and corrected. With notes critical and explanatory (1750: BL 1344g1); the pages mimic those in Theobald's first edition of Shakespeare. In 1765, the crypto-variorum format reaches an edition of Shakespeare: *The Plays of*

*William Shakespeare* ... with the Corrections and Illustrations of Various Commentators; To which are added Notes by Sam. Johnson (BL 11761c15).[33] 'Corrections ... of Various Commentators' then regularly appears on recensions of Johnson's text by George Steevens, Edmond Malone, Isaac Reed and finally the younger Boswell;[34] the words are an English version of *cum notis variorum* and its variants. Furness set out to replace the 1821 'variorum' edition, and his edition gave rise, with help from the Cambridge edition, to both the in-progress New Variorum Shakespeare and the page-arrangements and reference systems now so common in earnest editions of Shakespeare.

Such is the world's way that 'earnestness' (recall Attwater and Tillyard in the 1920s) cannot go unmocked, and mockery 'variorum Shakespeare' received before it began. Early printings of Alexander Pope's *Dunciad* (1728) are not elaborate, but Pope soon crowed to Jonathan Swift 'The Dunciad is going to be printed in all pomp ... with *Proeme, Prolegomena, Testimonia Scriptorum, Index Authorem,* and Notes *Variorum*' – full 'classic' panoply.[35] And the next year there appeared the elegant three-book *Dunciad Variorum* (1729: BL 11633g56), partly aimed at Lewis Theobald's *Shakespeare Restored* (1726) which mortally wounded Pope's first edition of Shakespeare (1723–5).[36] Pope wrote most of the pseudo-scholarly parerga and apparatus for *Dunciad Variorum*, imitating and ridiculing Theobald and 'slashing Bentley'. James McLaverty has persuasively argued that the *Dunciad Variorum* imitates the 1716 Geneva edition of Boileau (e.g., BL 12237h3), which like *Dunciad Variorum* has twin commentary blocks below the main text labelled 'Variations' and 'Imitations'.[37] The Boileau edition is in turn modelled on editions of classical authors, especially Parisian ones *cum notis variorum*, and has many features of Richard Bentley's 1713 Horace. As so often, the mocked (Theobald, Bentley), and the mocker (Pope) and the means of mockery (Boileau, Bentley, Pope) are endlessly joined.[38]

Though they became antagonists, Pope and Theobald each cared greatly about the appearance of their respective editions, and so did Edward Capell, the eighteenth-century's greatest editor of Shakespeare. Pope had the cultural and financial capital to control the appearance of his writings, their title-pages, their ornament and so forth.[39] Theobald's concern – joining text with scholarly debate – was practical (see above, p. 8). Capell, however, anticipated Johnson on how notes might distract the reader: 'every departure from it ["the establish'd text"] is at once offer'd to the eye in the most simple manner, without parade of notes which but divert the attention.'[40] Capell's interest was also aesthetic:

> A regard to the beauty of his page ... has induc'd the editor to suspend the operation of his plan in two of the poems ... the number of them [emendations and unsignalled readings from early texts] in each poem was so small, that it was thought the beauty of the edition would be more consulted, and the convenience of it but little impair'd, by throwing them thus together [i.e. in the Preface, rather than on pages of the text].[41]

Once upon a time in early modern and Enlightenment Europe, there were increasingly elaborate editions of Greek and Latin authors. Later, in England, John Milton's works were given the editorial attention and the page-design devoted to 'classic' authors. Elaborate classical editions, such as Richard Bentley's Horace, were then imitated in Lewis Theobald's edition of Shakespeare; before Theobald could print that edition, his great antagonist and victim, Alexander Pope, seized the design and stabbed 'piddling' Theobald, its intending imitator. Amid various inter-editorial conflicts, a rather old-fashioned, not quite 'classical', variorum edition of Shakespeare went its way from 1765 (Johnson) to 1821 (Boswell). In 1863–66, Cambridge scholars, working from Edward Capell's collations, offered an innovative text-layout. From Philadelphia, friendly city, there came H.H. Furness, who adopted the fledged classic(al) three-layer page-design – text, collation, two-columned commentary – for the works of Shakespeare. From Furness, from the Cambridge editors, from Theobald, from Bentley there arise our contemporaries, the Arden, New Cambridge and Oxford Shakespeares.

## NOTES

Place of publication is London unless otherwise indicated and printers/publishers are not cited; 'BL' precedes shelfmarks of copies consulted in the British Library, London; for citations of early modern works, see also note 11. An inferior version of this essay was presented at the Modern Language Association of America meeting, Washington, D.C., December 2000. This version is partly a contribution to what E.J. Kenney calls 'functional bibliography' (see n. 20). Thomas L. Berger, Bertrand A. Goldgar, Michael Harris, J. Paul Hunter, Joseph Levine, Anne Myers, J.F.S. Post, Alan Roper (who saved me from embarrassment), Cynthia Wall and Paul Werstine have improved this essay. Thank you. I thank, too, the patient staff of the British Library. They are (all) responsible for errors I did not make.

1  Samuel Johnson, 'Preface' to *The Plays of William Shakespeare* (1765) in *Johnson on Shakespeare*, ed. Arthur Sherbo, introduction by Bertrand H. Bronson, 2 vols (New Haven, Conn., 1968), 1, 100, referring to William Warburton's detractors. I might have quoted Johnson on his fellow editors: 'now we tear what we cannot loose, and eject what we happen not to understand' (1, 92).

2  E.M.W. Tillyard, *The Muse Unchained: an intimate account of the revolution in English studies at Cambridge* (Cambridge, 1958), p. 99.

3  Stephen Potter, *The Muse in Chains* (1937), pp. 69–70. 'Tillyard's title [see n. 2] implied that his memoir was a retort to Stephen Potter's [book] ... but he scarcely answered the latter's doubts about the value of university English studies, reiterated in Basil Willey's *Cambridge and Other Memories* [*1920–1953*] (1968)' (A.C. Partridge, *Landmarks in the History of English Scholarship 1500–1970* (Cape Town, 1972), p. 48). Praising Tillyard as a teacher, Willey also complains that 'walls of scholarship, variorum editions, complete letters and notebooks ... make general teaching seem imposture, and profitable learning almost impossible' (p. 35).

4  Furness to C.M. Ingleby, 6 August 1871, quoted in James M. Gibson, *The Philadelphia Shakespeare Story: Horace Howard Furness and the Variorum Shakespeare* (New York, 1990), p. 61.

5  The Arden page-layout does seem to be modelled on Furness's *Variorum*, admired by British scholars and reviewers alike, though learned authority appears to differ: '[I]t was the first Arden series that developed many of the features of design and layout best known to us today, when a second and third Arden series have been joined by editions under the imprints of the Oxford and Cambridge University presses whose design owes much to the Arden model' (Richard Proudfoot, *Shakespeare: Text, Stage and Canon* (2001), p. 4). That Arden, not Furness's variorum, influenced the Oxford and New Cambridge designs seems incontrovertible.

6  See *The Penn Monthly* and *The Athenaeum*, respectively, quoted in Gibson, p. 74. Furness grew more outspoken in his commentary as his textual views became more conservative (see Gibson, pp. 167–8, 170, 232 and 234).

7   R.G. White (ed), *The Works of William Shakespeare*, 12 vols (Boston, 1858–65: BL 11763c), 2, 1.

8   'Preface', *Johnson on Shakespeare*, 1, 103; see also the paragraph beginning, 'It is no pleasure to me, in revising my volumes, to observe how much paper is wasted in confutation . . .' (1, 99). George Steevens, who continued and expanded Johnson's edition, asserted, 'the true sense of a passage has frequently remained undetermined, till repeated experiments have been tried upon it, when one commentator, making a proper use of the errors of another, has at last explained it to universal satisfaction' (quoted in *The Critical Review*, 36 (Nov. 1773), p. 415).

9   William Shakspeare [*sic*], *Plays and Poems*, ed. James Boswell *et al.*, 21 vols (1821), 1, viii–ix. The New Variorum Shakespeare edition now in progress inconsistently includes or excludes earlier comment (e.g., on lexical, political and social-historical matters) now known to be inaccurate.

10   Chronologically: Peter Seary, *Lewis Theobald and the Editing of Shakespeare* (Oxford, 1990), Margreta de Grazia, *Shakespeare Verbatim* (Oxford, 1991), Simon Jarvis, *Scholars and Gentlemen: Shakespearean editing and the representation of scholarly labour, 1725–1765* (Oxford, 1995), Marcus Walsh, *Shakespeare, Milton, and eighteenth-century literary editing: The beginnings of interpretative scholarship* (Cambridge, 1997).

11   Early modern title-pages are prolix; for brevity and accuracy, I usually cite only author, a sometimes shortened title, place of publication and the British Library, London ('BL') shelfmark(s) of the copy or copies I examined.

12   The formula, like the edition it touts, bloats with time; another fairly simple one heads a Leiden Martial of 1567 (BL 1001a14): 'cum annotationibus aliquot vivorum doctorum perquam utilibus'.

13   Various titles and dates: Robert Clavell, *A* [or *The*] *General Catalogue of Books Printed in England* . . . (1675, 1681, 1696). Most of the advertised books come from Dutch presses with the balance from France, esp. the famous Delphine series.

14   Editions of Terence, texts popular with teachers, are instructive: a Venetian example of 1482 (BL IB21329) includes Donatus's *Vita* and his *interpetatio*; there follows in Venice, then Strassburg, then elsewhere a series of editions that accumulate commentaries by a succession of scholars. See n. 17, below.

15   David J. Shaw, 'The Brescia Press of A. and J. Britannicus and their Juvenal of 1501', *Gutenberg Jahrbuch 1971*, p. 91, n. 7 traces *modus modernus* to a contract of 1473.

16   Victor Scholderer, *Catalogue of Books Printed in the XVth Century now in the British Museum*, Part VIII (1935), p. xiii.

17   Perhaps the apogee of these editions is *P. Terentii Afri . . . Comoediae* (Paris, 1552: BL 11707i8) which has several forms of the *modus modernus*, marginal indications of topics and variant readings, huge compilations of scholarly commentary before, around and following the text. It concludes with an *Index* [truly]

*copiosissimus.* Madeleine Doran, *The Endeavors of Art* (Madison, Wisconsin, 1954), pp. 399–400, n. 31 calls this edition 'variorum', and so it is in all but title.

18  This system, still used, appears in Stephanus's editions of Plato and Aristotle as well as in early printed Bibles.

19  Current verse-division appears in New Testaments from 1551, in entire Bibles from 1553, in English translations from the Geneva (1560); see M.H. Black, 'The Printed Bible' in S.L. Greenslade (ed), *Cambridge History of the Bible: the West from the Reformation to the present day* (Cambridge, 1963), 408–75; pp. 436–7 and 442–3.

20  E.J. Kenney, *The Classical Text: Aspects of editing in the age of the printed book* (Berkeley and Los Angeles, 1974), pp. 152–3. Kenney further notes, 'numbering the verses on each page was not uncommon. … Numeration of the verse of individual poems by tens is found in an edition of Claudian published as early as 1510 … but this appears to be exceptional.' See n. 23, below.

21  In *The Works of Virgil* … Translated into English verse by Mr. Dryden (1697: BL 74k10), all the translated poems have line numbers which are used to key both the cuts illustrating the text and 'Notes and Observations on Virgil's Works in English' at the end of the volume. ('Notes and Observations' plainly derives from editions of Greek and Latin texts.) For a related, just earlier, Tonson publication, see the discussion of Patrick Hume's edition of *Paradise Lost* (n. 30).

22  Generally following this format are, for example, S.W. Singer (ed), William Shakespeare, *The Dramatic Works*, 10 vols (1826: BL 11761e19), J.M. Pierre's German-glossed English-language edition of various single Shakespearean plays, 8 vols (Frankfurt/Main, 1830–40: BL 11765aa3), J.P. Collier (ed), *The Works of William Shakespeare*, 8 vols (1843–4: BL 11764f18), and N. Delius (ed), *Shakspere's Werke*, 7 vols (Elberfeld, 1854–60: BL 2300h4), though Delius has an 'Index' (to glosses) keyed by act, scene, and line number within the scene – the last not in the text. H.H. Furness's variorum edition has line numbers within scenes from the first volume.

23  W.G. Clark, John Glover [and W.A. Wright] (eds), *The Works of William Shakespeare*, 9 vols (Cambridge, 1863–6), 1, ix (the first page of the 'Preface'). This edition gave rise to the lineated, one-volume 'Globe' edition (1864), still often cited, and influenced H.H. Furness and his edition's page-layout (see Gibson, p. 62).

24  Howard Staunton (ed), *The Works of William Shakespeare*, 4 vols (1864: BL 11765gg60; published serially and in other forms, 1857–60): the edition has no line numbers; beneath the text, there is a medial collation-line, quite selective, followed by notes mixing glosses with examples and discussion of other textual choices.

25  Economic and other considerations determined the layouts of Bentley's 1711 (conventional) and 1713 (innovative) editions. The text of 1711 (with 'between seven and eight hundred alterations of the common readings') had been set by late 1706 when Bentley began writing the notes, which thus appear at the volume's

end. Cheaper paper and typesetting costs led to the Amsterdam edition (1713), 'in all respects an improvement upon the first'; it was now possible to revise text and notes and to place text, collation and notes on the same page. See James Henry Monk, *The Life of Richard Bentley, D.D.*, 2 vols (1833), 1, 326, 313 and 188–9. The 1713 Amsterdam edition displays finely judged composition that makes each opening a harmonious, near-mirror-image composition of text, collation and commentary.

26 'Shakespeare stands ... in the Nature of a Classic Writer' (Lewis Theobald, *Shakespeare Restored* (1726), p. v) and cf. George Sewall's preface to *The Works of Shakespear ... The Seventh Volume* (1725: BL 78L13): '[O]ur own great Writers. ... are in some degree our *Classics*' (quoted in Jarvis, *Scholars and Gentlemen*, p. 50).

27 Theobald to William Warburton, 18 November 1731, in John Nichols and John Bowyer Nichols (eds), *Illustrations of the Literary History of the Eighteenth Century* 8 vols (1817–58), 2, 621.

28 John Milton, *Paradise Lost ... A new edition, with notes of various authors, by Thomas Newton*, 2 vols (1749: BL 641.l.5), vol. 1, sig. a2.

29 Each book of the poem is lineated by 10s down the inner margin of each page. Did Milton stipulate this lineation?

30 Hume's notes are a bibliographically independent addition to Tonson's 'Sixth Edition, Adorn'd with Sculptures' (1695, BL 644m16, which in fact contains the sheets of the 1688 folio 'fifth edition' of *Paradise Lost* [e.g., BL 643m10] with a new 1695 title-page). The notes are keyed by line number, and a true example of the 1695 *Paradise Lost* (e.g., BL 11631i19) has line numbers (by 5s down the left side of the text, recto and verso). In the *Dictionary of National Biography* entry for Hume, W.A.J. Archbold writes that the 1695 edition is 'said to have been the first to attempt exhaustive annotations on the works of an English poet'. The twelve-book *Paradise Lost* (1674) has no line numbers. Jacob Tonson was so proud of the highly profitable Milton folio editions that he holds a copy of one in his 'Kit-Cat Club' portrait by Kneller (1717: National Portrait Gallery, London) 3230.

31 See George Gascoigne, *A Hundreth Sundrie Flowres*, ed. G.W. Pigman III (Oxford, 2000), pp. lxii–lxiii and *passim.*

32 James McLaverty, 'The Mode of Existence of Literary Works of Art: The Case of the *Dunciad Variorum*', *SB*, 37 (1984), 82–105; p. 100.

33 'Illustrations' here means 'elucidations', making clear, shedding light. See 'Every age has its modes of speech ... which ... become sometimes unintelligible, and always difficult, when there are no parallel passages that may conduce to their illustration' (Samuel Johnson, 'Proposals for Printing, by Subscription, the Dramatick Works of William Shakespeare' (1756) (*Johnson on Shakespeare*, 1, 52)) and 'The notes ... are ... illustrative, by which difficulties are explained' ('Preface', *ibid.*, 1, 102).

34  'In 1803 Isaac Reed edited what he called the fifth edition of Johnson and
    Steevens. Under one convention the editions of 1773, 1778 and 1785 are referred
    to as Variorum; but under another, slightly more appropriate, Reed's editions of
    1803 and 1813 are called the First and Second Variorum, and Boswell's [1821] the
    Third' (J. Phillip Brockbank, 'Shakespearean Scholarship from Rowe to the
    Present' in John Andrews (ed), *William Shakespeare: his world, his work, his
    influence*, 3 vols (New York, 1985), 3, 723). For the record, editions deriving from
    Johnson (1765) and tagged as having 'Corrections … of Various Commentators'
    are: Johnson and George Steevens, 1773 (implicitly, the 'first edition'), 1778 'The
    Second Edition', 1785 'The Third Edition', 1793 'The Fourth Edition', 1803 'The
    Fifth Edition', 1813 'The Sixth Edition'. The last Johnson-derived edition (1821),
    the younger Boswell's memorial tribute to Edmond Malone, does not designate
    its place in a series.

35  Pope to Swift, 28 June 1728, in George Sherburn (ed), *The Correspondence of
    Alexander Pope*, 5 vols (Oxford, 1956), 2, 503.

36  On the wounding, see George Sherburn, *The Early Career of Alexander Pope*
    (Oxford, 1934), pp. 220 and 245. Pope's second edition (1728) includes at the end
    of vol. 8 a grouchy headnote (signed 'A.P.') before 'Various Readings or
    Conjectures on Passages in Shakespear [*sic*]', a list of readings not adopted from
    Theobald's *Shakespeare Restored.*

37  McLaverty, pp. 99–101. Jonathan Richardson Jnr, *Richardsoniana* (1776), p. 264,
    claims he undertook collating Pope's MSS 'on my having proposed to him the
    "making an edition of his works in the manner of *Boileau*'s"'. See D.F. Foxon, *Pope
    and the early eighteenth-century book trade*, rev. and ed. James McClaverty
    (Oxford, 1991), p. 32 n. 76 and David L. Vander Meulen (ed), *Pope's 'Dunciad' of
    1728: a history and facsimile* (Charlottesville, Virginia, 1991), pp. 47–8.

38  The mockery continued in the para-universe of burlesque: see, e.g., the 'Burlesque
    Annotations, after the manner of Dr. Johnson and Geo. Steevens, Esq. and the
    Various Commentators' in nineteenth-century editions of John Poole's *Hamlet
    Travestie.*

39  See Foxon, chapters 2 and 3. By 'appearance' and 'page', I do not mean format –
    folio, quarto, octavo, etc. – another point Foxon takes up (see esp. pp. 23–32 and
    63–4).

40  Edward Capell, *Prolusions* (1760), p. ii. cf. 'Preface' in *Johnson on Shakespeare*, 1,
    111 in the paragraph beginning, 'Notes are often necessary, but they are necessary
    evils' and Anthony Grafton, *The Footnote: A curious history* (1997), p. 217 on the
    'wonderful cacophony of scholarly voices' in variorum editions.

41  Capell, *Prolusions*, p. iv. Charles Jennens (ed), William Shakespeare, *King Lear*
    (1770) complained, 'he [Capell] was afraid his notes placed with the text should
    spoil the beauty of the book' (p. vii) and cf. Kenney, p. 155, on 'early printers' and
    their solicitude for their editions' 'appearance'.

# 2

# THE CONTINUING IMPORTANCE
# OF NEW BIBLIOGRAPHY

## *Giorgio Melchiori*

Though Heminge and Condell had assured the great variety of readers of the First Folio that they were offering them Shakespeare's plays 'cur'd, and perfect in their limbes ... absolute in their numbers, as [Shakespeare] conceived them', early editors felt free to have recourse to emendations whenever the reading of the Folio seemed corrupt. The earliest examples of this practice are Q4 (1622) of *Romeo and Juliet*, 'correcting' Q2, and Q2 (1630) of *Othello*, which is a rough collation of Q1 and F. An attempt to place editing on a much firmer bibliographical basis was made in the twentieth century, founded on an accurate study of early printing and playhouse practices, aimed at establishing the sort of copy that went to the printer in each single case. The New Bibliographers used such expressions as 'foul papers', 'memorial reconstruction', 'prompt copy', 'scribal transcript', but the definition that gained the greatest currency also among non-specialists was that of 'bad Quartos', for those early printed texts, notably of *Romeo and Juliet* (1597), *Henry V* (1600), *Merry Wives of Windsor* (1602) and *Hamlet* (1603), that were considered as 'stolen, and surreptitious copies, maimed, and deformed by the frauds and stealthes of iniourious impostors' alluded to by Heminge and Condell in their address to the Folio readers. The second generation of New Bibliographers extended the definition to other plays that had previously been considered early versions or source plays by different hands. It was argued that *The First Part of the Contention Between the Famous Houses of Lancaster and York* (1594) and *The True Tragedy of Richard Duke of York* (1595) were bad Quartos of *2* and *3 Henry VI* and, with some misgivings, *The Taming of A Shrew* (1594) was seen as a bad Quarto of *The Shrew* and even *The Troublesome Reign of King John* (1591) as some sort of memorial reconstruction of *King John*. A reaction to these excessive claims was inevitable. The simplest form of this reaction is represented by Eric Sams, who passionately rejected what he called 'the trumped-up charges of "Bad Quartos" (BQ) or "memorial reconstructions by actors" (MRA)' made against all the plays just mentioned above (Sams, 175). In fact, Sams aimed not so much at reconsidering the origins and transmission of individual printed play-texts, as at establishing a single Shakespearean authorship for them all. His method was that of finding verbal parallels between the texts he took into consideration and other plays for which Shakespeare's authorship was not in doubt.

With the advent of the computer this simplistic method was replaced by much more sophisticated approaches to the verbal analysis of Shakespeare's texts. Stylometry, neural computation and the like attempted to establish the different authorial hands present in plays. Their concern was with authorship and not with the way in which single plays came into being and reached the printed page. The earlier findings of the New Bibliographers were not seriously called into question.

The frontal attack aimed at discrediting the basic tenets of the New Bibliography came from a different quarter. The main argument used was that the notions of bad Quartos, foul papers, memorial reconstructions and the like were merely intellectual constructs, hypotheses for which there was no objective evidence. Several scholars questioned them in respect of single plays, but the most influential and closely argued was a paper by Paul Werstine in *Shakespeare Quarterly*, 1990: 'Narratives About Printed Shakespeare Texts: "Foul Papers" and "Bad" Quartos'. Werstine's main point is that 'the textual categories of "foul papers" and "memorial reconstruction"' are merely 'hypothetical constructs that have yet to be empirically validated with reference to any extant Shakespeare quarto' (Werstine, 81). He therefore takes to task Pollard, Greg, Dover Wilson and their followers for having contributed to transform mere conjectures into generally accepted facts, making in each case a 'single agent' (the foul papers of the original author or the reconstruction by actor–reporters) responsible for the copy that went to the printers. He concludes by accusing the New Bibliographers of being unaware of the fact that these texts were open to penetration and alteration not only by Shakespeare himself and by his fellow actors but also by multiple theatrical and extra-theatrical factors: scriveners, annotators, adaptors and revisers, as well as censors, and compositors and proofreaders (Werstine, 86). The accusation could hardly be more unfair: it is exactly through the work of the New Bibliographers that editors have been made aware of the interference of all these factors in early printed play-texts.

This caused serious disarray among editors, just at the time when new and wide-ranging editorial enterprises, such as the Oxford Shakespeare, the New Cambridge Shakespeare and Arden 3, were being undertaken. As soon as a plausible explanation of the process by which a play had reached the printing-house was suggested, the editor could be accused of creating fanciful 'narratives'. Werstine and his followers created an all-inclusive and all-purpose negative narrative intended to nullify all narratives by their predecessors. Theirs was not an *alternative* narrative, but simply the negation of all previous attempts at accounting for the state in which printed play-texts had reached us; the new school of textual studies, though pretending to take into consideration Elizabethan theatrical practices, in fact paid attention only to printing-house habits and practices. Their concern is with the *written* text rather with the real text, the text on the stage. Though there is a growing tendency to acknowledge the fact that Shakespeare plays were conceived not as literary works but as scripts within the framework of the newly developed entertainment industry, scholars and critics still find it difficult to take this notion fully into account. The instruments at their disposal were originally devised for exploring the written page: it needs an imaginative effort to realize that in the case of

Shakespeare such instruments are still perfectly valid, but must be used for a different purpose.

It was fortunate that one of my first editorial tasks had to do with a play that presumably was *not* presented on the stage, and certainly did *not* get into print in its own time, *The Book of Sir Thomas More*. In such circumstances my approach to it could not, in the first instance, be other than 'bibliographical'. But it was exactly this bookish approach that provided me with clear insights into: (a) the way in which a theatrical script came into being (rather than how it went into print); and (b) the numberless external factors interfering with its production, all of them strictly linked with the practical circumstances surrounding the origin and growth of the entertainment industry in post-medieval London.

What emerges most clearly from a study of the manuscript of *Sir Thomas More* is that it was not meant for the eyes of a literate reader in his study, but for the entertainment of an audience in the theatre. The art of entertaining can never be the result of an individual effort: it involves the skills of a number of people who contribute to the creation of the show, and must take into account the conventions of the time in a number of inter-connected fields, both general (moral, social, political, religious, etc.), and particular (acting space, acting time, visual elements and the like).

The case of *Sir Thomas More* is complicated by the drastic interventions in the script of the Master of the Revels Edmund Tilney. At all events it appears that Anthony Munday was responsible for preparing the copy of the play-text to be submitted to a company of actors and to the censor, and a comparison of this text with that of other manuscripts in his hand proves that this cannot have happened after 1593. This doesn't qualify Munday as the sole author of the play: at the time most plays for the public theatre were the result of collaboration among different authors, as appears clearly from Henslowe's *Diary*, where no payment for a play before 1598 is made to a single author but always to two or more together. Many of the numerous changes, additions or substitute passages by different hands in the manuscript seem due not to censorial interventions, but to be functional to the smooth running of the stage action or to the requirements of the company or of single actors. Such is the case of the introduction of a Clown's part or the refashioning of the central acts of the play (Melchiori and Gabrieli, esp. 28–9).

*Sir Thomas More* is certainly a special case, but is at the same time the best illustration of how the theatre business worked in Shakespeare's time. The lesson I learnt from it served as a guide in editing plays from printed texts. The contribution of the New Bibliographers was essentially that of showing how from a printed text it is possible to reconstruct the state of the original manuscript with all its accretions and corrections.

In order to establish 'the copy that went to the printer', they took into account, as far as possible, the process through which the manuscript of the play was put together, keeping in mind as well that writing paper was at the time an expensive imported commodity. Playwrights could not afford to waste it; they crammed up to forty lines on each side of a foolscap sheet and when it came to corrections, afterthoughts or insertions they either interlined them, creating problems of readability for the printer, or added them on separate slips of paper. Substantial additions had of course to be written on fresh sheets, frequently without a clear indication of where they should be inserted in the text. The New Bibliographers, rather than concerning themselves with the peculiarities and idiosyncrasies of individual printers, engaged in what was essentially detective work to discover the origin of a play-text before it went into print.

In turn the idea of memorial reconstruction is not a fanciful construct but the direct result of the study of the conditions of show business in the Elizabethan age. The trouble with this principle is that Greg, as well as later critics such as Kathleen Irace (1994), postulated that such reconstructions were due mainly to actors and therefore concentrated on the attempts to identify the 'culprits'. If it is true that some actors may have collaborated in the reconstruction of play-scripts by procuring for the compilers their single 'parts', is it not more likely that the actual reconstruction was the work of hacks in the pay of prospective publishers? Actors may have collaborated with their recollections of other parts of the plays in which they had appeared, but surely the texts of the so-called bad Quartos were put together by other hangers-on of the theatrical profession; also, the idea of 'reporters' sitting in the audience taking shorthand notes of the performance has been exploded. More likely, they were men who attended the theatre in the hope of becoming actors or playwrights.

Such men saw themselves as potential theatre poets; the evidence for this is in the fact that, in the early Quartos of *Romeo and Juliet* and *The Merry Wives of Windsor*, scenes which in the later versions are mainly in blank verse are reported in rhymed couplets: the compiler compensated for his faulty memory of those scenes with personal 'poetic' versions of his own devising (Elam, 355; Righetti, 16; Melchiori, 'Merry Wives', 37–41).

The question is: what particular version of a play were these people trying to reconstruct, since the texts presented on the stage could vary with each performance, subject as they were to all sorts of external pressures and interferences? Werstine has listed most of these possible external interferences, but there is reason to believe that many adaptations and/or revisions of play-texts are authorial. I suggest that in several cases the author himself provided, side by side with the full script meant for private occasions, a shorter acting version for the public stage, involving a substantial re-elaboration intended to streamline the development of the action and render the characters more straightforward. Recent performances of *Hamlet* based on the text of the first Quarto have been acknowledged as dramatically more effective than those of the longer texts, and the same can be said of the first Quarto of *The Merry Wives of Windsor*. I am satisfied that these 'bad' Quartos (as well as those of *Romeo and Juliet* and *Henry V*) reflect authorial acting versions of those plays. I must emphasize the word 'reflect': the compilers of the 'stolen and surreptitious copies' deplored by Heminge and Condell had no access to the complete play-scripts, so they based their reconstructions on the versions performed on the stage. Those early printed Quartos are indeed 'bad' insofar as they do not reproduce authorial texts: they simply reassemble, perhaps with the help of marginal members of the theatrical profession, the acting versions presented on the stage.

There is no justification for considering as 'bad' the other four Quartos (or Octavos) which have been classified under the same label: *2* and *3 Henry VI* may well be later Shakespearean rewritings of the early *First Part of the Contention* and *The True Tragedy*, and the same applies to *The Shrew* in respect of *A Shrew*. I would connect these plays rather with the practice of 'remaking' of which Shakespeare was a past master (Melchiori, 'Corridors', 168–9; Melchiori, 'Garter Plays', 21–4, 29–34, 51–5). He could even, on occasion, provide a new company with remakes of whole plays of his own; on the other hand I have no doubt that *King John* is Shakespeare's remake of *The Troublesome Reign*, whoever the author of the latter may be.

Obviously each single play is a separate entity with its own history and it would be foolish to try to establish general principles in assessing the transmission of dramatic texts. The editor of a Shakespeare play must proceed by suggestions, guesses, hypotheses: he can only look for clues in what is known of the external circumstances in which plays were written, produced and staged, but such clues can never amount to incontrovertible evidence or solid proof of the process through which any play assumed the form in which it reached us in print or in manuscript. No court of justice would be satisfied with the sort of merely circumstantial evidence that an editor can produce on the nature of a Shakespearean play-text, but fortunately editing is not a forensic activity and nobody is going to be sentenced for interfering with the course of justice by giving false evidence. When in 1910 W.W. Greg tackled the problem of the first Quarto of the *Merry Wives of Windsor*, developing the theory of memorial reconstruction by an actor, he was merely advancing a hypothesis which he later modified: his was an attempt at accounting for some features of the text – he suggested a method that did not exclude any number of possible alternative approaches (Greg, xxvi–xlii). The most authoritative of the New Bibliographers used the same discretion in dealing with other controversial early texts. They presented their theories as no more than guesses based on their previous editorial experience.

The new generation of critics does not seem to appreciate the importance of a direct experience in editing single plays; their criticism of the New Bibliographers is aimed at demolishing the theories of their predecessors without offering anything with which to replace them. What they most resent is that Greg's theories, though presented as mere hypotheses, had met with such wide acceptance. The trouble is that while the theories of the New Bibliographers were basically constructive, those of their critics are simply destructive, and the would-be editor is therefore left in a kind of limbo, not knowing what to present to readers and performers as an authentic text of a play.

A better grounded campaign, based on the concrete experience of editing, was the one waged by the so-called 'revisionists', led by the Oxford team of Stanley Wells and Gary Taylor, against the 'conflationists', under which name went the traditional editors who constructed their texts, when there existed more than one early edition of the same play, by assembling what they considered the best parts of each successive printing. There is no doubt that Stanley Wells is right in stating that 'The primary surviving texts of Shakespeare's plays represent those plays in various stages of composition' and that none of these texts 'necessarily represent in anything but in a definitive state the words that Shakespeare wished to be spoken or a larger action that he wished to be bodied forth' (in Elam, 340). The idea of producing a definitive edition of any Shakespearean text has been exploded, but the editor is still confronted with the problem of what to present to the reader. The idea that in some cases we have been fortunate enough to have both an early Shakespearean version of a play and a later version of the same revised by Shakespeare himself for performance in different circumstances is very sound. Wells and Taylor were quite right in including in their Oxford Shakespeare two different texts of *King Lear*, but in other cases, notably those of *Hamlet* and *Othello*, their determination to consider only the later versions appearing in the Folio as representing the final decision of Shakespeare about the form in which the plays should be presented on the stage for all future time seems unwise. Apart from the fact that the Folio appeared seven years after Shakespeare's death, so that one cannot be sure that all the revisions in it were actually due to Shakespeare himself, one should consider how many of such revisions were suggested not so much by authorial changes of mind, but rather by the pressure of external factors (Papetti, 45–50). For instance, how much did the death of Richard Burbage in 1613 influence the decision to leave out Hamlet's soliloquy at 4.4? How many of the additional lines in *Othello* found only in Folio are meant to compensate for the suppression of blasphemous expressions imposed by the Profanity Act of 1606 (Rossi, 14–22)?

We all know that no play was ever produced on the stage in exactly the form it had in the original authorial version. Every performance is an adaptation. I am inclined at this point to put in a plea in favour of conflated texts. Men of the theatre should be provided with as full texts, including variants, as are available in the original printings. It is their task to choose, select and cut in order to suit the circumstances in which the plays are to be staged.

What follows is a synthetic summary of my personal views on the nature of early editions of Shakespeare's plays. I do not call my conclusions 'verdicts', as Laurie Maguire does in the tables appended to a valuable study of *Shakespearean Suspect Texts* (Maguire, 230–322). In a way my list can be considered a supplementary contribution to that research, though frequently disagreeing with its conclusions, extended to those texts excluded from that survey because the early printings could not be considered 'bad'.

A few preliminary considerations:

(1) Collaborations: practically all the plays presented on the London public stage until at least 1598 were the result of collaborative work in different measure between the author or authors and actors and other members of the theatrical profession. I take 1598 as the dividing line because only in that year does the name of William Shakespeare appear for the first time on the title-page of a printed play.

(2) The practice of 'remaking' old plays for new or changed audiences.

(3) The inclusion/exclusion of 'pivot scenes', i.e. scenes which are expendable from the point of view of the development of plot or stage action but which in fact constitute the ideological centres of the plays in which they figure (Laroque).

(4) The occasional use of authorial foul or working papers, revealed by the presence in the text of different versions of the same speech, as in Q2 *Romeo and Juliet* 5.3 and in Q1 *Love's Labour's Lost* 4.3 and 5.2.

I list these plays, which I would call 'controversial' rather than 'suspect' or 'doubtful', in chronological order of first publication, taking into account also the later editions.

*The Troublesome Reign of King John* (Q1 1591): I believe that the Folio text of *King John* is a remake of the early play, and I doubt very much that Shakespeare had a hand in the 1591 Q (Melchiori, 'Shakespeare', 131–5).

*Titus Andronicus* (Q1 1594): a good text, probably collaborative; the 'fly-scene' present only in F is a pivot scene, part of Shakespeare's contribution to the script from the beginning, but excluded from the prompt-copy because theatrically expendable.

*The Taming of A Shrew* (Q1 1594): an early collaborative work re-made' by Shakespeare at a later date.

*1 Contention* (Q1 1594): not a 'bad Quarto' of *2 Henry VI*, but a memorial reconstruction of an acting version of a collaborative play; *2 Henry VI* is Shakespeare's remake of the play after he had written, or collaborated in the writing of *1 Henry VI*, as a link play completing the historical cycle on the reigns of the Henrys, begun before 1588 with the anonymous *Famous Victories of Henry the fifth*; this latter play (possibly originally in two parts) was in the late 1590s remade by Shakespeare into two plays: *Henry IV* and *Henry V*; owing to censorial intervention, the first of them was in turn largely rewritten with the addition of a Second Part.

*The True Tragedy of Richard Duke of York* (Q1 1595): a collaborative work, written originally as the second part of *1 Contention*, remade by Shakespeare later as *3 Henry VI*. See *1 Contention* above.

*Edward III* (Q1 1596): good text of a collaborative play to which Shakespeare contributed at least 1.2 and the whole of Act 2, replacing parts of the play suppressed and now lost, cp. Addition in Hand D in *Sir Thomas More* (Melchiori, 'Edward III', 171–7).

*Richard III* (Q1 1597): memorial reconstruction of an authorial acting version, possibly printed from a copy unrevised by the compilers. The following five Quartos (from 1598 to 1622) are based on Q1, with various interferences by the printers. F reproduces a fuller authorial version, possibly predating the abridged version presented in Qs.

*Romeo and Juliet* (Q1 1597): a 'bad' Quarto, i.e. a memorial reconstruction of an abridged acting version; Q2 (1599) reproduces authorial foul papers, possibly compensating for some gaps in them by recourse to Q1; Q4 (1622) is a first attempt at 'editing' Q2.

*Richard II* (Q1 1597): a good text with a major omission due to censorship. The abdication scene (possibly supplied not by the author but by members of the company) appears for the first time in Q4 (1608).

*Love's Labour's Lost* (Q1 1598): authorial foul papers, replacing a lost pirated edition. Cp. to Q2 *Romeo and Juliet* above (Melchiori, 'Frenchness').

*1 Henry IV* (Q1 1598): an authorial rewriting with additions of the first half of a one-play version (see *1 Contention* above), Q1 is based on a previous printing in the same year of which only a few pages are preserved; possibly it reproduces an imperfectly revised script incorporating pages from the early one-play version. Q2 to Q6 (1599 to 1622) are modelled on it, while F shows signs of further revision at least of speech headings (Melchiori, 'Shakespeare', 288–95).

*2 Henry IV* (Q1 1600): a new sequel to *1 Henry IV* (see *1 Contention* above), incorporating pages from the later part of the one-play version, printed from authorial foul papers but omitting several of the new passages. The latter are restored in F, which reproduces a transcript of the full text prepared for the printers with several scribal interferences (Melchiori, 'Henry IV', 189–202).

*Henry V* (Q1 1600): a 'bad' Quarto, i.e. a memorial reconstruction of an acting version of the play.

Three more 1600 Quartos (*Midsummer Night's Dream, Merchant* and *Much Ado*) are substantially good authorial texts.

*Merry Wives of Windsor* (Q1 1602): another 'bad' Quarto, a memorial reconstruction of a text abridged and rearranged for presentation on the public stage F presents one of the several stages through which the full text (possibly incorporating a previous court entertainment for a special occasion) must have passed in its early stage history (Melchiori, 'Merry Wives', 56–79).

*Hamlet* (Q1 1603): 'bad' Quarto – a memorial reconstruction of an abridged acting version, with changes suggested by the circumstances of presentation; Q2 (1604–5): the earlier original full authorial version for study rather than the stage, with some printers' excisions for political or other reasons; F: a revised text, or rather a late and possibly non-authorial intermediate stage in the process of adaptation from a 'literary' to an acting version (Papetti, 50–7; Clayton, *passim*).

*King Lear* (Q1 1608): substantially an early authorial version; F a revised authorial version.

*Troilus and Cressida* (Q1 1609): a good Quarto presenting an already revised version of an earlier original: the epistle prefixed to the second issue of Q1 and the accidental survival of the additional lines at the end of 5.3 in F reveal that the play was conceived as an open-ended tragedy, and transformed into a comedy by transposing to the end of the action Pandarus' speech (Melchiori, 'Shakespeare', 429–33).

*Pericles* (Q1 1609): A memorial reconstruction not of a collaborative work but of an authorial text; the compilers took advantage of the narrative of the play's action in George Wilkins' *The Painfull Adventures of Pericles Prince of Tyre*, which contains many 'verse fossils' from the original play-text (Melchiori, 'Shakespeare', 368–71).

*Othello* (Q1 1622): the first authorial version written before the Profanity Act of 1606 interfered with the structural function of the oaths; F is a thorough authorial revision compensating for such losses by the addition of a number of new speeches (Rossi, *passim*).

*The Two Noble Kinsmen* (Q 1634): I mention this only as an example of how collaboration between two authors was conceived in the Jacobean age, no longer a collective and communal undertaking but a systematic exploitation of the specific skills of each.

## REFERENCES

Clayton   '*Hamlet*: the Acting Version and the Wiser Sort' in Thomas Clayton ed. *The* Hamlet *First Published (Q1, 1603)*, (Newark, Del., 1992), 195–210.

Elam   'What Did Shakespeare Write?' *Textus* 9, ed. Keir Elam and Ann Thompson (1996) 339–56.

Greg   *The Merry Wives of Windsor* edited by W.W. Greg (Oxford, 1910).

Irace   Kathleen O. Irace *Reforming the 'Bad' Quartos. Performance and Provenance of Six Shakespearean First Editions* (Newark, Del., 1994).

Laroque   'Pivot Scenes as Dramatic Inclusions in Shakespeare's Plays', in *The Show Within: Dramatic and Others Insets in English Renaissance Drama (1550–1642)*, ed. François Laroque (Montpellier, 1992), 1: 155–66.

Maguire   Laurie E. Maguire, *Shakespearean Suspect Texts. The 'Bad' Quartos and their Contexts* (Cambridge, 1996).

Melchiori, 'Corridors'   'The Corridors of History: Shakespeare the Re-Maker'. *Proceedings of the British Academy* 72 (1986), 167–85.

Melchiori, 'Edward III'   Editor: *King Edward III* (New Cambridge Shakespeare, 1998).

Melchiori, 'Frenchness'   'The Frenchness of Boyet' in *L'Europe de la Renaissance: Cultures et Civilisations. Mélanges offerts à Marie-Thérèse Jones-Davies* (Paris, 1989), 269–83.

Melchiori, 'Garter Plays'   *Shakespeare's Garter Plays: 'Edward III' to 'Merry Wives of Windsor'* (Newark, Del., 1994)

Melchiori, 'Henry IV'   Editor: Shakespeare *The Second Part of King Henry IV* (New Cambridge Shakespeare, 1989).

Melchiori, 'Merry Wives'   Editor: *The Merry Wives of Windsor* (Arden 3, 2000).

Melchiori, 'Shakespeare'   *Shakespeare; Genesi e struttura delle opere* (Bari, 1994).

Melchiori and Gabrieli   Giorgio Melchiori, with Vittorio Gabrieli *Sir Thomas More* a Play by Anthony Munday and others, revised by Henry Chettle, Thomas Dekker, Thomas Heywood and William Shakespeare (The Revels Plays, Manchester, 1990).

Papetti   'Pre-texts: Polonius on Genre' in *Le Forme del Teatro IV*, ed. Viola Papetti (Rome, 1989), 45–60.

Righetti   'Uno, due, mille *Romeo and Juliet*' in Angelo Righetti (ed.), *Rileggere/Re-Reading Romeo and Juliet* (Verona, 1999), 9–18.

Rossi   'Othello One and Two: the Importance of Swearing' in Sergio Rossi ed. *The Tragedie of Othello, The Moore of Venice*, Atti del Convegno 25–30 Marzo 1884 (Milano, 1985), 7–22.

Sams   Eric Sams, *The Real Shakespeare: Retrieving the Early Years, 1564–1594* (New Haven, 1995).

Werstine   Paul Werstine, 'Narratives About Printed Shakespearean Texts: "Foul Papers" and "Bad" Quartos' *SQ* 41 (1990), 65–86.

# 3

## CORRECT IMPRESSIONS: EDITING AND EVIDENCE IN THE WAKE OF POST-MODERNISM

*Anthony B. Dawson*

### 'BIFOLD AUTHORITY'

Francis Bacon, in this as in so many things, markedly forward looking, says that the 'works or acts of merit' in relation to 'the books of learning' are two:

> First libraries, which are as the shrine where all the relics of the ancient saints, full of true virtue and that without delusion or imposture, are preserved and reposed; secondly new editions of authors, with more correct impressions, more faithful translations, more profitable glosses, more diligent annotations, and the like.
>
> (Bacon, 222–3)

His faith gives me courage, since, like most of the contributors to this volume, I am engaged in the work of diligently and profitably glossing, annotating and correcting a new edition of the most 'saintly', if not the most 'ancient' of authors; and no doubt this text will find its way into the 'shrine' with the other 'relics'. But in recent years, the ease and continuity suggested by Bacon's formulation have been vigorously challenged by scholars who dispute not only the difficulty of faithfulness and correctness but the very conditions of possibility that might be said to sustain such goals. That such a challenge was not unknown to writers like Bacon and Shakespeare might be inferred from the rather defensive phrase the former uses, 'and that without delusion or imposture', a phrase that no doubt resonates with anti-Catholic sentiment and an iconoclastic disdain for the worship of the saints, but which at the same time suggests the possible infiltration of error and uncertainty into the shrine itself. Not to mention, of course, that the very need for 'more correct impressions' allows post-modern bibliography, with its critique of the ideal of correctness and its insistence on the plurality and indeterminacy of texts, to enter the fray. As I will argue later, the text I have just finished editing, Shakespeare's *Troilus and Cressida*, goes much farther than Bacon in exploring the problems so belaboured by recent textual theory. This suggests the existence of lines of continuity between the Shakespearean theatrical scene and our own post-modern, bibliographical one, the latter both remembering and mis-remembering the former.

Bacon's model is optimistic and evolutionary. It imagines editors always improving on their predecessors, although a brief glance at the history of Shakespearean editing suggests a more contentious model, one in which the various contestants vie as much for precedence as for truth. Perhaps that's not quite fair; until recently truth, correctness, faithfulness, etc. were the dominant criteria by which editors conducted their work, the ideals they sought to realize. But personal and ideological interests could not fail to intrude and in doing so they opened the gap that post-modern bibliography has brought to our notice. In raising suspicions about the values that guided bibliographical work in the past, the 'new textualists' have not entirely abandoned the criteria of truth and correctness, nor have they done away with the concept of evidence; rather they have pluralized truth and refused to accept the sorts of relations that previous textual scholars understood to obtain between observable phenomena and the conclusions to which the 'facts' pointed. By asking different questions of the evidence, they spied new relations and came to quite different conclusions.

Before developing such general observations, however, I would like to turn my attention to an aspect of 'profitable' glossing that Bacon (for obvious reasons) neglects to mention, namely the role of performance in the editing of texts. I do so since it raises the question of evidence in a simple, raw form. Editing any Shakespeare text these days means confronting performance. At the very least this means providing something like a stage history or some kind of account of how one's text has fared in the theatre. More vexed than this is the expectation that one approach textual problems through performance. All early modern plays pose problems for the modern editor, but, as it happens, those posed by *Troilus and Cressida* are particularly intractable. Trying to solve them involves, among other things, paying attention to early modern performance conditions and to the relations between texts and performances as they then existed (insofar as one can hope to understand and interpret those relations). One also brings to bear what one knows or can surmise about modern conditions of performance, since a modern edition aims, among other things, to be useful to actors and students who might want to perform the play.

So, in determining the text, editors adduce the evidence of performance. This leads to a new kind of hermeneutic circle. One begins with printed texts (in the case of *Troilus,* Q and F). These printed versions derive directly or indirectly from manuscripts, which, in turn, subtend and in some cases derive from, perhaps represent, performance, though the only way we 'know' this (at least for Shakespeare) is through examining the printed versions. How do they subtend performance? First of all, the play begins life as a written document (in some ways of course it begins life – as the anonymous *Troilus and Cressida* epistle writer recognizes – as an idea in the 'brain' of the author, but I want to postpone that complicating factor for the moment). A version is written down, let's say by the author, who then reads what he has written to an assembly of actors. 'Parts' are written out, presumably by scribes. A playbook is (often haphazardly) prepared, 'plots' are scripted. A 'fair copy' might be produced, again by a scribe. Other hands (the revising author's, the bookkeeper's, those of actors) perhaps play a role in the marking up of the ms. that eventually reaches the printer. The printer represents, but of course does not accurately transcribe every detail of, the ms.

All of this inclines toward indeterminacy, but at the same time a modern text seeks typically to stabilize the changes wrought by the transmission process. The differences between Q and F derive from, and are evidence of, that transmission – but how does one adjudicate between them? One begins with the following facts: ms. produces (is prior to and necessary for) performance, ms. gets transformed into printed versions, printed versions are then studied for their hints about performance which both derives from and is a witness to the underlying ms. The printed text is a witness to the oral performance, the oral performance a witness to the written ms., and the written ms. has sustained both the oral performance and the printed text. Let's look at a simple example.

In 4.4. of *Troilus and Cressida*, after Troilus's last tearful line to Cressida, 'Distasted (F: 'Distasting') with the salt of broken tears' (47, TLN 2434),[1] F, but not Q, has a direction, '*Enter AEneus*' and immediately following, on the next line, both texts read,

> *AEneas within.* My lord, is the lady ready?

Now either Aeneas is 'within' or he is not. F has it both ways. In my view, the best explanation for the confusion is that *Enter 'AEneus'* is a bookkeeper's notation, probably marking the need for the actor to be there in readiness; alternatively, it could be an addition made for a revival with different blocking;[2] or even perhaps an error. Whatever the case, it is highly unlikely that Aeneas's entry is an authorial revision, since the whole dynamic of the scene depends on the pressure exerted by Aeneas's invisible presence and on the calculated delay of his entrance; indeed, he and Paris are still calling from 'within' at lines 97–8 (2488, 2490).

Most editors have simply followed Q. Gary Taylor, rethinking the play in theatrical terms for the Oxford edition, came to a different conclusion: 'No more than an appearance in a doorway is required; F's addition can hardly be accidental, whereas its failure to omit Q's following "*within*" ... could well be inadvertent, or indicative of theatrical uncertainty about this species of half-entrance' (*Companion*, 435). The magisterial 'can hardly be accidental' obscures the fact that in many of the extant playbooks there are errors and confusions, sometimes introduced by the bookkeepers themselves. Taylor's whole argument about F is that it derives from a theatrical ms.; and an examination of exactly such a ms., Heywood's *The Captives,* reveals that on several occasions the bookkeeper has written a direction at the bottom of a recto page that pertains to an action near the top of the following verso – i.e. as a kind of prompt to himself. The '*Enter AEneus*' could easily be a mark of that sort. Nevertheless, Taylor's point is worth considering further, because of what happens later in the scene.

As I said, the pressure of the scene derives partly from the felt presence of the intruders coming to get Cressida for the exchange, on the heels of the lovers' first night together. They arrive on stage at line 105 (2499), with the bizarre and universally rejected F stage direction '*Enter the Greekes*' (the only Greek in the crowd is Diomedes). Leading up to their arrival, we again hear Aeneas's voice, 'Nay, good my Lord?' and a line later, Paris calls 'Brother *Troylus*' (97–8), both marked '*within*' in QF. Troilus tells Paris 'Good brother come you hither, / And bring *Aeneas* and the Grecian with you' (98–9). All of this makes dramatic sense, since the pressure builds with the offstage voices and implied action, leading to the climactic entry. Of all recent editors, however, Taylor is the only one that pays attention to an anomaly in F: an '*Exit*' following Cressida's line, '... will you be true?' (100, 2493). Taylor comments that 'it seems impossible to explain away F's direction as an error, or an exit for Cressida'. He accordingly interprets it as 'a slightly misplaced exit for Paris' whom he has placed 'at the door' instead of 'within' for the line, 'Brother *Troylus*'. While it's true that the exit cannot apply to Cressida, who has to remain onstage, it could of course be an error; Cressida has nothing more to say in the scene and perhaps a bookkeeper going rapidly over the script took that fact as a sign that she leaves the stage. As for Paris's ever so brief entrance, again Taylor's comment is revealing: 'That Paris actually appears is suggested not only by the Folio exit ... but also by the way that Troilus addresses him in the following speech' (*Companion*, 435). But 'come you hither' hardly suggests that Paris is with Troilus on stage, or even visible to him or the audience. Quite the opposite in fact.

From my point of view, the deliberate rhythm of the scene requires that the physical presence of Aeneas and the others be delayed. That certainly is what is required by the Q text (usually regarded as a non-theatrical transcript), which here I think best represents Shakespeare's 'intention'. Perhaps this is a case where the theatre actually has, to use an old, discredited metaphor, 'contaminated' authorial intention: if the earlier '*Enter AEneus*' and this '*Exit*' do represent theatrical practice, then the eagerness of the actors to display themselves may have overbalanced the design of the scene. The evidence of '*Enter the Greekes*', however, suggests a more likely explanation. That direction seems like theatrical shorthand and probably derives from a bookkeeper more concerned with getting business worked out than worried about precision. As I suggested above, the bookkeeper is likely to have inserted '*Enter AEneus*' as a note to himself. The '*Exit*' at 100 also suggests the presence of a bookkeeper; while it may represent a printing house error, or, if it does apply to Paris, a textual trace of a different revival, it probably refers, mistakenly, to Cressida. This example, and there are several others like it, suggests that what lies behind F is a manuscript that has been (incompletely and haphazardly) annotated for performance, a point that has far-reaching ramifications for the task of editing.[3] From what we can tell by examining the extant playhouse mss, the kind of inconsistency discernible in F is not at all incompatible with the notion of its use as 'prompt copy'.[4]

In my example I have adduced several different kinds of evidence, some of which invoke performance as a grounds for reducing indeterminacy. But first there is textual evidence – what is actually there in the early printed texts. Then there is available knowledge about, in this case, mss actually used in the theatre and the activities of stage functionaries such as bookkeepers; this grounds speculation about the manuscripts behind printed texts. A third type of evidence is awareness of printing-house practices, and a fourth is claims about Shakespearean scene construction based on convictions about his theatrical know-how. All of this is in some ways circumstantial, but as I suggest below, this does not invalidate it.

I would be the first to grant that the idea of performance I am invoking is itself rather narrow and univocal. It doesn't take account of the shifts in daily practice that inevitably take place, the unpredictable changes that an actor might introduce during a specific performance. I mentioned the possibility of a different 'revival' as the source for some of the conflicting stage directions in the F text of *Troilus and Cressida*, but I didn't really take seriously the implication of performative instability. I am in one sense treating performance as determined by the presumed ms. source ('what Shakespeare wrote or "meant"'), leaving out what the epistle to *Tamburlaine* calls 'fond and frivolous gestures' (whether verbal or mimic), the unexpected extras, the clowns speaking more than is set down for them. The ephemeral in performance gives it its uniqueness and by its nature cannot be trapped in print or even in ms. – one need only compare a modern promptbook with a given performance. So it remains true that performance is in many ways unwritten, not genuinely textual. But for the purposes of editing we have to assume that in some ways it is. We imagine a performance that conforms to an imagined ms. source. I don't for the moment think there is anything wrong with this, or that it falsifies performance or text in any very important way.

## 'IMAGINARY RELISH'

Armed with the foregoing example and the sorts of evidence even a simple editorial choice entails, I turn now to the larger question of editorial desire. Jerome McGann, one of the founding fathers of the pluralist movement, begins his account of the textual condition with an analogy between textual and sexual intercourse, both of which he regards as forms of symbolic exchange: 'The sexual event itself – which is ... a model of the textual condition ... organizes a vast network of related acts of intercourse at the personal [and] ... social levels ... Love is and has ever been one of the great scenes of textuality' (3). The analogy, no doubt inspired by Barthes, is a wonderfully frictional one, suggesting both an immediacy and a carnality in our relationships with texts. Part of McGann's apparent intention here is to ground his understanding of textuality as ineluctably material, an aim that would link to his general emphasis on the concrete conditions of textual production (but note too the ambiguity in his thinking marked by the implied equivalence between an 'event' in time and an ontological condition – the 'sexual event' being 'a model of the textual condition'). His theory stresses the importance of transmission, of the text as a concrete social event in time, and of the crucial differences made by the 'most material levels of the text' (12) – not only its skin and bones, we might say, but its moles, freckles and even bruises.[5] And yet, in that opening analogy, he says of sex, and by implication of text, 'The climactic marriage of our persons is most completely experienced as a total body sensation almost mystical in its intensity as in its meaning' (3). Such marriages, he implies later in the book, have a clear textual counterpart: 'the most important "collaboration" process is that which finds ways of marrying a linguistic to a bibliographical text. We confront such marriages most forcefully when we read texts [such as many of Shakespeare's] which, while "written by" certain writers, were never "authorized" by them' (61). The wedding of linguistic and bibliographical in this image becomes intense, if not mystical, because it is embedded in the collaborative. The language here invokes materiality (the body, the bibliographic) only to leave it behind, and indeed a fruitful uncertainty about what exactly constitutes the material seems to govern much of what McGann has to say about editing and textuality. If we look hard enough and long enough at the material minutiae, he seems to imply, we can move past their intransigence and inertness into a quasi-mystical and yet still social space where 'to be human is to be involved with one another, and ultimately with many others' (3).[6]

Following McGann, W.B. Worthen, in his incisive account of the contradictions and dilemmas attendant on contemporary Shakespearean performance, especially with regard to the problem of authority and authorization, develops the view that there is no such thing as a 'work' that exists prior to either textual manifestation or performance. He quotes McGann's distinction between text, poem and work: 'The "text" is the literary product conceived as a purely lexical event; the "poem" is the locus of a specific process of production ... and consumption; and the "work" comprehends the global set of all the texts and poems which have merged in the literary production and reproduction processes' (McGann, 31–2).[7] Developing this view, Worthen builds an analogy between performance and McGann's idea of the 'poem'; he argues that 'performance is definitive of the process of cultural negotiation through which works have their continued existence' (15). Hence the 'authority' claimed by the theatre when it asserts its authenticity (i.e., its 'truth' to Shakespeare's text) misses the point. Far from tapping in to the authentic Shakespeare, performance (necessarily contingent, transitory, evanescent and collaborative) contributes instead to 'Shakespeare's' inauthenticity, or at least to his (its?) constantly changing, inessential 'nature' (McGann: 'The textual condition's only immutable law is the law of change' (9)). That is, there *is* no Shakespeare for performance to be true to, no work called *Hamlet*, but only textual events, of which this particular performance is one.

The pluralized understanding of performance and material text has frequently been linked to the idea of collaboration. Because theatre is a collaborative art, and the Elizabethan theatre in particular a place where singular authorship was not privileged in the way that it subsequently became, many scholars have concluded that even single-authored texts, such as those of Shakespeare, are inherently unstable, that the mere fact of collaboration undermines attempts to establish the authority of a particular material version of the work – as Worthen suggests about performance. McGann argues that because authorial intention rarely controls 'the state or transmission' of the text, 'literary texts and their meanings are collaborative events' (60). His conclusion from this is careful, extending only to the idea that an author's 'final intentions' cannot be the 'guiding criterion' for determining copy-text. Others who have used his work have not always been so cautious.

Leah Marcus, in *Unediting the Renaissance*, does not focus on the practical problems of editing, and is thus at liberty to extend some of McGann's ideas into a manifesto for a free-wheeling textual post-modernism. She criticizes the 'new bibliographers', Greg, Bowers and others, on ideological grounds – they tried to stabilize what was intrinsically unstable, and to protect the artist and his work against 'the depredations of history' (20). In contrast, she welcomes all the material versions of a given 'work', without worrying much about where they came from or trying to adjudicate between them. She regards the New Bibliographers as in retreat from history, despite their efforts to work out causes and effects of observable past phenomena. The implication of this kind of analysis is that history can be known only as a series of discrete and concrete events, that its variousness and multiplicity somehow undo the possibility of coherent diachronic comprehension. The mistake here, I think, derives from a confusion about the relation of evidence to what it can explain. It is perfectly true that complete and certain knowledge of historical reality is impossible. But that does not mean that reasonably plausible accounts of historical phenomena are impossible, nor does it suggest that evidence need not be carefully weighed in developing such accounts. The confusion, as I said, is about the nature of evidence. Drawing on a number of philosophical accounts, Michael Bristol develops a helpful distinction between 'veridical' and 'circumstantial' evidence in any 'forensic' inquiry, the former kind typically providing more assurance about the truth of a proposition than the latter. While the term 'circumstantial evidence' suggests a lack of credibility, Bristol shows that it frequently functions as a perfectly adequate guide to highly plausible conclusions. In Marcus's critique of the New Bibliographers, she appears to be holding them to standards which they would not apply to their own work, demanding veridical when they are content with circumstantial.[8] They are engaged in a forensic historical inquiry that aims at plausible, even likely, explanations. Most of the time, that is what 'truth' is.

The people whom Marcus calls the 'new philologists' have a different agenda and hence different questions to ask of the evidence before them. They are as invested in their ideas of discontinuity and rupture as the earlier textual scholars were in continuity and correctness. They are not especially interested in how particular texts came into being, nor in the temporal or causal relations between them, nor in their literary value, but rather in their cultural affiliations, especially as these may yield an analysis of power. 'Shakespeare' in this kind of analysis is a strategy for disseminating and maintaining cultural hegemony. Hence Marcus regards narratives that seek to explain how plainly inferior texts (from an aesthetic point of view), such as *Hamlet* Q1 or Q *Merry Wives,* came into being as a symptom of an ideologically driven, and oppressive, rage for order and hierarchy. Aesthetic value, she says explicitly, is an effect of power, an idea put about by 'professors of literature ... as a guarantor of their membership in an intellectual elite' (134).[9]

*Troilus and Cressida* might be said to stand as an allegory of many of the problems just rehearsed. The indeterminacy of the textual situation (the precise relations between Q (1609) and F have never been satisfactorily explained), the extreme opacity of the play's language, the oddity of its status as a performance-text,[10] invite an approach to the task at hand consonant with Marcus's project of unediting. And yet to me such a choice seems theoretically untenable. I am troubled by at least one implication of McGann's notion of 'work'. For to me, without some narrative that includes an idea of a *non-material* 'work' behind the manifest physical evidence contained in the actually existing versions, there is no coherent way to establish actual historical relations. One has to imagine a 'work' that is not simply equivalent to those two material objects Q and F.[11]

To put all this another way, *Troilus and Cressida* is both the material texts in which it has survived ('poems' in McGann's sense) and the conceptual object that emerged from Shakespeare's brain ('the work' in Tanselle's sense) and was transmitted by his hand to the paper on which it first found material expression. Shakespeare's 'conception' is in a sense both material and immaterial. It derives from a whole textual past, the books he read, the plays he had written and seen, the stories he heard. But there is also something 'mystical' about it, as there is about the strongly physical events such as sex and birth that McGann's analogies, not to mention the implicit metaphor in the word 'conception', evoke. The anonymous author of the Epistle that was hastily added to the 1609 quarto recognized this clearly: 'Eternal reader, you have here a new play, never staled with the stage, never clapper-clawed with the palms of the vulgar, and yet passing full of the palm comical – for it is a birth of your brain that never undertook anything comical vainly' (spelling modernized). The text is born in the brain of its comically talented author, but when it grows up it becomes a book. It is in one sense true that, as de Grazia and Stallybrass maintain, 'authors don't write books', i.e. they produce scripts that are then made into books by others.[12] But it is also true that they do 'write books' (*overheard at a conference: 'what are your working on these days?' 'Oh, I'm writing a book on the materiality of the text that contests the idea of authorship'*).

*Troilus* is thus not strictly an event, but a long narrative that begins well before Shakespeare's conception, continues and is refracted through his mental and physical work on it, and comes right down to the present and the various 'corrections' and 'glosses' (to recall Bacon's terms) of recent editors. Hence 'work' is a dialectical concept, one that includes both the immaterial idea that lies behind textual manifestations and the manifestations themselves. Without some such idea it would be impossible to edit at all, even to the extent of 'correcting' obvious slips or even typographical errors (the correction being based on a notion of what the author 'really' meant and what he must have written).

It seems to me that Shakespeare's 'authority' derives from some such dialectic. While 'authority' may be an ideological construct, it also designates real relations and a real history. On the question of how collaboration relates to authority, most scholars now believe that consideration of the theatrical conditions of Shakespeare's time, insofar as we can reconstruct them, should play some part in the determination of texts. That is, most of us agree that Shakespeare is not the exclusive, singular author of his plays as we know them. But to acknowledge that certainly does *not* mean that we have to give up the idea that he is the *primary* author, nor that, where we can make a coherent argument based on a sense of his dramatic instincts or disposition, we should not do so. Shakespeare's authority may be relative but it is not insubstantial.

It is true that editorial tradition has assumed the existence of a 'work' behind the texts, and accordingly has produced a canon of principles and criteria by which to go about the job of editing; so too the 'authority' of a given edition will derive partially from its adherence to that canon. While it may be true that traditional bibliography defined the transmission process too narrowly, the fact that the canon claims authority does not make it illegitimate; knowledge such as we lay claim to it depends on just such heuristic structures. And it also seems to me historically wrong to claim that the work is only a product of a range of texts and performances. Shakespeare after all was a real person who sat somewhere and wrote out something that was in some way 'in' his head. That changes, emendations, theatrical cuts and interpolations, errors, etc. all crept in between that act of writing and the Q or F texts, doesn't erase the original, now partially (but not wholly) inaccessible act of writing that took place. Hence, that initiating authorial act should constitute some kind of origin, even though it is not exclusive. Those who attack the idea of authority often tacitly assume that pluralizing authority undermines it completely. But it does not. It only means that we have to apply canons of accuracy, plausibility and approximation, more carefully.[13]

## THE AUTHOR'S DRIFT

The play itself keeps insisting on the perspectival nature of 'truth' and value. Ulysses, expatiating on 'reflection', the idea that knowledge depends on representations and replicas, traces what he calls 'the author's drift' (3.3.114). The phrase assumes an author, not (by the way) an invention of the Renaissance but an idea already well established in antiquity,[14] and it ascribes to that author an intention – a 'drift' or direction. 'Drift' includes both a random and a purposeful movement; instability and recursiveness are part of the process:

A strange fellow here
Writes me that man, how dearly ever parted,
How much in having, or without or in,
Cannot make boast to have that which he hath,
Nor feels not what he owes, but by reflection.

(3.3.96–100)

Ulysses's phrasing makes it clear that the existence of someone's 'parts' is indeed actual, however inaccessible such parts might be in themselves. He does not say that his hypothetical man has no 'parts' but rather that, without 'reflection', he cannot experience, nor even claim to have, what he actually has.[15] This is a germane paradox in the play, one accentuated by its being deployed at this moment as a manipulative strategy (Ulysses is playing a 'part'). Ulysses's tactics expose the political interest involved not only in constructions of value themselves, but even in the sceptical philosophical basis of such judgements. But, while the play stresses the difficulty of judgement and the uncertainty of knowledge, and recognizes the ways in which one's political desires can colour all philosophical position-taking, it does not empty out knowledge, honour or virtue as categories.

Shakespeare's texts, then, are in some ways prescient of the kinds of issues that post-modern bibliography has been insisting on. If we see those texts as events, then we are bound to regard those prior acts of conceiving and of writing also as events, and all of them together as part of a long narrative, beginning before Shakespeare and not over yet. The idea of a narrative might remind us of the continuities between modern academic practice and early modern theatrical culture, so that instead of insisting on absolute difference from the past, we might fruitfully start looking again at the kinds of deep-rooted connection invoked by Bacon's image of the shrine and its memorial relics.

## REFERENCES

Bacon   Francis Bacon, *The Advancement of Learning Book II*, ed. Hugh G. Dick (New York, 1955).

Bevington   William Shakespeare, *Troilus and Cressida*, ed. David Bevington, Arden 3 series (London, 1998).

Bradshaw   Graham Bradshaw, *Shakespeare's Scepticism* (Brighton, 1987).

Bristol   Michael Bristol, 'How good does evidence have to be?', in *Textual and Theatrical Shakespeare: Questions of Evidence*, ed. Edward Pechter (Iowa City, 1996).

*Companion*   Stanley Wells and Gary Taylor, *William Shakespeare: A Textual Companion* (Oxford, 1987).

de Grazia and Stallybrass, 'Love'   Margreta de Grazia and Peter Stallybrass, 'Love among the ruins: response to Pechter', *Textual Practice*, 11 (1997), 69–80.

de Grazia and Stallybrass, 'Materiality'   Margreta de Grazia and Peter Stallybrass, 'The materiality of the Shakespearean text', *SQ*, 44 (1993), 255–83.

Ellis-Fermor   Una Ellis-Fermor, *The Frontiers of Drama* (London, 1946).

Holderness, Loughrey and Murphy   Graham Holderness, Bryan Loughrey and Andrew Murphy, 'Busy doing nothing: a response to Edward Pechter', *Textual Practice*, 11 (1997), 81–8.

Long, 'John a Kent'   William B. Long, 'John a Kent and John a Cumber: an Elizabethan playbook and its implications', in *Shakespeare and Dramatic Tradition: Essays in Honor of S. F. Johnson*, ed. W.R. Elton and William B. Long (London, 1989), 125–43.

Long, 'Stage-directions'   William B. Long, 'Stage-directions: a misinterpreted factor in determining textual provenance', *Text*, 2 (1985), 121–37.

Long, 'Woodstock'   William B. Long, '"A bed/for woodstock": a warning for the unwary', *Medieval & Renaissance Drama in England*, 2 (1985), 91–118.

Marcus   Leah Marcus, *Unediting the Renaissance: Shakespeare, Marlowe, Milton* (London, 1996).

McGann   Jerome McGann, *The Textual Condition* (Princeton, 1991).

Pechter   Edward Pechter, 'Making love to our employment'; or the immateriality of arguments about the materiality of the Shakespearean text', *Textual Practice*, 11 (1997), 51–67.

Tanselle Thomas G. Tanselle, *A Rationale of Textual Criticism* (Philadelphia, 1989).

Vessey Mark Vessey, 'Erasmus' Jerome: the Publishing of a Christian Author', *Erasmus of Rotterdam Society Yearbook*, 14 (1994), 62–99.

Werstine Paul Werstine, 'Narratives about printed Shakespeare texts: "foul papers" and "bad" quartos', *SQ*, 41 (1990), 65–86.

Worthen W.B. Worthen, *Shakespeare and the Authority of Performance* (Cambridge, 1997).

## Notes

1 Line numbers refer to Bevington's edition and to the Folio 'through line numbers'; in quoting from Q, F, I haven't recorded accidental variants.

2 A few of the extant playbooks, such as *Woodstock*, contain markings that seem to derive from different productions – see Long, 'Woodstock'.

3 I discuss these in more detail in my forthcoming edition (Cambridge). My point here is to show how thinking about performance can affect editorial decisions.

4 As Long ('John a Kent,' 'Stage-directions'), Werstine and others have shown, terms like 'prompt copy' have frequently been used in misleading ways. I refer here only to the ms. used by the bookkeeper.

5 These are the kinds of elements that writers like de Grazia and Stallybrass emphasize.

6 His utopian vision of decentring and multiplying the 'text' in all its concrete manifestations seems to hold out the possibility of polymorphous enjoyment of endlessly unfolding textual partners. Do I go too far in detecting a hint of Marcuse's influence in this – a holdover from McGann's graduate student days in the 1960s perhaps?

7 Note the difference between this formulation and that of Tanselle, who regards the 'work' as a kind of platonic form standing behind and apart from its manifestations in different 'texts'. I think some version of Tanselle's idea is indispensable.

8 Greg *et al.* were aware that texts are approximations, or even editorial constructions; what they were working to achieve had an idealist ring not always pleasing to materialist ears, but their aim was to develop the most plausible conclusions arising from the evidence before them. What has really changed, as Bristol points out, is the forensic context, the kinds of questions that are being asked, and these depend ultimately on scholarly preference, on desire. See Pechter.

9 Such statements of course can be easily reversed – at present, professors with strong views about aesthetic value are likely to be at the margins, while their opponents enjoy the fruits of being in the 'intellectual elite'.

10 The play's early performance history is murky and has been much debated (see Bevington 87–90). Except for Dryden's completely transformed version, the play was not performed again till 1898.

11 Hence I agree with Tanselle's crucial distinction between 'texts of documents' and 'texts of works'. There has been a lot of debate about the so-called material text, helped along especially, though not initiated, by de Grazia and Stallybrass's 1993 article ('Materiality'). This led to an exchange in the pages of *Textual Practice* in which Edward Pechter argued that, because evidence in such inquiries is always inconclusive, the desires and predilections of the critic are what count. His own preference for the literary over the material drew replies from de Grazia and Stallybrass ('Love'), and Holderness, Loughrey and Murphy.

12 'Materiality', 273. They are quoting Roger Stoddard. In his reply to Pechter, Stallybrass makes the point explicit.

13 Tanselle: 'We should embrace the inevitable [i.e. the subjective element in editing] and concentrate on defining the role of judgement'.

14 See Vessey.

15 Many commentators have read Ulysses's words as an indication of total scepticism, but as Ellis-Fermor (77–8) pointed out long ago, that is not precisely the position he is taking. The whole passage is a meditation on Renaissance scepticism, and no doubt owes something to Montaigne. See Bradshaw, 38–9 and 154–6. But as Bradshaw points out, this kind of sceptical outlook is habitual with Shakespeare and noticeable in his work before there is evidence of his having read Montaigne.

# 4

## EARLY PLAY TEXTS:
## FORMS AND FORMES

### *H.R. Woudhuysen*

It may seem strange to offer Richard Proudfoot a brief essay which begins with blank pieces of paper, but he has always, especially in his labours for the Malone Society, been concerned with the material form printed books, manuscripts and documents take. Plays are usually transmitted on paper which may be marked or left unmarked by the printer or scribe. There are many possible reasons for not using a page or leaf, and the decision to leave paper unmarked may in itself convey some sort of meaning and have consequences for the text of a play. These preliminary investigations are almost entirely reliant on the four volumes of W.W. Greg's *A Bibliography of the English Printed Drama to the Restoration* (London, 1939–59). A wider context in which to look at the printing of plays would, of course, be more than desirable, but no one has as yet attempted to emulate Greg and to produce comparable bibliographies of, for example, poetry, sermons, news pamphlets or law books. I shall therefore begin by looking at blank leaves and move on to suggest, very tentatively, one or two possible effects their inclusion may have had on the printing of early plays. Various dates for the beginning and ending of such an account suggest themselves, but the period from the printing of *Gorboduc* in 1565 until the end of 1640, on the eve of the closing of the theatres and the publication of the second Jonson folio, supplies a huge amount of material, even when masques, entertainments, pageants, academic and Latin plays, collections, literary translations and Scottish printings are excluded. In addition to first editions, I have included later editions (but not issues or variants) printed before the end of 1640.

The page most frequently left blank in printed plays was the verso of the title-page. This was almost invariably the case from the mid-1570s; before then there are some blank title-page versos but quite a few contain printed matter, such as the play's argument, its prologue or a woodcut. In a few cases the text of the play itself may simply begin on the verso of its title-page. From 1575 until about 1605, with a few exceptions, it is relatively unusual for the versos to contain anything. Prologues and lists of roles were occasionally printed in that position: the second quarto of *The Two Angry Women of Abingdon* (1599) has both on the verso (Greg, 161(*b*)). From 1605 prologues are almost never printed there, although *The Two Noble Kinsmen* (1634) is a notable exception (Greg, 492(*a*)). Instead, lists of roles become more frequent and from about 1619 they become quite common. *The Lover's Melancholy* (1629) is the first play to print a list of the actors' names in this position (Greg, 420(*A*)); in subsequent years versos may contain both a list of roles and a cast list. *The Family of Love* (1608) has an address to the reader, a list of roles and a prologue on the verso (Greg, 263(*A*)). Also around 1605 the verso may contain other matter. The first play known to have a dedication on the title-page verso is the third quarto of *The Malcontent* (1605), containing Webster's additions (Greg, 203(*c*));[1] the next is the first issue of *The Devil's Charter* (1607)(Greg, 254(*A*I)). The only other instance of a dedication in this place seems to be the first edition of *A King and no King* (1619) (Greg, 360(*a*)). *Aglaura* (1638) has the licence in this unusual position (Greg, 541(*a*)), and three plays of the 1630s have woodcuts of one kind or another there (Greg, 107(*c*); Greg, 510(*A*); Greg, 525(*a*)). The 1634 edition of *The Faithful Shepherdess* seems unique in having commendatory verse on the verso of the title-page (Greg, 287(*c*)).

Nevertheless, the majority of title-page versos of plays printed between 1565 and 1640 are blank. A title-page without matter on its verso avoids the risk of show-through and, presenting a bold and clean front, would be suitable for advertising by the booktrade or at the theatre itself. Plays with blank title-page versos largely conformed to the dominant typographic practice of the time, so that the presence of matter on the verso may be of interest. The increasing frequency of lists of roles in such a prominent and easily found position suggests something about the help readers needed when navigating an unfamiliar plot. Of course, using the verso may also indicate a desire for economy, for paper is always expensive. In Peter Blayney's account of the printing and production of 800 copies of an imaginary play quarto he estimates the actual printing cost, including composition, correction and presswork, but before mark-up, at £2 16s. He reckons the price of the book's paper, which the publisher supplied, at only a shilling less.[2] Blank pages or leaves cost money: who took the responsibility for having them is by no means clear. One possible explanation, put forward by Don McKenzie, was that 'the printer was paid by the edition sheet (therefore the more the better) and that paper was a separate charge on the booksellers who supplied it'.[3] Even so, as we shall see, it is hard to reconcile printers' self-interested use of as much paper as possible with their obvious expedients to save space in the setting of plays.

Where the stationer was also the printer of the play, then its format and design were more or less in his own hands. Some authors – Jonson obviously springs to mind – might have had decided views about the way in which their work, if they still had an interest in it, should appear. Yet, even without the crucial evidence as to who was responsible for a book's design, Blayney was undoubtedly right to suggest that in his negotiations the stationer would generally leave the matter to the printer: 'If he has strong ideas about typography and layout he will explain his preferences at the outset, but otherwise will leave such matters to the printer's professional judgment'. He went on to say the printer knew, 'that the publisher is particularly concerned about costs'.[4] The printer also had to bear in mind that he paid his compositors by the sheet or forme, apparently irrespective of how much work the actual setting (and distributing) of type involved.

In other words, at this period a compositor was paid proportionately the same amount for 'setting' a blank page as for a page crowded with justified type.[5]

Blank pages or leaves were therefore not just expensive in terms of paper-use, but meant that the printer paid the compositor for work requiring almost no effort: this later came under the general category known as 'compositors' fat' or 'fat work', described by William Savage in his *Dictionary of the Art of Printing* (1841) as 'short pages, blank pages, and light open matter'.[6] Almost all accounts of the printing of plays take it for granted that smaller format editions – quarto and octavo – were relatively cheap to buy and of necessity were cheaply produced. In his essay on 'The Publication of Playbooks' Blayney argued that printed plays can rarely have made their publishers rich: the economics of the business meant that prices had to be kept down if there were to be any prospect of making a profit. Yet as Greg himself pointed out, 'In spite of economic reasons to be sparing in the use of paper early printers seem to have rather liked end blanks' (Greg, 4.cli). Blayney has noted that Nicholas Okes shared this preference, for he 'seems generally to have attempted to end the text either on the final recto of a gathering or on the verso before the final leaf'. The obvious explanation for this practice is that, as Greg put it, the end blanks 'served as a protection to uncased books', or that, according to Blayney, it allowed 'a blank to protect the print when folded or stitched copies were stored without wrappers'.[7]

The final blank served to stop damage to a book's vulnerable ending. If it ended with a whole blank leaf this could be folded over to cover the title-page of an otherwise unprotected book.[8] Greg noted that in the British Library copy of Dekker's pageant, *Troia Noua Triumphans* (1612), 'it is evident from the soiled condition of D1v and D2 (D2v being clean) that at some time the second of these leaves has been folded round the back of the volume to protect the title' (Greg, 302(A)).[9] Equally, according to Philip Gaskell, 'By the seventeenth century it was becoming common to protect the title-page with an initial blank leaf': in the next century this evolved into the half-title.[10] Again, Blayney has described 'leaving a blank leaf before the title' as Okes's 'usual custom'.[11] Blank leaves at both ends of a book would not only protect it but might be used as endpapers when it came to be bound,[12] but it would not usually be in the printer's or the publisher's interest to supply free material for the bookseller. Furthermore, the evidence suggests that printed plays were rarely sold already bound or that they were subsequently bound individually. On account of this, when plays were included in bound collections blank leaves were often discarded to reduce the volume's bulk.

It is not surprising that initial or end blank leaves do not often survive. Where a leaf is missing in all copies its contents can only surmised. Greg was always careful to describe initial or final leaves which he had not seen or which were not reliably reported as 'A1 blank ?' (Greg, 4.lxiii, cxlix–cli). The curious case of Joseph Webbe's version of Terence's *Eunuchus* (1629) shows he was right to be cautious. Several surviving copies of the book have two titles printed on the same sheet with different imprints: one for Nicholas Bourne, the other for the more obscure Philip Waterhouse. It was presumably for the stationer to decide whether to leave both title-pages or to remove one of them: where a title was removed a bibliographer might easily assume that the missing leaf was blank.[13] 'Blank leaves', Bowers noted rather mournfully, 'will create constant difficulties' in bibliographical descriptions, adding that 'Sooner or later, these missing blanks are likely to turn up to confound the bibliographer who has marked them as excised in the ideal copy'.[14]

Certainty about whether missing leaves were blank or not must be elusive, yet it is reasonable to assume that in the majority of cases such leaves preceding the title or following the play's end were probably blank. There are a number of cases where the play-text finishes on a final recto and the verso has a list of errata, an ornament or a colophon: although the verso is not blank, it was not essential that the matter printed there should survive, and it could be said to have protected the text of the play itself. A stronger case can be made for treating initial leaves which bear a signature, with or without ornaments, as blank.[15] The earliest known plays to have been printed with just a signature on the first leaf and a blank verso all belong to 1594: *Orlando Furioso, The Cobbler's Prophecy, I Selimus* and *The Massacre at Paris* (Greg, 123(*a*); Greg, 124(*A*); Greg, 130(*A*1); Greg, 133(*A*)). The first two were printed by John Danter for Cuthbert Burby, the third by Thomas Creede and the last by Edward Allde for Edward White. However, a decade before then the first quarto of Lyly's *Campaspe* (1584) bears a small leaf ornament on the recto of the first leaf of gathering A (Greg, 82(*a*)).

Actual blanks preceding the title-page in plays written for professional, public, court or inns of court performance do not seem to occur before 1594. In Greg's chronological order the first play which appears to have been produced with an initial blank (the leaf is missing in the unique copy in the Folger) is *Titus Andronicus* (Greg, 117(*a*)). This was followed by *A Looking-Glass for London and England* and *Friar Bacon and Friar Bungay* for which an initial blank survives (Greg, 118(*a*): A1 blank ?; Greg, 121(*a*)). In the case of *Friar Bacon* not only is the initial leaf blank but so is the verso of the last leaf. *Orlando Furioso* (1594) is the first play to have both its first and last leaves blanks (H4 blank ?), as does *The Cobbler's Prophecy* (1594). Danter, who printed both of these, also produced *The Old Wives Tale* (1595) which follows a similar pattern, leaving four (five, if the verso of the title-page is included) pages out of forty-eight blank (Greg, 137(*A*): A1 blank but for the signature 'A' and F4 blank ?). In the case of *I Selimus* (1594) the first and last leaves are blank, but so also is the verso of the penultimate leaf: out of the play's eighty pages five or six are blank. In octavos the proportion of printed to blank matter might be even higher. The first leaf of *The Massacre at Paris* is blank except for a signature 'A', and the last two leaves are blank: six or seven pages out of sixty-four are therefore blank (Greg, 133(*A*)).

Blank leaves at both ends of the book are relatively rare, although there are a few exceptions such as *Volpone* (1607) (Greg, 259(*a*)). It is more common to find the initial leaf and the verso of the final leaf blank. In a rough calculation, out of the 600 or so editions Greg described (excluding the categories mentioned above and title-page versos), about 380 have one or more blank pages.

New editions of plays rarely introduced new blanks, although this sometimes happened. The first five editions of *How a Man may Choose a Good Wife from a Bad* (1602–21) were all produced by different printers none of whom supplied any blanks apart from the title-page verso. When a sixth printer, John Norton, printed a new edition of the play in 1630 he included an initial blank (A1 blank ?), but lost it again reprinting the play in 1634 (Greg, 191(*a*)–(*g*)). In some plays the position of blanks might move around: for example, Creede's 1594 and 1598 editions of *A Looking-Glass for London and England* have A1 blank ?: when he printed the book again for the third time in 1602 and when Jaggard did so for the fourth time in [1605][16] I3v and ? I4 were left blank. In 1617 when Bernard Alsop printed the play from the 1598 edition, he followed its design exactly and left the blanks at the beginning (Greg, 118(*a*)–(*e*)). For the first edition of *Philaster* (1620), Okes left blank leaves at the beginning and end of the play; when he reprinted the revised text in 1622 he left only the last leaf blank (L4 blank ?). Augustine Mathewes supplied no initial or final blanks in his edition of 1628, but printed a list of roles on A3r, left its verso blank and, unusually, began the text of the play on A4r. Six years later, in another revised edition, William Jones again left A3v blank, but also supplied two entirely blank leaves at the end of the play. Edward Griffin's reprint of 1639 has no blanks except for the title-page verso (Greg, 363(*a*)–(*e*)).

Jones's 1634 edition of *Philaster* is particularly unusual because the demands of economy would suggest that the last gathering should have been printed as a half sheet. Printers regularly took advantage of just one half sheet (that is, of a sheet whose other half is not found in the same book): about 180 of the 600 plays contain initial or final half sheets but not both. If a whole sheet had been allowed for in the paper supply, then a half sheet would save money and the remaining paper could be used in another book. Yet the widespread use of blank pages and leaves argues that unused paper was seen as relatively disposable. Perhaps Jones simply miscalculated how much space the new material would take up or did not want to produce a book with text on its final verso. Mistakes of various kinds suggesting problems with space certainly occur. The first gathering of the unacted octavo play *Antigone* (1631) contains sixteen pages of which six (two versos and two leaves, one of which has only an ornament on its recto) are blank. Greg pointed out that this first gathering was 'printed last and that there was not enough preliminary matter to fill the whole sheet' (Greg, 450(*A*)). The verso of the last leaf of text is also blank as are the following two final leaves.

Padding of this kind suggests that printers sometimes wanted to make their books look more substantial than they were. This may well have been the case with another octavo, *The Massacre at Paris* [1594 ?], whose printer also set the text to make the play appear longer than it is.[17] There is some tendency with shorter plays, those with fewer than about two thousand lines, to include blank leaves, but not all such plays have them, and some may simply reflect inaccurate casting off. Among Shakespeare's works the first quartos of *Henry 5*, *The Merry Wives of Windsor* and *Hamlet* all begin or end with blank leaves (Greg, 165(*a*); Greg, 187(*a*); Greg, 197(*a*)). I have already mentioned the number of blanks in *Orlando Furioso*; the 1595 edition of *The Old Wives Tale*, which is not much more than a thousand lines long, consists of twenty-four leaves, of which the first is blank but for the signature 'A' and the last was probably blank (Greg, 137(*A*)). The 'A' text of *Dr Faustus* (1604) is about 500 lines longer but was also first printed as a book of twenty-four leaves with the last three pages blank (F3v and ? F4 blank); the third edition (1611) had the first leaf (A1 blank ?) and the verso of the last leaf blank (Greg, 205(*a*), (*c*)).

The presence of these blanks (even where they have not survived) might be taken to challenge received ideas about the relative value placed on printed plays. If they were the unconsidered trifles they are generally taken to have been, it is strange that printers or publishers were so often willing to leave blank paper in them. Blanks protected as well as bulked out their unbound, slim volumes. Perhaps it was felt that where a specific amount of paper was supplied for a particular job, it had to be used even if it bore no letterpress. However, the relative frequency in printed plays of single half sheets might argue against such a neat theory.

Yet elsewhere there is abundant evidence of a concern to save paper by what Moxon calls '*Bad, Heavy, Hard Work*'.[18] Plays offer considerable scope for compositors who wish to stretch or compress their copy. Scene headings, stage directions, entrances and exits can be set to make or lose space. Greg commented on marginal notes and the use of ornaments to separate acts or scenes: these last are perhaps most familiar from the later sheets of the first quarto of *Romeo and Juliet* (1597) (Greg, 4.clx–clxi; Greg, 143($a$)). He also drew attention to and generally noted what he called continuous printing, that is where 'metrical lines … remain typographical units, with a speaker's name, if necessary, in the middle' (Greg, 4.clx, cp. 1.xviii). Continuous printing was not just limited to verse lines, but could also apply to prose speeches, as in *The Isle of Gulls* or parts of *Westward Ho* (1607) (Greg, 235($a$); Greg, 257($A$)).

In the index of 'Notabilia' Greg was a little more explicit about the practice, observing that, 'In many plays, especially when the compositor is pressed for space, short speeches of two or three words may occasionally be found tucked in on the same line as the end of the previous speech, in verse and prose alike', but added that, 'No notice has been taken of this habit.' Greg divided the practice into regular and irregular use, noting 'The irregularity varies widely, from only occasional to almost regular' (Greg, 3.1639–40). Jonson was, of course, an enthusiast for continuous printing from the first quarto of *Poetaster* (1602) onwards (Greg, 186($a$)).[19] As a regular practice it added to the neoclassical dignity of the appearance of the text and contributed a sense of its literary quality.[20] It also saved paper. Where the practice is irregular, it was probably adopted, as Greg suggested for short speeches, out of expediency. A play may suddenly exhibit or cease to exhibit signs of continuous printing. This may be the result of its being set by a new compositor (or compositors), perhaps in a new printing shop, who favoured or eschewed the practice: Greg argued that this was the case with the Oxford play *The Raging*

*Turk* (1631) (Greg, 447(*a*)). More generally, irregular continuous printing tends to suggest compositorial anxiety about space.

It may occur quite suddenly, as in *The Widow's Tears* (1612), in which 'on K1–2$^v$ the speeches, though prose, are as a rule printed continuously' (Greg, 301(*A*)). On other occasions the practice may suddenly come to an end, as it does in the third quarto of *The Faithful Shepherdess* (1634), where it is abandoned after the foot of G2$^v$ in Act 4 (Greg, 287(*c*)). It is relatively rare for continuous printing at the beginning of a book to be abandoned later, although this occurs in the first quartos of *Michaelmas Term* (1607) and of *'Tis Pity she's a Whore* (1633) (Greg, 244(*a*); Greg, 486(*A*)). It is more common for continuous printing to be marked towards the play's end. For example, Greg noted 'a tendency towards the end to print speeches continuously': see the first quarto of *The Fawn* (1606), *The Ball* (1639), *A New Trick to Cheat the Devil* (1639), *The Night Walker* (1640) and so on (Greg, 230(*a*); Greg, 549(*A*); Greg, 561(*A*); Greg, 574(*a*)). Out of the 600 hundred editions of plays, over seventy betray some evidence of irregular continuous printing. In some of these cases it seems likely the compositor was trying to save space.

When there was an error of some kind in casting off books set by formes, irregular continuous printing would have been one way of dealing with this. Yet, to take a leading case, there is continuous printing in the first quarto of *King Lear* (1608) which was set seriatim. Twenty-five of the play's seventy-nine pages contain continuous printing, yet the quarto has an initial blank and a final blank verso. In other words, it shows both a desire to save space and a willingness to leave pages blank. The last three pages of text contain some fourteen examples of continuous printing, suggesting a decision to avoid using the verso of the final leaf. Ann R. Meyer has argued that inescapable crowding in the quarto and compositorial adaptation on the last page of the inner forme of its final gathering can account for differences between the Quarto and Folio texts in the play's closing moments.[21]

Continuous printing supplied one way of saving space; varying the number of lines to the page, so affecting its depth, was another. Greg did not discuss this practice in his introduction, but he did occasionally mention varying page depths in the entries themselves, although they are not indexed among the 'Notabilia'. Sometimes, as with *Lusty Juventus*, he used page depths to distinguish editions (Greg, 41(*a*)–(*c*)). He also noted additional lines which seem to be the result of proof correction in *Mother Bombie* (1594) and *Much Ado About Nothing* (1600) (Greg, 125(*a*); Greg, 168(*a*), 4.1673). In *2 Henry 4* (1600) two lines were omitted from F4$^v$ in the corrected state of the forme (Greg, 167(*a*)). Altered page depths, with or without changes in type size or fount, may be taken as evidence of shared printing or setting by two or more compositors. Again, the first quarto of *Romeo and Juliet* supplies a familiar example of this. Gatherings B–D contain thirty-two lines to the page, but E–K have thirty-six: the first part of the book was the work of John Danter, the second of Edward Allde. Greg noticed other plays with distinctive differences of page depth between gatherings. For example, in *All Fools* (1605), gatherings G and H have two more lines to a page than elsewhere and are set in a different type. In *Pericles* (1609) there are differences in page depth, type size and running titles between AC–E (37 lines, printed by William White) and BF–I (35 lines, printed by Thomas Creede) (Greg, 219(*A*);[22] Greg, 284(*a*)).

In other cases, sudden changes in page depths may represent attempts to deal with various problems: awkward settings, for example widows or beginning a new act or scene at the very foot of a page, could be avoided; matter could be added or taken away. Changing page depths are most often associated with problems of setting cast-off copy by formes.[23] Towards the end of a book the number of lines to a page might also be increased to save paper. The first two quartos of *Richard 3* (1597, 1598) collate A–M$^4$ with the last leaf blank (M4 blank ?) (Greg, 142(*a*), (*b*)). The third quarto of 1602, which wrongly boasted that it was 'Newly augmented', collates A–L$^4$ M$^2$: the new half sheet eliminated the final blank. Greg pointed out that 'The saving of half a sheet has led to the lengthening of the pages in the last three quires' (Greg, 142(*c*)). Something similar happened with the second quarto of *Eastward Ho* (1605). When first printed the play filled nine sheets; for the second edition it was crammed into eight. Towards its end the tendency to continuous printing increased and as many as forty-two lines were set to a page (Greg, 217(*a*), (*b*)). In both these cases the desire to save paper is fairly clear. The second quarto of *Romeo and Juliet* (1599) presents a paradox. Once again, Greg noted that some of the pages lengthen towards the end, although the verso of the second leaf of the last half sheet is blank. In other words it seemed better to set pages more deeply than to have letterpress on the book's final verso.

Greg recorded at least another nine first quartos of plays in which the page depth increases in the last few gatherings: there are more which he omitted to mention.[24] Some of these books lengthen their pages even when they make use of a final half sheet, whereas a whole final sheet would have made such lengthening unnecessary. Two of these nine, *Thierry and Theodoret* (1621) and *The Picture* (1630), begin with initial blanks: *The Picture* ends with a half sheet (Greg, 368(*a*); Greg, 436(*A*)). In *The Weakest Goeth to the Wall* (1600), which contains some marked divisions between sheets – A–E have thirty-six lines, F has thirty-five with a blank space at the foot of F4$^v$ and G–I has thirty-seven lines – the play's first leaf and the verso of its last leaf are blank (A1 blank ?) (Greg, 171(*a*)).

If these notes have any value I hope it will be to encourage further thought about the typography and physical form of printed plays. The central puzzle remains that there is conflicting evidence in their printing about the need to be sparing in the use of paper, the single most expensive item which went into their production. The presence of such quantities of blank leaves might also suggest that printed plays were not always considered to be entirely ephemeral items.

## NOTES

1  For the date of this edition, see Adrian Weiss, 'Watermark Evidence and Inference: New Style Dates of Edmund Spenser's *Complaints* and *Daphnaida*', *Studies in Bibliography*, 52 (1999), 129–54, p. 140.

2  Peter W.M. Blayney, 'The Publication of Playbooks' in *A New History of Early English Drama*, ed. John D. Cox and David Scott Kastan (New York, 1997), 383–422 at 408–9.

3  D.F. McKenzie, review of *Studies in Bibliography*, 15 (1962), in *Library*, 5/16 (1961), 65–8 at 66; he was referring to Robert K. Turner Jr.'s 'The Printing of Beaumont and Fletcher's *The Maid's Tragedy* Q1 (1619)', *Studies in Bibliography*, 13 pp. 199–220, in particular at 204.

4  Blayney, 'The Publication of Playbooks', 405.

5  *Ibid.*, 406–7; neither D.F. McKenzie, *The Cambridge University Press 1696–1712*, 2 vols (Cambridge, 1966), 1.72, Blayney's source for this argument, nor Philip Gaskell, *A New Introduction to Bibliography* (Oxford, 1972), discusses exactly whether compositors were paid for blanks. Payment by actual number of ens set seems not to have been introduced until the earlier part of the eighteenth century, see Gaskell, *A New Introduction to Bibliography*, 54–5, but cf. 173.

6  *OED* fat B. *sb.*[2] 5b.

7  Peter W.M. Blayney, *The Texts of 'King Lear' and their Origins*, vol. 1: *Nicholas Okes and the First Quarto* (Cambridge, 1982), 96.

8  Ronald B. McKerrow, *An Introduction to Bibliography* (Oxford, 1927), 123.

9  Cf. the slightly more complicated case of the Folger copy of *The Trial of Chivalry* (1605), Greg, 210(A1), reported in the corrections, 4.1676.

10  Gaskell, *A New Introduction to Bibliography*, 52.

11  *The Texts of 'King Lear'*, 378.

12  McKerrow, *An Introduction to Bibliography*, 123.

13  George Watson Cole, 'Blank Leaves or Alternative Titles', *Library*, 4/2 (1921–2), 272–4; cf. Fredson Bowers, *Principles of Bibliographical Description* (Princeton, NJ, 1949), 56–7; the books are *STC* 23898 and 23898a.

14  *Principles of Bibliographical Description*, 118.

15  Cf. Greg, 4.lxiii and Bowers, *Principles of Bibliographical Description*, 252. This seems to have been an exclusively English habit, see R.A. Sayce, *Compositorial Practices and the Localization of Printed Books 1530–1800: A Reprint with Addenda and Corrigenda*, Oxford Bibliographical Society, Occasional Publication 13 (1979), 17; it does not occur among the undoubtedly surreptitious books described by Denis B. Woodfield, *Surreptitious Printing in England 1550–1640* (New York, 1973).

16  See Laurie E. Maguire, 'The Printer and Date of Q4 of *A Looking Glass for London and England*', *Studies in Bibliography*, 52 (1999), 155–60.

17  Laurie Maguire, *Shakespearean Suspect Texts: The 'Bad' Quartos and their Contexts* (Cambridge, 1996), 280.

18  *Mechanick Exercises on the Whole Art of Printing*, ed. Herbert Davis and Harry Carter, 2nd edition (Oxford, 1962), 203, 343.

19  The play is included among the regularly continuously printed plays in the 'Notabilia'; the description in the main entry for it does not notice the practice.

20 See Zachary Lesser's discussion of the subject, 'Walter Burre's *The Knight of the Burning Pestle*', *English Literary Renaissance*, 29 (1999), 22–43.

21 'Shakespeare's Art and the Texts of *King Lear*', *Studies in Bibliography*, 47 (1994), 128–46; cf. *King Lear*, ed. R.A. Foakes, The Arden Shakespeare Third Series (1997), 122. Nevertheless the compositor of that final page of text in Q was prepared to sacrifice three lines to a terminal '*FINIS*'.

22 Cf. G. Blakemore Evans in *The Plays of George Chapman: The Comedies*, ed. Allan Holaday (Urbana, Ill., 1970), 228–9.

23 See, for example, William H. Bond, 'Casting Off Copy by Elizabethan Printers: A Theory', *Papers of the Bibliographical Society of America*, 42 (1948), 281–91, David J. Shaw, 'Setting by Formes in Some Early Parisian Greek Books', in *Book Production and Letters in the Western European Renaissance: Essays in Honour of Conor Fahy*, ed. Anna Laura Lepschy, John Took and Dennis E. Rhodes (London, 1986), 284–90.

24 See, for example, George R. Price, 'The Authorship and the Bibliography of *The Revenger's Tragedy*', *Library*, 5/15 (1960), 262–77, at 272.

# PART II

---

# EDITING AND
# FEMINISM

# 5

## 'TO FOSTER IS NOT ALWAYS TO PRESERVE': FEMINIST INFLECTIONS IN EDITING *PERICLES*

### *Suzanne Gossett*

In *Pericles* 4.3, a horrified Cleon asks his wife how she will account for the disappearance of Marina. Q1, 1609, the only undisputed source we have for the play,[1] prints (in prose) 'what canst thou say when noble *Pericles* shall demaund his child?' and Dionyza responds, 'That shee is dead. Nurses are not the fates to foster it, not euer to preserue, she dide at night, I'll say so' (G2r; 4.3.12–16).[2]

Proposed emendations to these lines go back to Q4, 1619, which read, 'Nurses are not the fates to foster it, nor euer to preserue'. In 1969 J.C. Maxwell reported marginalia by the nineteenth-century scholar H.H. Vaughan.[3] Vaughan's suggestion, 'That she is dead. Nurses are not the fates. To foster is not ever to preserve. She died at night, etc.,' assumes compositorial misreading of 'is' as 'it' and misplaced punctuation. The revision is coherent, ironically apposite to Dionzya's actions, and based on the facts and dangers of Jacobean childrearing and wet nursing. As emended the line picks up the repartee of the preceding brothel scene, where Boult twits the Bawd about her 'bringing up of poor bastards' and their fate in the brothel, where she has 'brought them down again' (4.2.13–15) – a special case of 'to foster is not ever to preserve.'

Given a single, deeply damaged text, discrepant sources or para-texts, and an early editorial history marked most notably by the Folio's outright rejection, an editor of *Pericles* is well advised to remember Dionzya's line, as emended, of course, by Vaughan. 'To foster is not ever to preserve' may mean that one does most for one's text by not preserving it ever, perpetually, (*OED* 1), nor on all occasions (*OED* 2), in its original form; less optimistically, like Dionyza it may suggest that despite attempts to restore and support the text, we must occasionally accept frustrating failures. Recent editorial history of the play is nicely exemplified by discrepant treatments of this crux. The Oxford 'reconstructed' text, edited by Gary Taylor and MacDonald P. Jackson, draws extensively on George Wilkins's 1608 novella, *The Painfull Adventures of Pericles Prince of Tyre*. The reconstruction is freely emended and claims to be closer than Q to the play's 'state when it left the hands of its author(s)'.[4] The New Cambridge edition is almost exactly the reverse. Challenging the 'received view of the 1609 quarto as essentially corrupt', unconvinced by theories of collaboration, the editors, Doreen DelVecchio and Antony Hammond, try to 'trust the text'. The result 'differs in hundreds of readings from other editions', primarily by rejecting emendations that go back to Malone.[5]

In the case of 4.3.14–15 the two editions run true to form. Cambridge refuses to emend, claiming that 'Most editors find "foster it" a difficult problem because there is no obvious antecedent for "it", but the pronoun here is the object of the verb used indefinitely'. They ignore the associated difficulties of 'Not ever to preserve'. Their parallel, *King Lear* 4.1.55, 'I cannot daub it further', demonstrates the inadequacy of offering an apparently grammatical explanation when an entire phrase rather than one element requires elucidation. Oxford, on the other hand, not only includes Vaughan's emendation but claims it for Taylor;[6] it is possible that he found it independently.

Both editions are weakest when they seem most definite. DelVecchio and Hammond argue primarily by analogy to Q1 *Lear* for their assertion that Q *Pericles* is based on foul papers. As Eric Rasmussen objects, they do not support this 'revolutionary conclusion' by 'detailed consideration of the hundreds of textual anomalies in the Quarto text'.[7] The one example they do offer adopts an unconvincing emendation from Sisson in a case where confusion seems to lie deeper than rough handwriting. In fact, to explain the differences between the two halves of the play they are ultimately driven to hypothesize that the first half is 'transcribed from the foul papers', the second half being 'much fouler'.[8] Given the 'fierce particularities' of extant dramatic manuscripts, Paul Werstine has deconstructed the concept of 'foul papers' as essentially metaphysical.[9] Most important, many of Cambridge's unemended lines continue to make no sense despite their contorted explanations.

Oxford's text, occasionally brilliant, is also unjustifiably assured. Apparently unwilling to accept the 'radical indeterminacy of identifying what kind of manuscript may lie behind a printed dramatic text' or analytical bibliography's inability therefore to 'isolate and quarantine the agents of transmission from the authentic/authorial Shakespearean text',[10] Taylor theorizes the specifics of the underlying *Pericles* manuscript. He names the actor–characters who reconstructed and reported this imperfect text and accounts for the correctness of the Gower passages by proposing that (1) the boy actor who played Marina and was responsible for the reconstruction, probably with a hired man, was apprenticed to the Gower actor and (2) the boy took – stole seems the right word – the Gower part.[11] Taylor belongs to a distinguished tradition: Kenneth Muir's theory about differences between Wilkins's novel and Q concluded with Wilkins inexplicably obtaining the rejected 'original sheets' for the Lysimachus–Marina scenes.[12]

Cambridge, Oxford and Muir are driven to hypothetical, unprovable and even unlikely conclusions to account for details that don't fit their overarching theories. The key terms for editing *Pericles* are indeterminacy, uncertainty, irresolvability;[13] the text demands a post-modern, post-structuralist approach. Each decision is local; a unified field theory is not possible. Fortunately, much recent textual scholarship has ceased attempting to attain absolute knowledge and 'ideal texts'. Peter Shillingsburg warns that editors must 'acknowledge that there are no objective procedures for editing texts and that the texts they produce are influenced by their critically based orientations and insights'.[14]

Barbara Mowat hypothesizes a 'large flow of manuscript copies of Shakespeare's plays' with 'idiosyncrasies that would inevitably have made their way into the printed copies'.[15] M.J. Kidnie has urged editors to resist supplementing stage directions, instead 'asking readers to interact with the dramatic text as necessarily unfixed and unstable'.[16]

While feminist-inflected editing must concede the elusiveness of *Pericles*, feminist 'orientations and insights' may nevertheless clarify the text. For example, inserted directions may look unnecessary, even mistaken. At 3.1.27 Cambridge directs without explanation that Lychorida exit after giving the child to Pericles, only to enter again with sailors carrying Thaisa at 'Here she lies, sir' (55). Presumably DelVecchio and Hammond think it inappropriate that a mere nurse or midwife be present as Pericles welcomes his infant. However, at 11 Pericles has addressed Lucina (in Steevens's famous emendation) as 'midwife gentle', and Tudor and Stuart midwives were recognized 'agents of respectability and upholders of sexual propriety. . . . dutiful, respectable, and well-appreciated members of their local community, leaders in the sisterhood of women'.[17] There is no reason why Lychorida cannot remain through Pericles's subsequent speeches and 'discover' the body in any of a number of ways at 'Here she lies'. Oxford, while keeping Lychorida on, adds a direction for Pericles to hand the infant back to her at this point because it would be 'awkward' for him 'to hold the baby during his emotional speech' to the apparently dead Thaisa.[18] Do they assume a man cannot emote with a baby in his arms? Pericles has received the infant from Lychorida in a nightmare version of the midwife's normal presentation. Rather than the formulaic, 'Father, see there is your child, God give you much joy with it, or take it speedily to his bliss',[19] he has been told to 'Take in your arms this piece / Of your dead queen' (17–18). Dramatic pathos is increased if he clutches the baby while speaking.

A number of complex cruces yield at least in part to feminist-inflected editing. For the first, textual fostering requires not preserving. In 2.1 Pericles, who 'would be son to great Antiochus' (1.1.27), finally mentions his own father. Examining the rusty

armour pulled in by the fishermen, Pericles recalls his dying
father's charge:

> Keepe it my *Perycles*, it hath been a Shield
> Twixt me and death, and poynted to this brayse,
> For that it saued me, keepe it in like necessitie:
> The which the Gods protect thee, Fame may defend thee.
>
> (C3v; 2.1.122–5)

Malone emended the last two lines to read:

> For that it saved me, keep it; in like necessity,
> The which the gods protect thee from! 'T may defend thee.[20]

All subsequent editors have accepted the adjustments to
punctuation. Staunton further modified 125 into the optative,
'may't defend thee', which is slightly preferable as the dying man's
speech is a series of imperatives (*keep it ... keep it ... may't*).[21]
Cambridge, retaining the original, reveal the weakness of their
procedure in their gloss, which slips in the crucial 'from' they
withhold from the text: 'This phrase needs explication, or
emendation. It could be freely paraphrased as: "from which
danger may the gods protect you, and your fame ... defend you."'
However, Pericles' father does not envision him saved by an
abstract fame, like a dead war hero, but concretely by the family
armour, the 'coat of worth' (132) with its 'brace'. Neither text nor
hero is fostered by Cambridge's rigidity.

In the next instances the text should be preserved. The startled
Marina asks her attacker, 'Why will you kill me?' Informed by
Leonine, 'To satisfie my Ladie', she muses, 'Why would shee haue
mee kild now? as I can remember by my troth, I neuer did her
hurt in all my life' (F3r; 4.1.69–70). Most editors since Malone
alter Q's punctuation to 'Why would she have me killed? Now, as
I can remember ...', so that Marina inquires about Dionyza's
motivation rather than expressing surprise at the change in the
woman who has fostered her for fourteen years. Yet Gower has
explained Dionyza's hostility as 'envy rare' developed as her
newly-adolescent daughter suffers by comparison (4.0.35–40).
The alteration reduces 'now' to a meaningless interjection, a

'discourse marker',[22] instead of a precise adverb of time; it eliminates one of the few references to Marina's fostering in a continuous 'family'; it weakens the connection to Dionyza's self-justification in 4.3.

Similarly, no change is necessary as Cerimon, looking at Thaisa's body, observes,

> Death may vsurpe on Nature many howers, and yet
> The fire of life kindle againe the ore-prest spirits:
> I heard of an *Egiptian* that had 9. howers lien dead,
> Who was by good applyaunce recouered.

(E4r; 3.2.82–6)

Versifying Wilkins, Schanzer and Edwards alter this to

> I have read
> Of some Egyptians who after four hours' death
> Have raised impoverished bodies, like to this,
> Unto their former health.

Schanzer claims that Q is 'manifestly corrupt', Edwards that Wilkins seems 'more authentic'.[23] To adapt from Wilkins is to shift attention from Thaisa to Cerimon. The revisionists apparently assume the 'Egiptian' is male. Yet the passage picks up the play's central concern with women who die and are revived. Thaisa is presumably in the kind of 'Syncope or swounding' from which Edward Jordan describes young women suffering in *Suffocation of the Mother* (1603): 'all the faculties of the body fayling, it self lying like a dead corpse three or four houres together, and sometimes two or three whole dayes without sense, motion, breath, heate, or any signe of life at all.' In *Microcosmographia: a Description of the Body of Man* (1615) Helkiah Crooke warns that 'it is impossible almost to perceiue whether such women do yet liue or no, and doubtlesse many are buried in such fits (for they will last sometimes 24. houres or more, and the bodies growe colde and rigid like dead carkasses) who would recouer if space were giuen'.[24] Gail Paster's work on the coldness of women suggests there is no need to redirect the passage.

What might be entitled 'the shadow of sisterhood' in the plot begins with a notorious crux. As he consigns baby Marina to Dionyza, Pericles swears:

> till she be maried,
> Madame, by bright *Diana,* whom we honour,
> All vnsisterd shall this heyre of mine remayne,
> Though I shew will in't.

(E4v; 3.3.28–31)

In 1793 Steevens emended to 'unscissored shall this hair of mine remain'; many editors adopt Malone's further modification, 'though I show ill in it'. Considering that at Diana's altar Pericles announces the imminent marriage of his daughter and promises that

> now this ornament
> Makes me look dismal will I clip to form,
> And what this fourteen years no razor touched,
> To grace thy marriage day I'll beautify

(5.3.74–7)

the emendation is logical. The apparently repetitive vow Pericles makes upon learning of Marina's 'death', 'He swears / Never to wash his face nor cut his hairs' (4.4.27–8), occurs only 'three months' (5.1.22) before he discovers the presumably fourteen-year-old Marina in Mytilene. The emendation is supported by Twine and by Wilkins, who has Pericles vow 'solemnely by othe to himselfe, his head should grow uncisserd, his beard untrimmed, himselfe in all uncomely. ... till he had married his daughter at ripe years'.[25] 'Ill' looks follow from 'unscissored' hair. Dyce suggested that 'will' arose 'merely from the original compositor having repeated the w';[26] it also could have arisen from mishearing by the reporter, or even from an error in expansion of shorthand notes.[27] In the theatre the words would be indistinguishable.

Despite the neat solution there are reasons to suspect deeper corruption here. Obviously, if the emendation is correct the second vow reiterates the first unnecessarily. Thus it is tempting to think that the two vows, one after the wife's death and one

after the daughter's, were originally distinguished. Did Pericles
swear the first time, 'willfully', that his daughter would remain his
only heir, *all* 'unsistered' because like Leontes he would refuse to
remarry, and only the second time to disregard his appearance, to
remain unwashed, unshorn and in sackcloth?[28] This was Lillo's
solution as early as *Marina* (1738). The play, unlike Twine and
Wilkins, eliminates the (male) child born to Pericles and Thaisa
after their reunion, but it has an overt interest in dynastic
continuity, beginning in Antioch where Pericles seeks a wife
'From whence an issue I might propagate' (1.2.71).

Editors have methodically discounted the play's persistent but
buried concern with sisterhood and especially with Philoten, who

> Would euer with *Marina* bee.
> Beet when they weaude the sleded silke,
> With fingers long, small, white as milke,
> Or when she would with sharpe needle wound,
> The Cambricke which she made more sound
> By hurting it or when too'th Lute
> She sung, and made the night bed mute,
> That still records with mone, or when
> She would with rich and constant pen,
> Vaile to her Mistresse *Dian* still,
> This *Phyloten* contends in skill
> With absolute *Marina.*

(F1v; 4.0.20–31)

Since Malone editors have emended to make Marina – 'she', not
'they' – the one who weaves with long white fingers. For Malone,
'to have praised even the hands of Philoten would have been
inconsistent with the general scheme of the present chorus';[29]
'she' in 21 parallels 23 and 26. But removing the image of the two
girls weaving together alters the relationship. In 5.0.5–8 Gower
again praises Marina's needlework, whose 'art sisters the natural
roses' – *OED*'s earliest citation of 'sister' as a verb. The
association of 'sisters' vows', needles and embroidery, and singing
recalls *A Midsummer Night's Dream* 3.2.204–17, where the quasi-
identity of young girls is similarly destroyed by competition for

men. Emilia's description of her relation to Flavina in *The Two
Noble Kinsmen* belongs to a similarly edenic past; it concludes
that 'true love 'tween maid and maid may be / More than in sex
dividual' (1.3.81–2). The surviving text of *Pericles* submerges the
relation of Marina and Philoten, who dies along with her parents
but whose guilt is never demonstrated. A production at Ashland,
Oregon in 1999 mutely stressed 'would ever with Marina be'
rather than 'contends'. Philoten, eavesdropping, burst into tears
as her mother complacently tells Cleon that 'to foster is not ever
to preserve'. Neither 'all unsistered' nor 'all unscissored' is merely
or clearly an error; an editor must print one, but either could be
justified.[30]

Issues of uncertainty and feminist reading intersect in a
difficult editorial dilemma, whether to alter 4.5 (traditionally 4.6;
Oxford Scene 19). Whereas sometimes Q's text seems confused or
nonsensical, its version of the interview between Marina and
Lysimachus is coherent. Lysimachus's suggestion that his sin was
merely hypothetical, 'Had I brought hither a corrupted mind /
Thy speech had altered it' (107–8) and his subsequent insistence
that 'I came with no ill intent' (113), play easily as the awkward
and embarrassed lies of a young man who expected to find the
usual false *virginities* (26) he jocularly calls for on entering. He
doesn't believe the Bawd's claim that the new girl was 'never
plucked yet' (45–6), casually begins conversation with Marina by
asking how long she has been at her 'trade', but backtracks to
'mendacious revisionism'[31] as he realizes what kind of a woman
he has encountered. Demands to modify the scene arise because
Marina's brief lines seem inadequate to bring about the
governor's conversion, and alteration is apparently supported
by the existence of more extensive speeches for Marina and
different attitudes for Lysimachus in Wilkins's *Painfull Adventures.*

To follow Wilkins is to change both characters. By virtue of her
longer speeches Marina appears more assertive, more 'feminist'.
Rather than encountering her casually, Lysimachus glimpses
Marina from his window and determines that 'since shee must
fall, it were farre more fitter, into his owne armes, ... than into
the hote imbracements of many'; later he confesses that 'I hither

came with thoughtes intemperate, foule and deformed, the which your paines so well have laved, that they are now white'.[32]

There are four possible bases – frequently conflated – on which one could decide to incorporate material from Wilkins: playability; theories about the text or its transmission; the emotional logic of the scene; and attitudes towards the social content. Theatres often expand the encounter. When the Oxford editors disagreed, Taylor arguing that Q is 'theatrically intelligible' but Jackson preferring Wilkins's outline, they resolved on expansion because of 'a long-standing tradition in the modern theatre', coupled with the immediate demands of the Stratford, Ontario company.[33] Nevertheless, the criteria for theatrical modifications, like Shillingsburg's for editors, are always ultimately aesthetic. David Thacker at the RSC used different bits of Wilkins than does Oxford.[34]

Theories of transmission that assume Wilkins's novella is a better report than Q and contains 'verse fossils' of a superior original permit, though they do not require, insertions. Philip Edwards argued that Wilkins gave the correct version of the scene, which the reporter of Q had misunderstood. For Edwards, if Q's treatment of Lysimachus were correct the young man would have to be a 'tester', like the Duke in *Measure for Measure*. Instead, 'Wilkins is basically correct in reporting a humbled and ashamed Lysimachus confessing his errors. ... In preserving the apologia and omitting the confession, Q has arguably altered the balance of the play'. This judgement, however, also reveals itself as essentially aesthetic. In his edition Edwards did not incorporate material from Wilkins in 4.5, but he did insert 'A straggling Theseus born we know not where' in 2.5. as 'too good to lose'.[35]

The Oxford editors, believing Wilkins to be a collaborator as well as often a better reporter than the person(s) responsible for Q, import three substantial passages into 4.5. This reconstruction contradicts Taylor's textual theories – if Marina were the reporter, why would she misreport this key scene? It violates Oxford's guidelines, which called for making 'much more' use of Wilkins in his share of the play, Acts 1 and 2 or Scenes 1–9.[36] It is based on questionable assumptions about conditions of dramatic

production and about early modern social attitudes. Nevertheless, it is appealing.

To resolve the 'impasse' between the conviction that Wilkins
'better represents Shakespeare's intentions' and the 'implausibility
of any hypothesis which would explain Q's accidental omission
and alteration of this material', Taylor hypothesized a Master of
the Revels 'particularly sensitive to allusions to the promiscuity
of courtiers', citing plays, including *The Second Maiden's Tragedy*
(1611) and *Eastward Ho* (1605), in which 'passages containing
such material were censored'.[37] However, contemporary King's
Men's plays such as *Measure for Measure* (1604), *Philaster*
(1608–10) and *The Maid's Tragedy* (1610–11) contain equally
lubricious courtiers and men in authority.[38] *Eastward Ho* invited
royal wrath because of its satirical take on the Scots, and both
Richard Dutton and Janet Clare treat *The Second Maiden's
Tragedy* as an exceptional case, where censorship was invited by
the depiction of regicide and by parallels with the Frances Howard
scandal. Furthermore, Buc began licensing (and censoring)
printed plays after 1607, Tilney continued licensing (and
censoring) performances until 1610, creating more uncertainty:
who would have censored the 1608/9 *Pericles*?[39] Oxford suggests
that an anomalous 'Exit' direction in *The Two Noble Kinsmen* may
indicate that the Jailor's Daughter's 'denunciation of adulterous
courtiers and proud ladies' was intended to be cut;[40] instead her
speech, remaining in the text, actually weakens their hypothesis.
Dutton and Clare disagree about the oppressiveness of dramatic
censorship, but even she concludes that 'There are no consistent
political, moral or cultural criteria to be discerned'.[41]

Implicit in discomfort with Q's version of 4.5. is an objection
to the double standard that silently accepts Lysimachus's
behaviour and the pure heroine's apparently contented betrothal
to a man who frequents brothels. Yet both are consistent with
early modern sexual ideology. In Marston's *Dutch Courtesan*
(1605) Freevill is prepared to 'resign' the courtesan he has been
maintaining because he is about to marry the pure Beatrice, who
is happy to have him. The play implicitly supports Freevill's
pragmatic position: 'I would have married men love the stews as

Englishmen love the Low Countries: wish war should be maintained there lest it should come home to their own doors' (1.1.65–8).[42] In *Philaster* the Spanish prince Pharamond's unsuitability as a husband for princess Arathusa is demonstrated by signs that he will be unable to make the required transition from bachelor freedom to married fidelity. While on an official visit to meet his intended, the prince finds that 'the constitution of my body will never hold out till the wedding', and he is caught with the court's light lady in his chamber.[43] In a sinister variant, Ilford, in Wilkins's *Miseries of inforst Mariage*, learning of his father's death, announces his intention 'shortly to goe to Church, and from thence do faithfull seruice to one woman'. His friends object, 'Its impossible, for thou hast bin a whoremayster this seauen yeare', but Ilford replies, 'Tis no matter, I will now marry, And to som honest woman to, and so from hence her vertues shall be a countenance to my vices'.[44] Surely Lysimachus is less scandalous than Leontes and Posthumus, who win back wives they have seriously injured, or Bertram and Angelo, who attempt seduction and lie to their sovereigns.

What should a feminist editor do with 4.5? From an 'exclusively political perspective' Valerie Wayne prefers the reconstruction because 'it presents a more articulate Marina. ... Rather than the silent or whimpering symbol of virginity's charm that an earlier generation of critics celebrated her for being, she becomes an important agent in the play's critique of those in power'. Wayne points out that all editing carries 'a politics'; however, 'when critics and editors challenge existing hierarchies, our politics become more visible'. For 4.5. Wayne would actually prefer a stronger challenge than Oxford's. Objecting to their imposition of a series of stage directions based on Wilkins, '*weeps*', '*kneeling*', '*He lifts her up with his hands*', '*He wipes the wet from her eyes*', she reveals the subjectivity of all editorial intervention by asking, hypothetically, 'Is it possible to adapt Marina's resistance in Wilkins without also importing her tears and abjection?'[45]

The quandary articulated by Wayne reveals the essential problem of editing *Pericles*: all our commitments, including our sexual politics, may have textual consequences. Steevens objected to Marina's denunciation of Boult after Lysimachus leaves, especially the lines 'Thou art the damned doorkeeper to every / Coistrel that comes inquiring for his Tib' (4.5.168–9), as 'too knowing in the impurities of a brothel'.[46] Anne Barton complains that the passage shows 'uncharacteristic venom and masculinity' and contrasts with Marina's apparent inability to understand the Bawd's professional instructions at 4.2.116–20.[47] Oxford, on the other hand, omits two later lines from the same speech, 'O that the gods / Would safely deliver me from this place!' (181–2), because the invocation disrupts the logic of Marina's argument. Yet both the speech and the interruption are justifiable. Marina has learned quite a lot about the brothel between 4.2 and 4.5. She does not 'commit willingly', but her strategy with Lysimachus has precisely followed the Bawd's advice: 'To weep that you live as ye do makes pity in your lovers. Seldom but that pity begets you a good opinion, and that opinion a mere profit' (4.2.111–14). Equally understandably, under intense stress, she breaks her train of thought to pray for assistance. Oxford removes a sign of weakness; Steevens and Barton would remove one of strength.

Accepting indeterminacy, the Arden 3 *Pericles* does not massively reconstruct 4.5. It is ultimately impossible to know whether Wilkins accurately reports the original text, now surviving only in a distorted form, or whether he had second thoughts as he wrote it up; whether cuts were introduced to make the text fast paced and playable;[48] or whether 4.5. is a poor report, either by a group of players recording a performed 'minimal text' or by a venal player.[49] Perhaps 4.5. is merely 'typical of Shakespeare's frequent carelessness about details'.[50] Or perhaps *Pericles*' mysterious appeal, its consistent success on the stage, is tied to its very indefiniteness, an openness that has invited differing solutions, a Marina strong or overwhelmed, a Lysimachus loving or infected with the pox,[51] a Pericles saintly or derelict, a wife and daughter both dead and alive. The play begins with a riddle, and it remains one. All a feminist editor can hope, in the end, is that offering a well-fostered child will preserve it, if not ever, at least until the next edition.[52]

## Notes

1  All subsequent quartos are derived from Q1. Taylor and Jackson treat George
   Wilkins's *The Painfull Adventures of Pericles Prince of Tyre* (1608) as a 'reported
   text' of the play, but they admit it is 'of variable accuracy and value' (Stanley Wells
   and Gary Taylor, *William Shakespeare: A Textual Companion* 1987, 557). *Painfull
   Adventures* is reproduced in Geoffrey Bullough, *Narrative and Dramatic Sources of
   Shakespeare*, vol. 6 (1966), 492–546. For the evidence for attributing *Pericles* 1–2
   to George Wilkins, persuasively developed in the work of David Lake, M.A.W.
   Smith and MacDonald P. Jackson, see the Introduction to my Arden 3 edition,
   forthcoming.

2  Line numbers and modernized citations are from the forthcoming Arden 3
   edition.

3  J.C. Maxwell (ed.), *Pericles*, rev. ed. (Cambridge, 1969).

4  *Textual Companion*, 559.

5  Doreen DelVecchio and Antony Hammond (eds), *Pericles, Prince of Tyre*
   (Cambridge, 1998), vii.

6  *Textual Companion*, 578.

7  'The Year's Contributions to Shakespeare Studies: Editions and Textual Studies',
   *Shakespeare Survey 52* (1999), 316.

8  DelVecchio and Hammond, 206–8.

9  See 'Editing after the End of Editing', *Shakespeare Studies* 24 (1996), 47–54.

10  Paul Werstine, 'Plays in Manuscript', in *A New History of Early English Drama*, ed.
    John D. Cox and David Scott Kastan (New York, 1997), 492; W. Speed Hill,
    'Where are the Bibliographers of Yesteryear?' in *Problems of Editing*, ed. Christa
    Jansohn (Tübingen, 1999), 112.

11  Gary Taylor, 'The Transmission of *Pericles*', *PBSA* 80 (1986), 193–217.

12  Kenneth Muir, *Shakespeare as Collaborator* (1960), 74.

13  More negatively, Walter Cohen calls the textual problems 'insuperable' in his
    introduction to the Oxford text for the *Norton Shakespeare*.

14  Peter L. Shillingsburg, *Scholarly Editing in the Computer Age* (Athens, Ga., 1986),
    93.

15  Barbara Mowat, 'The Problem of Shakespeare's Text(s)', in *Textual Formations and
    Reformations,* ed. Laurie E. Maguire and Thomas L. Berger (Newark, Del., 1998),
    136.

16  Margaret Jane Kidnie, 'Text, Performance, and the Editors: Staging Shakespeare's
    Drama', *SQ* 51 (2000), 470.

17  David Cressy, *Birth, Marriage & Death: Ritual, Religion and the Life-Cycle in Tudor
    and Stuart England* (Oxford, 1997), 60.

18  *Textual Companion*, 572.

19  Cressy, 62.

20  F.D. Hoeniger (ed.), *Pericles* (Arden, 1963), has 'The which the gods protect thee from, may defend thee!' He cites Pericles's earlier line to the fishermen, 'May see the sea hath cast upon your coast' (2.1.55), and notes that '*may* without pronoun was common usage in Shakespeare's day'. It is more likely that the earlier syncopation results either from Pericles's breathlessness or from transmission problems beginning in the immediately preceding speech.

21  Howard Staunton (ed.), *Plays*. 3 vols (1858–60).

22  Norman F. Blake, 'Pragmatics and the Editing of Shakespeare', in *Problems of Editing*, ed. Christa Jansohn (Tübingen, 1999), 113.

23  Ernest Schanzer (ed.), *Pericles* (New York, 1988), xxiii; Philip Edwards (ed.), *Pericles* (London, 1976), 198.

24  Cited Gail Paster, 'The Unbearable Coldness of Female Being: Women's Imperfection and the Humoral Economy', *ELR* 28 (1998), 421 and note 17.

25  Bullough, 524.

26  Alexander Dyce (ed.), *The Works of William Shakespeare*, 2nd edition, vol. 8 (1866), 95.

27  Adele Davidson, 'Shakespeare and Stenography Reconsidered', *AEB*, ns 6 (1992), 87.

28  On the basis of scansion editors since Malone have moved *all* to accompany *honour*. Hammond and DelVecchio retain the unemended lines but treat the second vow as 'ironically' recalling the first (145).

29  Edmund Malone, *Supplement to the Edition of Shakespeare's Plays*, vol. 2 (London, 1780), 94.

30  I discuss this point further in 'You not your child well loving: text and family structure in *Pericles*', in the Blackwell *Companion to Shakespeare, Volume IV: The Poems, Problem Comedies, Late Plays* (Oxford, forthcoming).

31  Simon Palfrey, 'Lodged with the sign: *Pericles*' brothel', unpublished paper, Shakespeare Association of America (1999), 11.

32  Bullough, 533, 536.

33  *Textual Companion*, 558–9.

34  Roger Warren, *Staging Shakespeare's Late Plays* (Oxford, 1990), 226–7.

35  Edwards, *Pericles*, 182–3, 162.

36  *Textual Companion*, 558.

37  *Textual Companion*, 559.

38  Richard Dutton cites other plays, for example Webster's, that 'revolve around the politically and sexually corrupt standards of the court': *Mastering the Revels: The Regulation and Censorship of English Renaissance Drama* (London, 1991), 197.

39 See Richard Dutton's chapter on censorship in John Cox and David Kastan, *A New History of Early English Drama* (New York, 1997), especially 302–3.

40 *Textual Companion*, 627.

41 Janet Clare, *'Art Made Tongue-Tied by Authority': Elizabethan and Jacobean Dramatic Censorship* (Manchester, 1990), 211; cf. Dutton, *Mastering the Revels*, 248.

42 John Marston, *The Dutch Courtesan*, ed. David Crane (London, 1997), 10. Witgood, in Middleton's *A Trick to Catch the Old One*, similarly leaves his courtesan to marry the virginal Joyce.

43 Robert K. Turner (ed.), *Philaster*, in *The Dramatic Works in the Beaumont and Fletcher Canon*, ed. Fredson Bowers, vol. 1 (Cambridge, 1966), 416.

44 George Wilkins, *The Miseries of Enforced Marriage*, ed. Glenn H. Blayney (Oxford, 1963), ll. 1667–79.

45 Valerie Wayne, 'The Sexual Politics of Textual Transmission', in *Textual Formations and Reformations*, ed. Laurie E. Maguire and Thomas L. Berger (Newark, N.J., 1998), 197; also Valerie Wayne, 'Political and Textual Corruption in *Pericles*', unpublished paper, Shakespeare Association of America (1999), *passim*.

46 Samuel Johnson and George Steevens, *The Plays of William Shakespeare*, 4th edition, vol. 13 (London, 1793), 567.

47 Anne Barton, *Essays, Mainly Shakespearean* (Cambridge, 1994), 168.

48 See Kathleen Irace, *Reforming the Bad Quartos: Performance and Provenance of Six Shakespearean First Editions* (Newark, Del., 1994).

49 Andrew Gurr, 'Maximal and Minimal Texts: Shakespeare versus the Globe', *Shakespeare Survey* 52 (1999), 85; Gary Taylor, 'Transmission'.

50 Marco Mincoff, *Things Supernatural and Causeless: Shakespearean Romance* (Newark, Del., 1992), 31.

51 Margaret Healy, 'Pericles and the Pox,' in *Shakespeare's Late Plays: New Readings*, ed. Jennifer Richards and James Knowles (Edinburgh, 1999), 97.

52 Audiences at the Folger Shakespeare Institute, the Harvard Humanities Institute, and the Columbia Shakespeare Seminar responded generously to versions of this material. I would like to thank particularly Peter Blayney, Paul Werstine, Leslie Thomson and Valerie Wayne for talking through the issues with me.

# 6

## EDITING DESDEMONA

*Lois Potter*

'My story being done,' says Othello, describing his courtship of Desdemona, 'She gave me for my pains a world of sighs' (1.3.159–60). That Desdemona should sigh rather than speak seems right: this is the Desdemona known to Brabantio, 'a maiden never bold' (1.3.95), and it is also the Desdemona traditionally known to most theatre-goers. In fact, however, she sighs only in the 1622 Quarto of *Othello*. In the Folio of 1623, Othello still remembers her as silent, but now he claims to have received 'a world of kisses'. What a difference a year makes. It is the difference between Brabantio's initial account of Desdemona and Othello's own narrative, which, as her father says, makes her sound as if she were 'half the wooer' (1.3.176).

Until recently, most editors were certain that the Folio was the better, possibly the revised, text of *Othello*, but the line about Desdemona's 'kisses' has always been one of the exceptions. In 1709 Nicholas Rowe, following the Folio, printed 'kisses' without comment (presumably he had not noticed the Quarto reading), but Pope in 1725 adopted 'sighs', adding the exclamation: 'The lady had been forward indeed to give him *a world of kisses* upon the bare recital of his story'.[1] Virtually every edition since Pope has made the same choice, often without feeling the need to explain it at all. (The one exception is the Signet Classic edition by Sylvan Barnet, which follows the Folio even in this reading and gives no note.) It was thus an exciting moment when, in 1986, the Oxford

editors restored the Folio 'kisses'. They made their choice partly
on grounds of consistency, since they took the Folio to be a
revision of the Quarto, and partly because they found the reading
of 'sighs' as 'kisses' 'difficult to explain as an error'. The editors do
not call Desdemona 'forward'; rather, they suggest that she 'may
be thought of as impulsively affectionate.'[2] Not only is an
impulsively affectionate Desdemona more to the taste of
contemporary readers than a sighing one; directors and audiences
feel much the same. Since the appearance of the Oxford edition,
I have heard Othello say 'kisses' in the theatre at least twice.[3] No
one seems to have been shocked.

The choice between Desdemona's sighs and kisses is only the
most obvious example of how a textual decision becomes a
comment on character, a comment that is in turn embedded in
cultural history. Given the subject matter of *Othello*, it is not
surprising that such blurring of textual and moral judgements
constantly occurs in the history of its editing. It was perhaps most
vicious in the debate between two scholars of the previous
generation, Alice Walker and M.R. Ridley. Though their editions
appeared almost simultaneously – Walker's New Shakespeare
*Othello*, co-edited with J. Dover Wilson, in 1957, and Ridley's
Arden 2 *Othello* in 1958 – Walker's *Textual Problems of the First
Folio* (1953) had already stated the same views that she repeated
at greater length in her part of the introduction and notes to the
edition. Not only did Walker strongly prefer the Folio over the
Quarto, she believed that it was the earlier of the two texts. But in
stating these two points, she constantly falls into moral language:
the Quarto is 'a licentious transcript of a late acting version of
*Othello*' and many of the passages in which it differs from the
Folio are simply 'vulgarizations' for which an actor or
unintelligent transcriber is to blame.[4] She often argues in favour
of a Folio reading simply because it is more consistent with her
pre-existing conception of a character. For instance, making two
huge assumptions at once, she rejected Othello's 'Zouns,' which
occurs only in Q (3.3.157), because 'Restraint is the dominant
trait in Othello's character. Had it not been, the play would not
have been a tragedy.'[5] Following an alteration which originated

with Warburton, she chose to spell 'rites' as 'rights' (1.3.258), arguing that Desdemona is seeking not the 'rites' of love, but 'the privileges ('rights') of sharing the hazards of war'. Faced with the 'world of kisses', she blamed the 'inexplicable error' of the compositor.[6]

Although Walker's moralistic language, assumptions about character consistency, and distrust of the actors make her arguments highly vulnerable, she was not wrong about the interpretative implications of the textual problems for which she found such dogmatic solutions. Ernst Honigmann's Arden 3 edition agrees with her in taking the Folio to be the better text, but since he regards it as a revision of the Quarto, whereas for her the Quarto is a perversion of the Folio, he naturally sees the movement from earlier to later version as constructive rather than destructive. In his study of *The Texts of 'Othello' and Shakespearian Revision*, he goes so far as to suggest that some of the Folio revisions were intended to 'protect Desdemona'[7] – that is, to make her less forceful, less susceptible to accusations of immodesty, less 'forward' (to use Pope's term), than in the Quarto.

Certainly, in 1.3, the scene in which she first appears, there are several examples that seem to confirm Honigmann's viewpoint. All occur in the brief exchange about where Desdemona should lodge during Othello's absence (1.3.241–3). The Duke suggests that she stay at her father's house; Brabantio says, 'I'll not have it so,' and Othello retorts, 'Nor I.' In the Quarto, Desdemona at once intervenes with her own 'Nor I'; the Folio's 'Nor would I there reside' sounds less impulsive. When she asks the Duke for permission to speak (1.3.244–7), the Quarto places a dash at the end of her speech; either she trails off helplessly or else the Duke interrupts her:

DES

    most gracious Duke,
    To my vnfolding lend a gracious eare,
    And let me finde a charter in your voyce,
    And if my simplenesse. –

DU

What would you – speake.

In the Folio, however, the Duke seems to have more respect for her; she is allowed to finish her sentence, and she expresses herself coherently:

And let me finde a Charter in your voice
T'assist my simplenesse.
DUKE
What would you *Desdemona*?

Two other variations seem to have the same motivation. In the Quarto Desdemona says that her heart is subdued even to Othello's 'vtmost pleasure' (1.3.252); she says in the Folio, with less obvious sensuality, that what subdues her heart is 'the very quality' of her husband (usually interpreted as his military life and career). When she has finished, in the Quarto, Othello supports her with a general request: 'Your voyces Lords: beseech you let her will, Haue a free way'. In the Folio, Othello's response, apparently directed to the Duke alone, is, 'let her have your voice' (1.3.262). He no longer asks the entire Senate to vote on a private matter; moreover, by omitting the reference to 'her will', with its potential sexual meaning, he also avoids giving his wife any 'will' at all, even as he goes on to say that his own sexual 'affects' are 'weak and defunct'. When the Duke (in Q) or the First Senator (in F) tells Othello, 'You must away tonight' (278), the Quarto Desdemona has another impulsive interjection: 'To night my Lord?' This line is absent in the Folio. As one might expect, Walker is scornful of Q's 'utmost pleasure' ('Othello's pleasure has nothing to do with the argument') and considers Desdemona's 'To night my Lord?' (1.3.279) a similar 'misrepresentation of Desdemona'.[8] One could argue, then, that the Folio shows a consistent pattern of trying to make Desdemona less susceptible to charges of talking too much, too vaguely and too impulsively.

But the pattern of 'protecting Desdemona' becomes less clear in later scenes. In 2.1, when Desdemona is next described, it is Cassio who speaks, and his lines, as recorded in the two editions, show the same ambivalence over her sensuality. Having spoken of her as divine, he suddenly breaks into a prayer to 'Jove' to protect Othello (2.1.79–82),

> Q:    That he may blesse this Bay with his tall Shippe,
>        And swiftly come to *Desdemona's* armes.
>        Giue renewd fire,
>        To our extincted spirits.
>        And bring all *Cypresse* comfort.

> F:    That he may blesse this Bay with his tall Ship,
>        Make loues quicke pants in *Desdemonaes* Armes,
>        Give renew'd fire to our extincted Spirits.

Here, though the Promethean figure in both passages is Othello, and Desdemona is largely the passive recipient of his ardor, it is the Folio reading that most vividly sexualizes her. There is obviously some confusion in the text of F, perhaps because of the stage direction for Desdemona's entrance following 'Spirits', which resulted in an abrupt ending from which the final line must surely have been omitted by mistake. Honigmann, though he retains the Folio's 'love's quick pants', rejects the interpretation given by Partridge in *Shakespeare's Bawdy*, on the grounds that 'Cassio later rejects sexual imagery applied to Desdemona (2.3.14ff.).' But the line is certainly physical, whether one takes F as an improvement of a rather lame line in Q or Q as the toning-down of a too-vivid image in F. Similarly, when Desdemona makes her brief appearance at 2.3.248, just after Othello has dealt with the drunken fight, her line in Q is 'What is the matter?' but in F she asks, 'What is the matter (Deere?)'. Walker thought it out of character for Desdemona to use this endearment in public, so she transferred it to the following line and made Othello call her 'dear sweeting'. Honigmann retains the Folio reading, without comment. 'Dear', in the late twentieth century, hardly seemed to need one.

Walker's and Ridley's editions are, respectively, Folio-based and Quarto-based. It is tempting to argue that they are also gender-based, and to be disappointed that Alice Walker, the only woman of her time to be involved in the editing of a major Shakespeare play for a major series, should pin so many of her arguments on a reading of Othello and Desdemona that was already beginning to seem old-fashioned in the late 1950s. By contrast, M.R. Ridley's edition sometimes seems to foreshadow the feminist approach to *Othello* that would soon begin to find a voice. But this is because Ridley's decision to base his Arden 2 text on the Quarto forced him to argue the opposite view to Walker's at every opportunity. Given some of the Quarto readings already discussed, this meant that he was virtually obliged to assume a Desdemona who was more sensual than most critics had recognized. In the 'rites'/'rights' debate, Walker had declared that editors who choose 'rites' show 'a misunderstanding of Desdemona.' Ridley retorted that 'to retain "rites" is to "misunderstand" a Desdemona of Dr Walker's creation, not of Shakespeare's.'[9] Yet his own language about other parts of the play shows annoyance with some of Desdemona's behaviour. He particularly disliked her backchat with Iago in 2.1: in the first place, it was unrealistic for a young woman to talk like this when she must surely want to rush down to the harbour herself; moreover, it was disturbing to see how easily she took to repartee with Iago. Ridley's note has a considerable affect on later editions, particularly those for schools. In the New Swan Shakespeare (1976), Gāmini Salgādo annotates Desdemona's 'I am not merry,' pointing out that this aside 'explains in advance what might otherwise seem rather odd behaviour for a newly married woman waiting anxiously for her husband's safe arrival.'[10] The Macmillan school edition of 1984 insists that her semi-flirtatious manner, though it 'does not cast doubt on her innocence,' nevertheless 'may suggest an aspect of her social behaviour that is relevant to later events.'[11] (The editors do not indicate the nature of this relevance, perhaps because they are reluctant to give away the ending to a first-time reader.) Both editions acknowledge that Desdemona is easy to misunderstand – is, in fact, embarrassing. Honigmann, also taking note of Ridley but no longer offended by the episode, comments on its dramatic effectiveness not only in showing Iago's ascendency but in establishing that 'Desdemona understands sexual innuendo' (2.1.117–64).

Surprisingly, neither Ridley nor Honigmann took the opportunity to discuss an emendation for which there is some evidence. The line, 'O, fie upon thee, slanderer!' (2.1.113), which marks Desdemona's entry into the dialogue with Iago, is unattributed in Q, though indented to indicate a new speaker; it is only in F that it is given to Desdemona. Steevens noted that it might as well belong to Emilia as to Desdemona,[12] and, as J.P. Collier was the first to point out, a handwritten insert in the Duke of Devonshire's copy of Q1 also ascribes the line to her, in what looks like, as Collier calls it, 'a hand-writing of the time'.[13] Kenneth Muir and M.A.J. Allen, the editors of *Shakespeare's Plays in Quarto*, used this copy, now in the Huntington Library, but were noncommittal about the possible date of the handwritten notes. While any attribution by Collier must be treated with suspicion, the existence of this emendation is more interesting than its authenticity. Spoken by Emilia, the line is only one more example of her verbal sparring with Iago. Spoken by Desdemona, it makes her seem to encourage Iago's misogynistic jokes, as of course she continues to do later in the scene. Honigmann deals with the problem by offering an attractive and actable reinterpretation of the entire episode, though one that implies rather subtle ensemble playing: Desdemona's reason for asking how Iago would praise her (2.1.117) is that she 'wants to stop the marital bickering and places herself in the firing line'.

The second episode that bothered Ridley occurs in 4.3 ('the Willow Scene'). The absence from the Quarto of much of this scene – including Desdemona's song, much of the surrounding dialogue, and Emilia's long final speech – is, of course, the most striking difference between the two texts. As it appears in the Folio, this scene can hardly be said to 'protect' Desdemona, who, with no prompting, suddenly says, 'This Lodovico is a proper man' (4.3.34). This line seems, oddly enough, to have given no trouble to eighteenth- and nineteenth-century critics. Convinced that Desdemona was totally pure and innocent, they found it an interesting example of the strange thoughts that can come into the head of such a woman. For Samuel Johnson, it was psychologically acute, part of the process by which Desdemona 'endeavours to change her train of thoughts';[14] two authors quoted in the *Variorum* found it moving, or, as one said, 'An exquisitely subtle touch' which shows Desdemona trying, 'with her perfect innocence, to imagine what guilt is.'[15]

Ridley, however, found Desdemona's line so tasteless that he wondered whether it might belong instead to Emilia, whom he saw as a counterpart to Juliet's Nurse ('ancient damnation') in her encouraging the young woman to take a casual view of sexual immorality. In this view the willow scene might be treated as a temptation of Desdemona by Emilia, comparable (though opposite in its outcome) to Iago's temptation of Othello. Desdemona's final couplet –

> Good night, good night. God me such usage send
> Not to pick bad from bad, but by bad mend!

(4.3.103–4)

either shows her complete rejection of this temptation or, more ambiguously, suggests that it *is* a temptation, and one which, if she had lived longer, she might not have resisted. Honigmann, in Arden 3, puts Ridley's suggestion into practice, transferring the speech prefixes so that it is Emilia rather than Desdemona who brings up the subject of Lodovico.

A suggestion that Honigmann makes but does not put into practice is that lines 4.3.63–6 (in which Emilia jokes that she wouldn't commit adultery 'by this heavenly light' but in the dark) were marked for cancellation by Shakespeare but printed by mistake. His evidence is that Desdemona twice asks Emilia whether she would do such a deed for all the world. 'After what has happened not even someone as slow-witted as Emilia [Honigmann's feelings about Emilia are similar to Ridley's] could make a joke of Desdemona's marital fidelity – so out goes the joke, to be replaced by an alternative version, one that bypasses Desdemona's own sexual behaviour.'[16] This is a difficult argument, because what looks to us like duplication might be necessary redundancy, or an aspect of the two women's characterization. John Jones, who believes that F is a careful revision of Q, sees repetition, particularly in the play's two final acts, as an example of deliberate improvement. By expanding ordinary human exchanges, he argues, Shakespeare helps to fill in what might be called the missing 'middle' of the play, providing a breathing space in the plot and a moral space between the absolutes of good and evil.[17]

On the other hand, it is generally agreed that sometimes (as in *Love's Labour's Lost*) Shakespeare's passages for deletion were 'marked very lightly or not at all' – perhaps because he thought that he might want to use the lines elsewhere – so that the deletion went unnoticed.[18] Though it has not before been suggested that duplication might have happened in Cassio's first scene on Cyprus, it might be worth considering the possibility that one or the other of Cassio's hyperbolical speeches (perhaps 55–66) was marked for cutting but printed accidentally. As the scene now stands, there is something very arbitrary (even more so than Desdemona's sudden mention of Lodovico in 4.3) about Montano's question to Cassio: 'But, good lieutenant, is your general wived?' (2.1.60). It is too early in the scene for Montano to know that a ship with two women on board is about to put in, and Cassio has hardly had time to say anything. Two directors in 1999 showed their awareness of this problem by offering independent emendations at this point. At the Royal Shakespeare Theatre, Stratford-upon-Avon, Michael Attenborough changed Montano's line to 'But is it true your general's wiv'd?', suggesting that this had been a topic of gossip even before Cassio's arrival. At the Oregon Shakespeare Festival in Ashland, Tony Taccone, using a text prepared by dramaturg Barry Kraft, cut Montano's question and transposed Cassio's hyperbolic speech to an earlier point, so that his reference to 'the divine Desdemona' (1.3.73) could motivate Montano's puzzled 'What's she?' and the reply that makes it clear that Othello is now married.

Editorial practice often produces readings which, like forgeries in painting, seem to their inventors in keeping with the original but shriek of their own period to later eyes. Jennens's proposed emendation to the perennial problem of Iago's reference to Cassio as 'almost damned in a fair wife' (1.1.20), though dating from 1774, turns the villain into a fop who exclaims (with regard to

Emilia's many admirers and his own jealousy), 'A fellow's almost damn'd in a fair wife!'[19] Thomas Hanmer rewrote Desdemona's 'That death's unnatural that kills for loving' (5.2.42) as 'That death's unnatural; what! kill for loving!'[20] Opinions will probably differ over Honigmann's alteration to one of Desdemona's lines in the same scene. When Othello warns that she is 'on thy death-bed', both texts agree that she replies, 'I [usually modernized as 'aye'], but not yet to die.' Honigmann's emendation – 'I? – but not yet to die!' (5.2.52) is an attempt to deal with what he finds a 'strange' reply. As I understand it, Desdemona's reply is similar to Fluellen's when Pistol says 'Base Troyan, thou shalt die': 'You say very true, scald knave, when God's will is' (*Henry V*, 5.1.33–4).[21] But a Desdemona capable, even on her deathbed, of such helpless knee-jerk witticisms may sound even more 'strange' than the original line or Honigmann's version of it.

Honigmann's current view of the texts of *Othello* involves revision but in two directions: some F readings result from revisions of an earlier MS, but Q must be based on a different, cut version of that MS, since a number of lines in Q are virtually meaningless without the fuller text that is preserved in F. There are indications that some Q readings predate those in F. In Iago's soliloquy in 2.3, he declares that Desdemona may do what she likes with Othello, 'Even as her appetite shall play the god / With his weak function.' The lines obviously recall and distort Othello's words about his 'weak and defunct' affects, so it is likely that the reference to 'her appetite' is a similar distortion of the words that immediately preceed them in the Quarto, but not the Folio: 'Let her will have a free way.' The same seems true of the most important case, the willow scene. Although the editors of the Oxford *Complete Works* and John Jones, in *Shakespeare at Work*, argue persuasively that Shakespeare revised Q into F by adding the song and 'building up Emilia's role in the closing scenes,'[22] the Quarto text sounds abrupt and some of its lines refer to other lines present in F but not in Q. For instance, as Honigmann points out, Desdemona's prayer, with its reference to 'uses', present in both texts, acquires its full meaning as a response to Emilia's 'let them use us well' (F only) and is unlikely to have existed without it.[23] It is sometimes suggested, as by Honigmann, that the willow song had to be cut from Q1 because the voice of the boy actor who created the role broke sooner than expected. But this theory does not explain the absence of Emilia's final speech. If the song and speech were added, the decision to provide such rich material for two boy actors might reflect a new and more Fletcherian sensibility in the theatre. If, as I tend to think, they were cut, we have evidence, consistent with the other examples I have been discussing, that, from the beginning, this intimate scene between two women, in which both talk rather freely about the possibility of being attracted to men other than their husbands, was an embarrassment.

An embarrassment to whom? To the author initially, if it were he who cut them. But then to others. Awareness of the textual problems in *Othello* came as early as 1630, when the publisher of Q2 produced the first 'conflated' edition of the play, drawing readings from both texts. In the important 1.3 variants, the 'editor' voted as follows: 'Nor I' (Q1); 'very quality' (F); 'Your voices Lords, etc.' (Q1). Desdemona gives Othello 'sighes' (Q), not 'kisses'; and in 2.3 she asks 'What is the matter?' (Q), without the Folio's extra endearment. In other words, whoever altered the copy text for this volume made some decisions that 'protect' Desdemona and others that do not. Perhaps *decisions* is the wrong word, since the editor's basic text was probably Q1 and some of the Q readings may have been retained without conscious choice. The point is that Q2, as far as we can tell, works in both directions – making Desdemona sometimes more sensual and sometimes less so. In that respect its changes resemble those in the Folio. The kind of purity Brabantio describes at the beginning is tied to a timidity, or modesty, that would seem to make ordinary existence virtually impossible – 'her motion / Blushed at herself' (1.3.96–7). By contrast, Iago, even when praising her, makes her sound as if she was excessively 'easy' ('Th'inclining Desdemona') and overflowing with sensuality ('as fruitful / As the free elements': 2.3.335–7), and Cassio, as Honigmann notes, even when rebuking Iago for his innuendos, talks of her in the same language that he might have used of a prostitute.[24] Describing the heroine in polarized terms has often been seen as the result of a general male inability to come to terms with female sexuality. The nature of the difference between the Q and F readings suggests that the difficulty is not confined to the play's characters. This would be true even if some of the problems were due (as Honigmann suggests) to the compositor's difficulty with Shakespeare's handwriting. This compositor, as Richard Proudfoot says, has recently been identified as 'John Leason, the inexperienced typesetter dubbed "Compositor E" by Charlton Hinman'.[25] It is tempting to imagine his feverish adolescent imagination transforming 'sighs' into 'kisses'. But he could hardly have come up with such a reading unless he thought of Desdemona as someone for whom 'kisses' might seem the appropriate word.

Honigmann's Arden 3 edition is, as he describes it, 'less committed to either Q or F than previous editions, exercising more freedom of choice'.[26] Of course, the phrase 'freedom of choice' is now as loaded as Walker's language of 'corruption', but we also have the freedom to choose not to make the predictable play on words or to draw the predictable conclusions from it. Honigmann's point is that most Q/F variants matter very little: we do not need to polarize the two texts, and particularly not along moral lines. What is important is precisely the fact that the authorial/editorial activity that created their differences works in both directions – sometimes making Desdemona more sensual and sometimes less so. The textual evidence, in all its contradictoriness, suggests that someone – probably the author, but possibly not only him – was uncertain about how to achieve a balance between Desdemona's sexuality and her innocence. It is the reversal of the problem of depicting 'honest' yet dishonest Iago; precisely because her role is so small compared to his, even minimal changes to her lines affect her characterization. As the various editorial comments on 1.3, 2.1 and 4.3 indicate, these passages remain points at which the tension over the character becomes apparent. Of course, insofar as Shakespeare needs to make Desdemona's behaviour sufficiently ambiguous to justify Othello's suspicions, it could be argued that he is not so much protecting Desdemona as protecting Othello. Yet it is worth remembering that Henry Jackson, who saw the play in Oxford in 1610, referred to a Desdemona who, 'although she pleaded her case very effectively throughout, yet moved (us) more after she was dead, when, lying on her bed, she entreated the pity of the spectators by her very countenance.'[27] It is important both that he speaks of her as having moved her audience to sympathy and that he remembers her as having held her own in speech.[28] For one spectator, at least, the balance was right.

## NOTES

1  *Othello*, ed. Alexander Pope, in *Works of Shakespeare in VI Volumes*, vol. 6, 1725–6.

2  Stanley Wells, Gary Taylor, John Jowett and William Montgomery, *William Shakespeare: A Textual Companion* (Oxford, 1987), 479.

3  Allentown, Pennsylvania, in 1996; Ashland, Oregon, in 1999.

4  *Othello*, ed. J. Dover Wilson and Alice Walker (New Cambridge edition, Cambridge, 1957), 125, 124, 132.

5  Alice Walker, *Textual Problems of the First Folio* (Cambridge, 1953), 139.

6  *Othello*, ed. J. Dover Wilson and Alice Walker (New Shakespeare edition, Cambridge, 1957), 153.

7  E.A.J. Honigmann, *The Texts of 'Othello' and Shakespearian Revision* (London and New York: Routledge, 1996), 35, 98.

8  Walker, *Textual Problems*, 141.

9  *Othello*, ed. M.R. Ridley, Arden Shakespeare (London: Methuen & Co., 1958), 36.

10  William Shakespeare, *Othello*, The New Swan Shakespeare, ed. Gāmini Salgādo (Harlow: Longman, 1976), 44.

11  William Shakespeare, *Othello*, The Macmillan Shakespeare, ed. Celia Hilton and R.T. Jones (1984), 94.

12  *The Plays of William Shakespeare*, 12 vols (Johnson–Steevens edition, 1778), X: 485.

13  J.P. Collier, *The Works of William Shakespeare*, 8 vols (London, 1843), vol VII, 532.

14  *The Plays of William Shakespeare*, (Johnson–Steevens edition, 1778), X: 592.

15  Edward Rose, *Sudden Emotion: Its Effect upon Different Characters as Shown by Shakspere* (1880–82), quoted *Variorum*, 429.

16  Honigmann, *Texts*, 35.

17  John Jones, *Shakespeare at Work* (Oxford: Clarendon Press, 1995), 261–3.

18  Honigmann, *Othello*, 361.

19  Charles Jennens (?), *Othello* in *Five Plays of Shakespeare*, 2 vols (London, 1773), 2: 3.

20  *The Works of William Shakespeare*, vol. 6, ed. Thomas Hanmer (Oxford, 1744).

21  *Henry V*, ed. T.W. Craik, Arden 3 (London: Routledge, 1995).

22  Stanley Wells, Gary Taylor, John Jowett, William Montgomery (eds), *The Oxford Shakespeare* (Oxford, 1986), 925; Jones: see note 17, above.

23  Honigmann, *Texts*, 11–12.

24  Honigmann, *Othello*, note on 2.3.20.

25  See Richard Proudfoot, *Shakespeare: Text, Stage and Canon* (London, 2001), 19.

26  Honigmann, *Othello*, 359.

27  Geoffrey Tillotson, '*Othello* and *The Alchemist* at Oxford in 1610', *Times Literary Supplement*, 20 July 1933, 494.

28  See Paul Yachnin's comments on this passage in *Stage-Wrights: Shakespeare, Jonson, Middleton, and the Making of Theatrical Value* (Philadelphia: University of Pennsylvania Press, 1997), 26–35.

# 7

# WHO IS PERFORMING 'IN' THESE TEXT(S)?; OR, *SHREW*-ING AROUND

## *Barbara Hodgdon*

As I edit *Taming of the Shrew*, I am haunted by voices: those of the Arden 3 General Editors; those of previous editors; those of textual, literary and performance critics, including reviewers; those of past performers; those of imagined performances. I also hear voices coming from texts other than Folio's (F1) – not just the Anonymous *Taming of a Shrew* (1594), with its puzzling 'completion' of *Shrew*'s 'incomplete' Sly frame, but also those of an expanded 'textual consciousness'[1] that includes other filiations and interfaces, embraces a corporate (and corporeal) textuality: John Fletcher's *The Woman's Prize, or the Tamer Tamed* (ca.1611) and John Lacey's *Sauny the Scott, or The Taming of the Shrew* (1698). By the mid-eighteenth century, David Garrick's *Catherine and Petruchio, Alter'd from* SHAKESPEAR's *Taming of the Shrew* (1754) joins the conversation, eventually silencing them all; only in 1844, with J.R. Planchè's 'Elizabethan-style' performance at London's Haymarket Theatre, was something like F1's *Shrew* (1623) re-heard.[2] I rehearse this genealogy as background to what I want to do here: trace how what I will call editorial orality and editorial re-performance have shaped (de-formed?) *Shrew*'s modern editions. For not only have protocols of editorial literacy suppressed *Shrew*'s theatrical literacy; they also have substituted one performative literacy for another.[3]

# NOISES OFF

Since the instances I rehearse involve extra-dialogic stage directions (SDs), listen, first, to some editorial rationales – a kind of frame. Although these incorporate some shifts in thinking since the New Bibliography, they also retain features of that older tradition and so can stand as broadly descriptive of the practices governing the twentieth-century editions which I discuss.

✦ Gary Taylor: 'Shakespeare could rely on this first special readership [professional colleagues and personal friends] to 'edit' his manuscript, at least mentally and perhaps physically, as they read it. He could also rely on those readers to bring to their reading much specialist knowledge about the conditions and working practices of the contemporary theatre. ... The written text of any such manuscript thus depended upon an unwritten para-text which always accompanied it: an invisible life-support system of stage directions, which Shakespeare could either expect his first readers to supply, or which those first readers would expect Shakespeare himself to supply orally. The earliest editions of the plays all fail, more or less grossly, to supply this unwritten text; modern editions, more or less comprehensively, attempt to rectify the deficiency by conjecturally writing for him the stage directions which Shakespeare himself assumed or spoke but never wrote'.[4]

✦ Stating that his editorial goal in adding stage directions is to aid the reader who lacks visual imagination, Stanley Wells explains that he 'start[s] from the basic premise that the editor needs to identify points at which additional directions, or changes to those of the early texts are necessary to make the staging intelligible ...'. Wells seeks consistency as the principle governing such additions or changes, but aside from several vague references to McKerrow, he offers no theorized rationale.[5]

To say the least, these are intriguing narratives. Although he hints at the theatrical collaboration that Jeffrey Masten so elegantly outlines and theorizes, Taylor nonetheless maintains Shakespeare's authority: indeed, his notion of a lost orality attributed to Shakespeare seems patterned on notions of *Ur*-texts, or Q0s. In his account, this 'unwritten para-text' becomes a rationale for editorial (performative?) behaviours in which the editor acts as the absent author's all-too-representable 'other', supplies his – or their – lost orality, turns it into writing, fixes it all down. Taylor, however, does go on to say that although filling 'such lacunae is necessarily hazardous, it is necessary if we are to relish the texts as scripts for theatrical performance [even though the] filling which modern editors concoct might not always be to Shakespeare's taste'.[6] Wells's more direct, more practical advice aims at readerly understanding, with a view to comprehending stage action: here, Wells's imagined reader figures that curious category, the 'general reader' – a phrase which appears to mean those-who-read-novels-not-plays (or, perhaps, even a newspaper or magazine). Yet if this imagined reader is incapable of discerning action from dialogue, what makes Wells think that she/he will read SDs carefully? Are italics really that powerful?

Neither Oxford's nor Arden 3's protocols specify what theatre space editors might imagine when, supplying the missing orality, they write these presumably necessary SDs, yet the implicit assumption is that they are thinking of 'Shakespeare's theatre'. To be sure, Arden 3's *Editorial Guidelines* advise consulting reprints before 1700 and seventeenth- and eighteenth-century adaptations on the grounds that they offer insight into 'details of *language in passages they retain*' and that the adapters read the plays with a sense of contemporary idiom; what gets elided is that many of those adaptations took place on proscenium stages. In general, those *Guidelines* bracket off performance *as* performance, separating it physically and spatially from the text as part of the Introductory matter: 'later stage history – which may be a record of the play's "afterlife," "appropriation" or cultural history'.[7] Each of these terms – 'afterlife', 'appropriation', 'cultural history' – suggests an 'original' theatrical life for the play, one tied to early modern playing. Presumably, then, something approximating this (ideal?) performance lies at the heart of textual editing: its aim is to produce an edition that understands the past and makes it more accessible to contemporary readers (academic and 'general') and theatrical practitioners. Look, now, at what actually has happened in the case of *Shrew*.

## PLAY HOUSE [4.1]

PETRUCHIO

Go, rascals, go, and fetch my supper in.    *Exeunt Servingmen*
    *Sings* Where is the life that late I led?
      Where are those –
Sit down, Kate, and welcome. ***They sit at a table.*** [Folger]
          Soud, soud, soud, soud.
       **[Food, food, food, food!]**
    *Enter Servants with supper.*
**Why, when I say? Nay, good sweet Kate, be merry.**    5
Off with my boots, you rogues, you villains, [!] w **W**hen?
    *Sings* It was the friar of orders grey
      As he forth walked on his way –
***Servant begins to remove Petruchio's boots.*** [Folger, Bevington]
Out, you rogue, [!] y**Y**ou pluck my foot awry.
Take that, [!] ***He strikes the Servant.*** [Rowe]
    a**A**nd mend the plucking of the other.    10
Be merry, Kate. Some water here: [!] w**W**hat hoa. **[ho !]**
    *Enter one with water.*
Where's my spaniel Troilus? Sirrah, get you hence
And bid my Cousin Ferdinand come hither.
             ***Exit a Servant.*** [Capell]
One, Kate, that you must kiss and be acquainted with.
Where are my slippers? Shall I have some water?    15
Come, Kate, and wash, and welcome heartily.
      ***A Servant offers water, but spills some.*** [Bevington]
You whoreson villain, [!] w**W**ill you let it fall?
***He strikes the Servant.*** [Capell]
KATHERINA
Patience, I pray you, [.] '**t****T**was a fault unwilling.

PETRUCHIO

    A whoreson, beetle-headed, flap-eared knave: [!]

    Come, Kate, sit down, I know you have a stomach.      20

    Will you give thanks, sweet Kate, or else shall I?

    What's this? Mutton?

1 SER.

    I [**Ay**].

PETRUCHIO

    Who brought it?

PETER

    I.      25

PETRUCHIO

    'Tis burnt, and so is all the meat.

    What dogs are these? Where is the rascal cook?

    How durst you villains bring it from the dresser

    And serve it thus to me that love it not?

    There, take it to you, trenchers, cups and all: [!]      30

      *He throws the meat, etc. about the stage.* [Rowe]

    You heedless joltheads and unmannered slaves. [!]

    What, do you grumble? I'll be with you straight.

                  *Exeunt Servants.* [Dyce]

This re-lineated, marked-up, re-marked, polyvocal passage is designed to reveal both editorial orality and editorial performativity as well as to show up *Shrew*-edition-as-palimpsest, F1 made (overly?) accessible. Here, modernized punctuation introduces pauses (**periods** in place of commas, thus slowing down the comic mechanism) as well as exclamatory emphases (!!!) that occur *ad lib* throughout modern *Shrew* editions as (prescriptive) signifiers of 'comedy' (This is funny! Amazing! Look at me!); potentially, both kinds of changes travel into theatrical performances.[8] One editorial change I do not indicate prescribes yet another dimension of orality: most modern editors (H.J. Oliver [Oxf[1]] excepted) print lines 22–5 ('What this, mutton? ... I') as a single verse line. In choosing not to do so, I resist, Kate-like, Arden 3's mandate for turning prose into verse – or, in the case of Sly, vice versa. I have included F1's 'Soud, soud, soud, soud' (retained by many modern editions) as well as the editorial emendation, 'Food, food, food, food' in order to point to contradictory editing practices. Conjecturing that 'soud' represents Petruchio humming, Oliver retains it, thus conveying a kind of 'print orality'; other modern editions emend to 'food' on the grounds that the *OED* has no satisfactorily applicable definition.

What I'm primarily interested in, however, are the SDs. Here, marking their provenance foregrounds details of historical transmission, the origins of which consistently are elided in the text 'proper', appearing (usually) only in collations or (rarely) in textual commentaries. Strictly speaking, only that deriving from Dyce (1857) at line 32 represents a *necessary* clarification of F1, which directs the servants to (re)enter a few lines later (as in many early modern texts, whatever the provenance of the copy, entrances are more likely to be marked than exits). The two SDs peculiar to the Folger edition (Mowat and Werstine 1992) as well as Bevington's '*A Servant offers water, but spills some*' (1992) subscribe to a similar logic, one that aids Wells's general reader. Although many of the added SDs appear in *A Shrew*, *the Shrew*'s 'evil twin', all are credited, in modern editions, to eighteenth-century editions (Rowe[1] 1709; Capell 1768).[9] I take this as evidence of a widespread move to separate 'suspect text' from 'true original'. Even the most extravagantly performative of them – Rowe's '*He throws the meat, etc. about the stage*' – or a version of it, as in '*He throws the food and dishes at them*' (Thompson, Cam[2] 1984; Folger) appears in all but Oliver's Oxf[1], which also has a testy note (one function of commentary is to criticize previous editors) about directing a servant to go get Cousin Ferdinand. Claiming that such an exit spoils the joke – which is that no such cousin exists and both Petruchio and the servants know it – Oliver argues that introducing this as well as some of the other SDs reduces Petruchio's irrationality by giving his anger a rationale when it most lacks reason: he may, for instance, spill the water himself.[10]

Oliver's comment is a rare departure from an editorial tradition that re-plays this scene as it was staged in the eighteenth century. As though buying into what the academic theatre critic

Hamlet says to the itinerant players (with characteristically bad timing), other modern editors have suited the action to the word. Certainly the dialogue does *speak* these actions, but does dialogue always (consistently?) *prescribe* behaviours? However one might address that question, the editorial choreography here gives Petruchio performative behaviours very different from those in F1: it makes him – irrevocably, one might say – a man who hits people.[11] Elsewhere, of course, F1's *Shrew* does direct physical violence, but such instances are associated with Kate, who binds Bianca, strikes Petruchio and beats Grumio, or with Vincentio, who beats Biondello, the only instance of *staged* masculine violence. F1's Petruchio, however, is a man of violent words, not blows – a braggart, a 'mad-brained rudesby' who speaks of macho-romantic exploits (*Suppose*-ings?). He threatens Grumio but finally only '*rings him by the ears*'; he says he will strike Kate if she hits him again (in the so-called wooing scene, more properly a 'keen encounter' like that between Richard III and Lady Anne), but there are no SDs indicating that he actually strikes either his servants, his bride-to-be or his wife. Grumio, of course, does tell an exaggerated tale of being beaten – creating the persona of 'suffering servant' for Curtis's benefit. But that, together with Gremio's report of Petruchio's behaviour at the wedding, is another (editorial) story.

By importing other performances, other printed texts, modern editions reveal a Petruchio who owes his stage life less to 'Shakespeare' than to Rowe. Indeed, the frontispiece of Rowe's 1709 edition shows an engraving of this scene. But what it records is not 'Rowe' but *Shrew* as the engraver knew it, whether as performance, print or both: that is, the scene as it appears in Lacey's *Sauny the Scott*, where Petruchio throws the meat and Sauny (Grumio) stands ready to catch it.[12] Curiously enough, the cover illustration for Ann Thompson's 1984 *Shrew* (Cam²), the play's first so-called feminist edition, features a drawing by C. Walter Hodges of this scene on an 'Elizabethan' stage, complete with cowering servants and Petruchio's signature property, his whip – not introduced *in print* until 1788, where it appears ('*whip for Petruchio*') opposite Petruchio's entrance to the wedding scene in the promptbook for John Philip Kemble's performance of Garrick's *Catherine and Petruchio*). Even more intriguingly, Thompson's edition adds two SDs to Petruchio's and Kate's initial meeting: after Petruchio threatens to cuff Kate if she strikes again, '*He holds her*' – constraining Kate physically for thirty-one lines before directing '*He lets her go*' after 'with gentle conference soft and affable'.

What are the implications of editorial re-performances – figured in older bibliographical traditions as 'theatrical contagion' – which work to create normative fantasies of Petruchio as brutal servant-beater and, with a causally related reading, to mark him as one who displaces onto his servants the physical abuse he 'intended' for Kate? (After all, as Lady Mary Chudleigh writes in 'Verses to the Ladies', 'Wife and servant are the same, / And differ only in the name'.[13]) Obviously, this added choreography plays into feminist readings and performances, where the what-shall-we-do-with-*The Shrew* problem raises its perennial head. Yet it is Rowe and modern editions, as much as if not more than 'Shakespeare', who are responsible for the play's 'hard opinions', for its problematic theatrical reputation. It would seem that Stephen Orgel's claim – 'actors are the original poststructuralists, assuming ... that the author does not control the play, the interpreter does'[14] – needs extending to include *Shrew*'s editors. For, as we have it in all modern editions, *Shrew* is a print intervention that, in papering over one performance history with another, occludes or at the very least blunts any invitation to play house like F1's Petruchio. 'Don't tell me what to do', says F1(Kate-like); 'Oh, you'll love it', says the editor.[15]

## 'WHERE'S THE WEASEL'?

Peter Holland tells a story of taking his seven-year-old son Adam to a performance of *Shrew*, preparing him beforehand by summarizing the plot. At the interval, Holland asked if Adam was enjoying the play. 'Oh yes,' he replied, 'But where's the weasel'? Just as it may be easy enough to confuse one rodent with another, it is also easy to confuse one Kate with another.[16] Here, then, is another instance of Rowe's performative hand (never for the first time) incorporated into *all* modern editions.

PETRUCHIO

    'Twas I won the wager, though you hit the white,

    And being a winner, God give you good night.

                  *Exeunt Petruchio **and Katherina***

HORTENSIO

    Now, go thy ways; thou hast tamed a curst shrew.

LUCENTIO

    'Tis a wonder, by your leave, she will be tamed so.

                          ***Exeunt omnes***

Taking the happy couple off as bride and groom, Rowe ended the play with their exit. Many critics have followed his lead; many, too, fantasize, for the pair, a sexy night of (offstage) wedded bliss. Pope (1723) appended *A Shrew*'s Sly ending; Theobald (1733) took it out again and also restored the final two lines, finishing with an '*Exeunt Omnes*' to clear the (proscenium) stage. F1, however, looks like this:

PETRUCHIO

    'Twas I won the wager, though you hit the white,

    And being a winner, God give you good night.

                        *Exit Petruchio*

HORTENSIO

    Now, go thy ways; thou hast tamed a curst shrew.

LUCENTIO

    'Tis a wonder, by your leave, she will be tamed so.

Following Rowe (who does note that F1 and Q *omit* Kate's exit), all modern editions suppress this exit direction. Moreover, only Ann Thompson notes the change in her textual commentary. Is there any rationale for restoring F1's reading of this significant non-exit? At every other point in F1 where Petruchio and Kate leave the stage together, the SD reads '*Exeunt*', even after the wedding, where it is squeezed in: '*Exeunt P.Ka.*' Although SDs are notoriously dodgy signs, it seems reasonable to argue, if only on the grounds of consistency about 'couple exits', that F1 'speaks true' – whether that 'truth' comes from a compositor's 'voice' or from whatever oral para-text may have been spoken during the play's first rehearsals. If obeyed, what's the result? Several potential performances are 'in' this text, which appears to give Kate prime (and pride) of place, turning her into a (theatrical?) marvel, a 'wonder' – a kind of Epicoenean figure, a (silent) epilogue, boy actor as womanly man or manly woman. And, of course, it resonates with other 'Shakespearean' plays, notably *The Winter's Tale*.[17]

Curiously enough, it is not necessary to (re)embrace F1 to uncover traces of such a 'hidden' performance – nor is it necessary to discard editorial traditions that rely on seventeenth- and eighteenth-century enactments to imagine it. In Lacey's *Sauny the Scott*, after a Barber enters and pulls Peg's (Kate's) aching tooth, she appears to die and, toward the end, is brought in on a bier: returning to life, she wins the wager for Petruchio, speaks a scolding single line to the other women, for which she receives Petruchio's praise, and the play concludes with song and dance. But an even more intriguing moment occurs in Garrick's *Catherine and Petruchio*, generally thought to 'gentle' the strictures of Shakespearean taming – achieved, at least in part, by having Petruchio '*Goe forward with Catherine in his Hand*' and speak her lines on the duty the subject owes the Prince. Here, it is he who has the last words: 'How shameful 'tis when Women are so simple / To offer War where they should kneel for Peace; / Or seek for Rule, Supremacy and Sway, / Where bound to love [not serve], to honour and obey' – which would seem to confirm that Kate has indeed been ventriloquizing him all along. But the moment I find most interesting occurs slightly earlier in Garrick's staging, in which the sun–moon exchange and Kate's mistaking Vincentio as a maiden lead directly to the final 'proofs' of Kate's taming. Here, it is Baptista, not Vincentio, she misrecognizes; addressing her father, she kneels to ask pardon for her mad mistaking. Baptista tells her to rise and asks, 'How lik'st thou Wedlock? Ar't not alter'd Kate?' to which she replies, 'Indeed I am. I am transform'd to Stone' – and Hortensio then comments, 'Here is a wonder, if you talk of Wonders'. Somewhat uncannily,

Garrick staged both *The Winter's Tale* and *Catherine and Petruchio* the same year (1756), and the Prologue, which he spoke, and which is printed in the facsimile *Catherine and Petruchio*, addresses both plays.

If, as Masten argues, what we want is 'more Shakespeare, the more the better', perhaps in the case of *Shrew* one need look no further than – or, perhaps more appropriately, look back to – F1.[18] For editors have regularly put in its place another play, one that re-speaks the oralities and re-performs the behaviours that have marked other performances. To come to a quick (and by now obvious) point, the *Shrew* we have been reading (and in most cases seeing) all these years is a selective editorial collaboration with those performances – and their texts. Yet, how would *Shrew*'s textual and performative history read if editors had also imported the penultimate moments of Garrick's play, described above? Since they did not, in effect the (famous, or infamous) mutuality of *Catherine and Petruchio*'s ending continues to sustain and support editors' marital fantasies – and, consequently, our own theatrical and socio-cultural performances.

Finally, let me sketch out a possible Folio-only performance of *Shrew*'s ending. After all, given Arden 3's protocols, which (somewhat ironically, given my argument here) warn editors to refrain from introducing their own interpretations into textual commentary and from including too much present-day theatrical evidence, which might date an edition, this may be my only chance at such imaginings. Leaving Kate onstage, with Hortensio affirming that only Petruchio has left – 'Now, go *thy* ways, *thou* hast tamed a curst shrew' – and Lucentio expressing amazement – ''Tis a wonder, by your leave, she will be tamed so' (this line, which has always puzzled me with its 'thy' and 'thou', now makes better physical sense) – positions her as a near-allegorical figure, the 'perfect' wife. Such a performance 'feels like' an element which might be understood, through the conventions of the court masque, as directing the spectator's gaze towards the ruler's presence, newly revealed – a presence which Kate's speech of (*Suppose*-d) submission has just invoked. Here, however, that convention occurs within the frame of a 'domestic' masque, one which unveils – and celebrates – Kate's new identity. If read in this way, what appears to be on offer also unsettles fixed perspective – as well as monolithic meanings. For it suggests that it is Kate, not the lordly or monarchical Petruchio, who is *Shrew*'s closural organizing presence, its means of resolution – and, perhaps, of disrupting patriarchal authority. And as all eyes – onstage as well as off – are drawn to her, what they see is indeed something to wonder at. Whether she has been tamed or not, I also want to imagine, still remains ambiguous, in question. Given such body-play, the present-day theatrical – and editorial – practice (here, where one physically places the *AS* moments in relation to *TS* in an edition is a crucial decision which potentially keys theatrical practice) which appends *A Shrew*'s closural frame, safely enclosing *The Shrew* as a masculinist power fantasy, would seem, not just to un-fashion Folio but to undercut its potential for requiring onlookers to awake their faith, for letting such a wonder – whether 'played' by a boy or by a woman – seem familiar.

## NOTES

1   See Joseph Grigely, *Textualterity: Art, Theory, and Textual Criticism* (Ann Arbor: University of Michigan Press, 1995), pp. 47–9.

2   Planchè's staging used two locales: the exterior of the ale-house and the Lord's bedchamber, in which all the action took place (he used placards affixed to the wall to indicate other locales). The Act-drop was never lowered; the characters from Induction occupied one corner of the stage throughout; at close the Lord gave a signal to his servants to remove Sly, and as this was being done, without a word spoken, the curtain fell.

3   On theatrical literacy, see Jeffrey Masten, *Textual Intercourse: Collaboration, Authorship, and Sexualities in Renaissance Drama* (Cambridge: Cambridge University Press, 1997).

4   Stanley Wells, Gary Taylor, John Jowett and William Montgomery, *William Shakespeare: A Textual Companion* (Oxford: Clarendon Press, 1987), p. 2.

5   Stanley Wells, *Re-Editing Shakespeare for the Modern Reader* (Oxford: Clarendon Press, 1987), pp. 68, 76–7. On the issue of consistency, William B. Long points out that only printing and print culture demand such regularity; they are not factors in the theatrical marking of authorial papers, where notation only occurs in response to an actual staging problem. He notes difference between professionals and amateurs – the latter adding more advisory SDs than the

former, who did as little as possible to whatever sort of copy they received in the theatre. See William B. Long, 'Stage-Directions: A Misinterpreted Factor in Determining Textual Provenance', *Text* 2 (1985): 123–5.

6  Wells and Taylor, *A Textual Companion*, pp. 2–3.

7  *The Arden Shakespeare, Series 3 Editorial Guidelines* (June 2000), p. 23.

8  Although I do not subscribe to the notion that F1's punctuation represents 'authorial signs', as does Neil Freeman, it nonetheless seems reasonable to assume, following Ben Jonson's lead, that punctuation marks signal pauses for breath. Jonson is cited in Laurie E. McGuire, *Shakespeare's Suspect Texts: The 'Bad' Quartos and Their Contexts* (Cambridge: Cambridge University Press, 1997), p. 114. For me, the value of F1's punctuation is that it works to estrange a particular strand of modernization and invite re-examining the relationships between printed dialogue and oral speech. *Shrew*'s modern editors also mark frequent asides – another sign of 'comedy'.

9  In *A Shrew*, Ferando (Petruchio) threatens to cut Sander's (Grumio's) nose, verbally attacks the servant charged with pulling off his boots, and a SD reads '*He beats them all. They cover the board and fetch in the meat*'; shortly thereafter, Ferando '*throws down the table and meat and all and beats them*'. After Ferando and Kate exit, another SD reads '*Manent servingmen and eat up all the meat*'; and when Ferando returns, '*He beats them all out* again' clears the stage before she shares his taming strategy.

10  H.J. Oliver (ed.), *The Taming of the Shrew* (Oxford: Clarendon Press, 1982), p. 184, commentary.

11  Ralph Alan Cohen describes a staging he directed in which he relied entirely on F1's SDs. Cohen notes the 'origins' of the additional SDs but does not draw the conclusions I suggest here. See 'Looking for Cousin Ferdinand: The Value of F1 Stage Directions for a Production of *The Taming of the Shrew*', in Laurie E. Maguire and Thomas L. Berger (eds), *Textual Formations and Reformations* (Newark: University of Delaware Press, 1998), pp. 264–80.

12  *Sauny the Scott* has the SD '*Throws meat at 'em, Sauny gets it*' – the excuse, this time, is that the meat is poisoned and will produce choler. Garrick's *Catherine and Petruchio* also has '*Strikes him*'; '*Servant lets fall the* Water' and '*Throws the meat, &c, about*'.

13  Chudleigh's verses are inscribed by Elizabeth Brockett on the opening leaves of her First Folio (Folger First Folio #23). My thanks to Sasha Roberts for this information.

14  Stephen Orgel, 'What is a Character?' *Text* 8 (1995): 105.

15  Adapted from Peggy Phelan, 'Incarcerations', paper delivered at a University of California, Berkeley Symposium, February 2001.

16  As I have argued elsewhere, looking at the Kate who speaks her final obedience is like comparing those before and after photos in weight loss ads: one searches the

one for signs of the other. See 'Katherina Bound: Play(K)ating the Strictures of Everyday Life', chapter 1 of *The Shakespeare Trade: Performances and Appropriations* (Philadelphia: University of Pennsylvania Press, 1998), pp. 1–38.

17   Leaving the rest of the company onstage rather than directing a general exit also reinforces the point that Kate is a stand-out among those who occupy a more mundane world.

18   Masten, 'More or Less: Editing the Collaborative', paper delivered at the 2000 Shakespeare Association of America meeting; my thanks to Masten for a copy of his paper.

# PART III

---

# EDITING AND STAGE PRACTICE

# 8

## TO EDIT? TO DIRECT? –
## AY, THERE'S THE RUB

*George Walton Williams*

We stand now at a point of transition in the editing of Shakespeare's plays, and we may note this transition in the two series of plays published in the Arden edition, the 'Second Arden' and 'Arden 3'. Briefly, where the Second Arden edition (1946–88) placed academic scholarship first, Arden 3 (1995–) is giving equal attention to the theatrical presentation on stage. Professor Peter Holland, reviewing the first volumes of Arden 3, has exactly expressed this transition:

> As the Arden 2 series became the repository of academic orthodoxy and peer-group communication, [the Presses of Cambridge and Oxford Universities created] new rival editions both foregrounding their concerns to 'pay attention to the theatrical qualities of each play and its stage history'.[1]

Arden 3 has followed their example, he concludes, and he praises the edition of *Titus Andronicus*, in which the editor, Jonathan Bate, 'seizes the play's many opportunities for exploring the possibilities of significant staging with such glee that the Shakespeare editor is revealed in a totally new guise as a theatre director whose medium is the page not the stage.' Antony Hammond, the editor of *Richard III* for the Second Arden, one of the last plays to appear in that series, has squarely faced the problem: 'Editors must make "a conscious decision" as to whether they are editing "the poem" or "the play"'.[2]

As an indication of the former view of academic orthodoxy, I may cite from the late Professor Harold Jenkins's correspondence:

> The editor's business is to present and explain the text; how this is to be presented on the stage is a matter for the director and how it has been presented in various productions is a matter for the theater historian; and it seems to me that there is a good deal of confusion nowadays about what an edition ought to do.[3]

That is the view of one of the General Editors of the Second Arden. We may set against that authority the dictum of the General Editors of Arden 3:

> Both the introduction and the commentary are designed to present the plays as texts for performances, and make appropriate reference to stage, film and television versions, as well as introducing the reader to the range of critical approaches to the plays.[4]

Professor Holland's approval of the editor as director is a position I wholeheartedly endorse. I argue that every editor should be a director, whose page is his stage. Some editors are reluctant to accept that responsibility; they are fearful of infringing upon the domain of the director. They should not be. Directors are constantly infringing upon the domain of the editor. Directors always edit. They substitute modern words for old-fashioned words; they omit obscure classical or topical allusions; they reassign speeches – in short they do not hesitate to edit the play before an actor has set first foot on the stage. But the response of the editor is not a matter of retaliation; it is simply an opportunity of exercising the options. Editors should adopt the equivalent directorial attitude in their work: where a stage direction printed in Quarto or Folio is wrong, misleading or ambiguous, the editor must present it in the edition – as the director would on stage – correctly, clearly and unambiguously. (The present practice of some editors is to print in the edited text the Folio direction, knowing it is incorrect, and then in the commentary notes to give a correct form and an explanation. That's villainous. Let the editor print in the edited text a correct form, and in the commentary notes the incorrect form and an explanation why it is unsatisfactory.)

A simple example: Folio *Richard III* contains the direction (1.1.41.1):

*Enter Clarence, and Brakenbury, guarded.*                    (44)

This is perfectly clear and entirely unambiguous: it means that those two noblemen have come onstage under guard, that they are prisoners. No reader could misunderstand it. It is, however, wrong, as the play makes instantly clear. What history says and the play shows – in the same words – is

*Enter Clarence, guarded, and Brakenbury.*

There is no mystery here. Richard's speech immediately following the entry explains the direction: 'What means this armed guard / That waits upon your grace?' Forty-five lines later, Brakenbury identifies himself as the official from the Tower in whose charge Clarence has been placed. Is that sufficient? My reply is that it is not; or, if sufficient, not the proper way to present the matter. The direction should be able to stand on its own, giving instruction that is not contradicted or corrected by the dialogue.

The policy should be simply this: where the original direction is wrong, the editor should emend so that the printed text presents what is theatrically right, while what is wrong is preserved in the footnote. Retaining an erroneous and unactable direction in the edited text produces an edition which does not present the play as a text for performance.

All editors will agree that the dramatist's dialogue is primary. There is little of the director's work on the spoken word that an editor can accomplish on a printed page. But, on the other hand, directing the acted word by means of stage directions printed in the text is a task that an editor can and regularly should perform. The addition of invented editorial directions is a subject of personal taste, but some editions can be made more 'spectator-friendly' by the help that a sensitive editor – one with an eye on the stage – can provide. A free-wheeling director can easily overstep the borders of editorial propriety in reworking Shakespeare's plays; and the equivalent editor can be too specific in imposing his/her editorial inventiveness on the requirements of directing. Some critics have thought the stage directions of J. Dover Wilson, for example, excessive – so helpful as to be intrusive.

This paper has noted the problem of a stage direction printed in the original Folio. I want to concentrate now rather on those directions not printed in an early text but implied in the dialogue, where the dialogue contains 'action-directions', directions imbedded in the dialogue.[5] Supplying such directions where there are none is the way in which the editor demonstrates that he or she has visualized the stage action; and by which he or she transmits that vision to the spectator–readership. We may notice here three (of many) different sorts of directions to be supplied. The first and most important – when, as often, Quarto and Folio provide no printed help – is the direction that tells the reader which actors are on stage and which are not. This is the basic and essential requirement, the editor's first responsibility as director. In *Henry VI*, Part 3, for the seizure of Rutland in 1.3.1–9 most editors have found the Folio directions not only inadequate, but positively misleading:

| | |
|---|---:|
| *Enter Rutland, and his Tutor.* | 399 |
| *Enter Clifford.* | 402 |
| CLIFFORD | |
|    Chaplaine away … | 403 |
| CLIFFORD | |
|    Souldiers, away with him. | 407 |
| TUTOR | |
|    Ah *Clifford*, murther not this innocent Child, | |
|    Least thou be hated both of God and Man.    *Exit* | 409 |

As the Folio text stands, the Tutor (or Chaplain), having passionately pled to save the child's life and having asserted that he will die with him, makes an exit unmotivated, solitary and apparently tranquil. But this is intolerable: the exit at 409 necessitates some violent action. Soldiers must hale the Tutor away, as they were ordered to do. But that there should be soldiers to hale him away necessitates that soldiers should be on stage to do so; they must be brought on. The most suitable moment for their entrance is with Clifford (402). The editor with directorial eye must therefore print: 'Enter Clifford [with Soldiers].' And 'Exit [Tutor, haled off by Soldiers]'.[6]

A particular kind of exit direction unmarked in the earliest prints has received some attention recently. Professor Proudfoot has termed these 'advanced exits'. These are exits that can properly be supplied by editors in the middle of a scene for a character to make an early exit before the general exeunt that follows later or at the end of the scene. The editor can justify such an early exit if there is a line in the dialogue making such an exit appropriate, a line in which the speaker bids farewell or in which he is bid farewell. So in *Henry VI*, Part 2, at 2.4.100–4, Eleanor, Duchess of Gloucester, who has been found guilty of witchcraft and treason, is brought onstage 'in a white Sheet' (to show her shame), a prisoner of 'the Sheriff . . . and Officers'. The Sheriff tells us that his office and commission end when he transfers his prisoner to the custody of Sir John Stanley, who will take her to the Isle of Man for detention there.

ELIANOR

  Sherife farewell, and better then I fare,             1280

  Although thou hast beene Conduct of my shame.

SHERIFE

  It is my Office, and Madame pardon me.

ELIANOR

  I, I, farewell, thy Office is discharg'd:           1283

  Come *Stanley*, shall we goe?                      1284

At line 1283, the Sheriff and his Officers are discharged, his commission is ended, and the responsibility for Eleanor is transferred to Stanley. As the Sheriff and his Officers have now no further function, they may appropriately leave; new business begins at 1284 with Eleanor's turning to Stanley. The Arden 3 editor supplies '*Exit Sheriff with Officers and Commoners*'.[7] The dramatic advantage of this early exit, before they would leave at the Folio final '*Exeunt*', is that the crowded company clear the stage, leaving it free for a final dialogue between Eleanor and Stanley, a passage of quiet after the excitement of the preceding lines, which has required a full and busy stage. The final Folio '*Exeunt*' at the end of the scene signifies now only Stanley and Eleanor, instead of those two and the Sheriff and the numerous company.

A comparable instance earlier in the same play: at the end of 1.4.76–80, York and Buckingham confer privately on the subject of the disgracing of Gloucester; they congratulate themselves that they have discovered matter that will assure his political ruin.

BUCK

    Your Grace shal give me leave, my Lord of York,      707
    To be the Poste, in hope of his reward.

YORKE

    At your pleasure, my good Lord.      709
    Who's within there, hoe?

                *Enter a Servingman*

    Invite my Lords of Salisbury and Warwick
    To suppe with me to morrow Night. Away.

                        *Exeunt*     714

In terms of simple politeness, one does not invite guests to a supper in the presence of someone who is not also to be invited. More to the point in terms of simple politics: as the business to be discussed at that supper is no less than the high treason of the overthrow of the Lancastrian rule, the beginning of the Wars of the Roses, it is not likely that York would wish Buckingham to be privy to the conspiracy. The Arden 3 editor, taking York's 'At your pleasure' as a speech of polite dismissal, provides an early exit at 709 for Buckingham, who is eager to be on his way to bring the bad news to Gloucester. As in the preceding example, the change of address indicates a change of business and so a change of character involvement.

This sort of early exit functions to reduce the number of actors on stage, so decreasing the busyness of the scene and replacing it with a diminution of *foci* of activity, perhaps concluding with a single character who is allowed a final couplet or a long soliloquy, or, if concluding with two characters as in these examples, a quiet dialogue differing in tone from the animation that has gone on before.[8]

As a second consideration of directing the play on the page, the editor must decide how the actor should speak one particular group of speeches – specifically the 'aside'. R.B. McKerrow's *Prolegomena for the Oxford Shakespeare* (1939) addresses this problem. McKerrow describes two types of speeches 'aside': (1) 'those which are intended as reflections of the speaker for the benefit of the audience ...'; and (2) those 'when the characters on the stage are formed into two groups, one perhaps ... hidden ... commenting on the first group' (p. 55). These provide good starting points. To go further: the first type is a form of speaking that is spoken directly or indirectly to the audience (or privately to (an)other character(s)) as a specific contrast to a speech being made for public hearing in the context of the principal action on stage. It usually defines the remarks of a single character. The term 'aside' appears in Folio directions only some seventeen times, of which about half are in one play, *Pericles*; the direction is clearly not something that Shakespeare thought necessary to include in his text. He could depend on his actors to speak their speeches in a manner appropriate to the character they were representing and to the context of the action. Much has been written about discontinuing the vigorous custom of the last century in generously providing indications that speeches should be spoken 'aside'. Many modern critics hold that some speeches, traditionally marked 'aside', should be spoken aloud, so that they can be heard, even by the characters who, it was thought, should not be hearing them. So Hamlet's opening line – 'A little more than kin, and less than kind' – which since the time of Theobald's second edition (ed. 1740) has been marked 'aside', is treated as normal speech in the Arden and other modern texts.[9] The question of what should be spoken aloud or aside is so closely involved with the personality of the actors and their conception of their roles that this paper does not propose to enter that debate; it is hardly profitable for an editor to attempt to generalize when so many particulars of the director's craft impinge.

McKerrow's second type of article should perhaps be encouraged. That is, the form of speech which editors have come to call 'apart', though McKerrow does not use that term. No more does the Folio. That term does not appear at all in the directions of the Shakespeare Folio; but it does occur in the dialogue, e.g. 'Stand all apart' (*Richard III*, 4.2.1). Another term, 'They stand aloof', occurs twice in stage directions (*3 Henry VI*, 3.3.111.1, *Two Noble Kinsmen*, 5.1.136.7). (That form might have some currency now, if it did not come with irrelevant modern associations.)[10] 'Apart' is a useful term and it should be more widely used. The 'apart' can be an indicator of a longer condition or separated dialogue. It may involve several characters, and it can suggest a line of stage action parallel to the main line of action continuing on stage. It represents, like the 'aside', a divergent, not necessarily antagonistic, stream of action.

A most complicated system of 'apart' situations is that in *Henry VIII*, 3.2.1–203 (a presumed Shakespearean section). The opening sequence is conversation among Norfolk, Suffolk, Surrey and the Chamberlain (1–75). These four discuss the machinations of the Cardinal in conversation which constitutes the main (as it is the only) business of the scene. When the Cardinal and Cromwell enter, in the second sequence (76–104), the Cardinal and Cromwell, oblivious to the presence of the four lords on stage, converse, and their conversation becomes the main business of the scene. The business of the four lords is 'marginalized'; 'They stand apart' – as in Arden 3 (adapting Collier's 'They stand back' (ed. 1853))[11] – commenting on what they overhear from their own separated vantage, for the principal business of the scene has shifted from them and their conversation to the conversation of the Cardinal – including two soliloquies of the Cardinal after Cromwell has left him. The third sequence (105–10) is very brief: the King enters with Lovell, reading from a schedule. The four lords continue their discussion 'apart' while the King enters and reads. In the fourth sequence (110–35), the King recognizes that the lords are present (but not the Cardinal); his business with them becomes the principal business of the scene, and the Cardinal's role, which has been the principal business, now becomes marginalized and he must stand 'apart' while the lords and the King discuss him, describing his strange behaviour. At the King's command, Lovell recalls the Cardinal from his musings

(135 SD), and the Cardinal joins the main action of the scene, the conversation between the Cardinal and the King (the fifth sequence 136–203). Though the lords (and Lovell) do not contribute to this dialogue, they are no longer 'apart', having been brought into the main business by the action of the King.

An editor, seeking to be helpful, will indicate the status 'apart' first of the lords and then of the Cardinal. A plethora of 'aside' markers confuses, and those directions do not sufficiently clarify or make specific. Communicating his or her vision of this complicated staging – three separated groups of seven (or eight) characters on stage at the same time – is the job of the editor.

The third directorial function of the editor is to describe what the actors may do on stage. As this is primarily a responsibility of the stage director, the editor may well wish to be cautious in supplying directions. As a general rule, when the dialogue makes it clear what the actors are to do, the editor is well advised to do nothing. To supply no direction. As Hammond argues: add stage directions 'only if the action in question is not immediately and unambiguously evident from the surrounding dialogue'.[12] On those occasions, however, when the dialogue is ambiguous and the editor wishes the situation to be unambiguous, a direction is justified. An editor might say it was necessary. But, as Professor Russell Brown writes elsewhere in this volume: 'Annotation of what is unspoken ... calls for a close engagement with the texts as well as an evocation of theatre performance' (p. 172).

Two instances of this situation appear in the sequence of the kisses of Romeo and Juliet at the Capulet feast. When the lovers meet at the feast, as is well known, their first utterances to one another take the form of a Shakespearean sonnet (1.5.93–106). The final couplet of that sonnet is followed by another line of Romeo's (107). Editors obeying an earlier tradition, perhaps assuming that Romeo's speech should not be interrupted, have tended to place the kiss after Romeo's line, but the kiss is the punctuation of the sonnet – no punctuation more suitable – after the final couplet ('sake'/'take') and the fourteenth and last line of the sonnet, line 106.[13] The 'Thus' in line 107 becomes then in modern directing not anticipatory, but recollective.[14] This bit of stage business, as it is crucial to the text and the tone of the play, and as it is the subject of some critical disagreement, should be favoured with an editorial stage direction. Fortunately, most modern editions have recognized that the proper location for the direction is as the Arden has it.

JU

    Saints do not move, thogh grant for praiers sake. 105

RO

    Then move not while my praiers effect I take.    106 [*Kiss.*]

    Thus from my lips, by thine my sin is purgd.    107

JU

    Then have my lips the sin that they have tooke.    108

RO

    Sin from my lips, o trespas sweetly urgd:

    Give me my sin againe.    [*Kiss* ?]

JU

    You kisse bith booke.    110 [*Kiss* ?]

NUR

    Madam your mother craves a word with you.    111

Four lines later is the second problem of the kissing, at the end of a quatrain (lines 107–10), and here editorial and directorial judgments differ, and differ understandably. The first question here must be answered by directors and by editors alike: is there a second kiss at line 110? The absence of a direction here in an edition will leave the question to be answered by the reader who might not realize that there was an option. The absence of a direction to kiss on stage will answer the question decisively for the spectator; the presence of the action 'They kiss' will answer the question as decisively. But if there is to be a second kiss at this point, where should the direction be placed? Once again, this stage action seems of importance sufficient to warrant specific editorial assistance.

    The Arden editor and many others place the direction for a second kiss after line 110a; other editors place it after 110b. The decision is open to debate. Either placing has its advantage. To the present writer, it appears that the direction should follow 110b, Juliet's line, at the end of and punctuating the quatrain.[15]

The rhyme ('tooke'/'booke') defines the moment of intimacy which the calling of the Nurse rudely interrupts. Such an interruption at a tender moment is an ancient cliché, but the cliché still works (as any class B Hollywood film will testify), and Shakespeare, knowing its effectiveness, used this interruption as a foreshadowing of the more important interruption by the Nurse at Romeo's leave-taking in 3.5.36.1 – in exactly the same tender situation by the same boisterous figure.

But each director has one choice only. Editors must make that same choice, but they may explain in the commentary why they have made that choice and what the other choices are. Professor Holland again: it is important 'for an editor to alert readers and potential directors to the differing possibilities of the scene consequent on his [or her] emendation.... . Editors will need to make users aware of all those moments where there are no right answers'. But when editors are satisfied that a particular emendation of a direction is required for a full presentation of their particular interpretation, such editors are obliged to print that choice. Dr. M.J. Kidnie has in a recent article phrased this necessity well:

> Editors exert a great deal of intellectual labour weighing up a variety of staging options before choosing which one to print. The very difficulty, however, of the decision-making process implicitly validates the editorial activity, and behind assertions of the editorial responsibility to the author and the reader lies the conviction that the intellectually – even morally – upstanding editor is the busy editor.[16]

And while it is true that introducing such a direction – the editor's choice of 'which one to print' – may be prescriptive, failing to specify in that context will be equally prescriptive in the opposite direction. Hammond has argued in another context that 'when more than one staging solution is *viable* (even when ... one particular one was most likely), interpretation should not be narrowed by introducing prescriptive directions'.[17] The position of this paper is that, like directors, editors must indicate on the page as guidance to their reader/audience the instruction that they think 'most likely' – especially in matters of entrances and exits. Editors much be convinced of the rightness of positions they take, and at the same time they must be equally convinced of the possibility that their positions are not right but are wrong, and they must be ready in their commentary notes to explain the suitability of their choices and the consequences of alternate positions.

Elsewhere in this volume Professor Foakes – with a commendable absence of timidity – offers a clear and patiently thought-out example of this policy (pp. 136–7). Noting the lack of detail in the (Q/F) first entry direction for King Lear, he supplements for 'a modern reader' with terms that fully exhibit his particular interpretation of how that entrance should be staged. That is his editorial responsibility as a director; as his additions clearly contribute to the visual sense of the scene they will be appreciated by many readers.

Professor Proudfoot has called attention to this kind of situation:

> [When] editorial SDs are not merely hinted at or implied but defined and dictated by the text [, to] omit them is to run the risk of seeming not to understand the text, or even the whole mode and character of Elizabethan dramatic discourse. As we know, in the theatre directors and actors may do anything: our job as editors is to supply them with the initial aid of an exact and thoughtful reading of an accurate text. Not to offer editorial SDs is a purism which reduces the activity of editing to one of mechanical reproduction and runs the risk of privileging the editor over his users.[18]

One critic wants editors to be gleeful; another, to be morally upstanding; and a third, to be exact and thoughtful. There are no better prescripts, but I want them to be also observant and watchful, looking at the stage that should always be before the mind's eye.

## NOTES

1. *Times Literary Supplement*, 28 April 1995, pp. 3–4.

2. Antony Hammond, 'Encounters of the Third Kind in Stage Directions', *Studies in Philology*, 89 (1992), 96 (slightly edited).

3. Personal correspondence; kindness of Professor Honigmann.

4  P. xv. Quotations of the text are from the Folio, with the Through Line Numbering of Charlton Hinman; citations to an edition are to the individual volumes in Arden 3 or to the Arden *Complete Works*, revised edition (2001).

5  E.A.J. Honigmann, 'Re-enter the Stage Direction', *Shakespeare Survey*, 29 (1976), 117–25. Stanley Wells, 'The Editor and the Theatre: Editorial Treatment of Stage Directions', in *Re-Editing Shakespeare for the Modern Reader* (Oxford, 1984), 56–78. Hammond, pp. 71–99, esp. 75. Linda McJannet, *The Voice of Elizabethan Stage Directions* (Newark: Univ. of Delaware, 1999): the 'performance cues in the dialogue' (p. 203).

6  John Cox and Eric Rasmussen (Arden ed. 2001); more guardedly, their exit is 'Exit [guarded]'.

7  Ronald Knowles (Arden ed. 1999), who has (quite rightly) chosen to bring on 'Commoners' at line 17 to provide a visual fulfilment of the 'giddy multitude' of line 21. For further comment, see my 'Early Exits: An Open Letter to Editors', *Shakespeare Quarterly*, 51, (2000), 205–10.

8  It is perhaps worth mentioning that in both these instances, the close of 'Act 1' and the close of 'Act 2', the scene-ends provide powerful contrast to what immediately follows: the secret whispering of York at the end of 'Act 1' and the muted shameful dialogue of prisoner and keeper at the end of 'Act 2' are both followed by outbursts of noise: the noisy hallooing of the falconers (2.1) and the brazen interruption of the sennet (3.1). These deliberate contrasts at scene-ends – one is tempted to say 'act-ends' – display a youthful playwright already a dexterous master of one of the tricks of stagecraft.

9  Honigmann, p. 120.

10  Though these terms are rare in the canon, they are found often in other plays of the period (see Alan Dessen and Leslie Thomson, *A Dictionary of Stage Directions in English Drama 1580–1642* (1999)). Dessen and Thomson suggest that 'apart' can signify 'elsewhere on the stage'.

11  Gordon McMullan (Arden 3 ed. 2000).

12  Hammond, p. 92. Professor Foakes points to the directions that the actor Edward Alleyn added to his part in *Alcazar*.

13  Brian Gibbons (Arden ed. 1980). The text is quoted from Quarto 2; the lineation is the Arden.

14  A parallel situation in *Henry V*, 5.2. 272–3 (3262–3): 'therefore patiently, and yeelding. You have Witch-craft in your Lippes'. The first sentence is very close in tone to the first sentence in *Romeo and Juliet*, and the second is close in language ('move not'/'patiently'; 'thy lips'/'your lips'), the kiss occurring between the sentences in both plays.

15  So closing the quatrain, as the first kiss closed the sonnet. Some editors announce that the quatrain is the beginning of a second sonnet, though how they are privileged to have that information is not clear.

16  Margaret Jane Kidnie, 'Text, Performance, and the Editors; Staging Shakespearean Drama', *Shakespeare Quarterly*, 51 (2000), 456–73; esp. p. 473.

17  Hammond, p. 96.

18  Correspondence, April 2000.

# 9

## RAW FLESH/LION'S FLESH: A CAUTIONARY NOTE ON STAGE DIRECTIONS

### R.A. Foakes

Now that we have *A Dictionary of Stage Directions in English Drama 1580–1642*, compiled by Alan C. Dessen and Leslie Thomson (1999), the evidence is available to support further investigation of their nature and usage. The focus of the compilers is on 'that theatrical vocabulary found in tens of thousands of stage directions that constitute the primary evidence for what we know (or think we know) about the presentation of such plays to their original audiences'.[1] Alan Dessen has explored the nature of the signals provided by terms used in many common stage directions, terms that were part of a commonly accepted theatrical vocabulary,[2] and thinks we should not improve on them or standardize what is found in early texts. I want to take issue with his argument, and suggest that modern editors should expand and explain more than is customary in such scholarly editions as the Arden Shakespeare. I also go further than George Walton Williams, who thinks of stage directions in editions of Shakespeare's plays as 'correct' or 'incorrect' (see p. 112). It seems to me that the matter is more complicated, as can be seen if we attend to the surviving evidence of the way plays were staged at the Rose theatre.

The *Dictionary* shows that the basic vocabulary includes such terms as 'above' (300 instances), 'alarm' or 'alarum' as a call to arms (400, often with 'excursions'), 'ascend' (60), 'aside' (550), attire(d)' (90), 'banquet' (100), 'descend' (100), 'discover' (200), 'disguise(d)' (230). 'Enter' and 'exit' must be the best known terms in what formed a code readily interpreted by playwright, actors and readers. But familiar as they are, it is notable that the meaning of some remains imprecise; we do not know exactly what 'above' suggested to a reader, or what happened on stage when alarms and excursions were called for. In addition to this basic vocabulary are many other words and phrases that turn up less frequently, and a number that are rare, such as 'bastinado', 'brand' for a torch, 'dag' for a pistol, 'dart' for a spear and the unique 'gentle Astringer' who enters in Shakespeare's *All's Well that Ends Well.*

This last direction appears to be Shakespeare's own, but it is notoriously difficult to identify the authorship of most stage directions, which could have originated with the playwright, the acting company, or a scribe or printer. Clearly stage directions vary in kind, and Antony Hammond has distinguished six classes, three of which have to do with basic matters: getting on and off the stage, or entries and exits; speech-prefixes; and structural divisions, as into acts and scenes. A fourth category consists of directions implicit in the dialogue. The two classes he found most interesting are those relating to properties and stage effects, and all formal directions relating to 'whatever the words leave out'.[3] Some such separation of directions into different kinds might help in distinguishing between a basic common theatrical vocabulary and less common terms imported for special effects or peculiar in some way. There was also evidently a shared conventional way of placing and presenting directions, which as readers we take for granted. Thus speech prefixes are conventionally placed to the left of the text, and stage directions positioned in the centre if long, to the right if short. These conventions have been studied by Linda McJannet, who claims that, whatever their content, stage directions 'observed a set of shared conventions when it came to the *form* in which directions of various kinds were cast'.[4] The widespread acceptance of basic conventions of vocabulary and form explains why surviving play-scripts show that 'nothing was done to an author's directions unless the players felt it to be necessary'.[5] The extant manuscript playbooks are often sparsely marked-up, with no concern for regularity or thoroughness, and few theatrical alterations.

Okay – but hold on a moment – isn't there something odd about prompt-books being casual in their treatment of directions, and interested only in entries, some exits, and some effects or properties, while little concerned with the last class, those relating to action, to whatever the words leave out? Antony Hammond, taking his evidence mainly from Middleton's *Second Maiden's Tragedy* and from Webster's marginal annotations in the printed text of *The White Devil*, found that an authorial manuscript was more likely to contain directions of a kind that 'assist a reader to visualize the play', so he concluded that most of what happened on stage is not to be found in stage directions, and that 'action on the Elizabethan stage was much more elaborate than can be demonstrated from virtually any of the surviving texts'.[6] Authors such as Webster in 1612 and Jonson in his 1616 Folio went to some trouble to supply readers with directions to assist them in visualizing the action, but they were exceptional in doing so. In the public playhouses of the 1590s it would appear, if Hammond is right, that prompt-books required only a minimum of basic stage directions, and that anything more in printed texts was likely to have been provided by the author.

If this seems odd, it may be because the playhouses continued to operate using a method we know was employed at the Rose. The staging of a play there was indicated less by the text than by the 'plot' hung, apparently, where the bookkeeper and actors could see it. One of the extant plots is of special interest in this respect, that of George Peele's *The Battle of Alcazar*, relating to performances in 1598–99 or later. The plot of this play was drawn up for a revival long after the play was written (about 1589), and several years after a quarto was published in 1594 claiming to present the play 'As it was sundry times played by the Lord High Admiral his servants'. The printed text is short at just under 1,600 lines long, and was called an 'abridgement' by W.W. Greg. It was studied by Bernard Beckerman from the point of view of performance, and he noted that 'The stage directions for most scenes in the Quarto are too vague to tell us much about the intended staging'.[7] For most scenes perhaps, but, as Beckerman observes, there are anomalies, most notably at the beginning of the play.

The plot has been damaged, and lacks the fifth act. It has no act divisions, and is divided by rules into scenes, but it has a series of dumb-shows with a presenter that in effect serve as act-divisions, two of which, 'Actus secunda. Scæna prima' and 'Actus 4', are so marked in the Quarto. The plot merely numbers the dumb-shows that begin what the author may have thought of as the first four acts. In the Quarto the play begins with two dumb-shows: in the first, Muly Mahamet shows his two young brothers 'the bed, ... and they betake them to their rest', after which a Presenter speaks; then in a second dumb-show, Muly enters again with two murderers, who 'draw the curtains, and smoother the yong princes in the bed. Which done, in sight of the unkle they strangle him in his chaire, and then goe forth', and the Presenter speaks again. Nothing of this is to be found in the plot, which merely names the actors who are to appear, including two pages to attend Edward Alleyn, who played Muly Mahamet the moor. The elaborate directions in Q, which include the phrase 'in sight of the unkle', suggesting an author visualizing the uncle perhaps being strangled facing the audience or showing his terror, presumably were written by Peele. It could be that they are not in the plot because the stage was set up with a curtained bed for the opening of the play, and the actors knew what to do. Evidence for the later dumb-shows is more elaborate in the plot than in Q. For the second, the plot calls for Nemesis to enter 'above', then three ghosts and 'to them lying behind the Curtaines 3 Furies', one with a whip, one with a 'blody torch' and the third with 'a Chopping knife'. The properties required are also listed in the margin. Nemesis and the Furies are mentioned in the text of the Quarto, but the only direction is '*Three ghosts crying* Vindicta'. The third, very elaborate dumb-show in the plot, which calls for Nemesis, Furies with scales, three ghosts, vials of blood, and much fetching and carrying, is omitted altogether from Q. The fourth, which again is detailed in the plot, requiring dead mens' heads and bones in dishes and the appearance of Death and three Furies, is abbreviated in Q to the single direction, '*Enter to the bloudie banket*'. The plot lacks the final act, and Q has a substantial entry for the last dumb-show calling for 'Fame like an Angell' to hang crowns on a tree, for a blazing star and fireworks, and for the crowns to fall one by one. It seems as if the printers of Q had a manuscript containing the author's directions for the dumb-shows of the first and last acts, but not the other three.

Greg believed that Q was 'drastically cut down' by omissions and 'by the suppression of spectacular shows', for staging by a small cast, but Beckerman has shown that the two texts agree structurally, and that there is little difference in the number of actors required (Beckerman, 121). Beckerman agreed with Greg, however, that Q 'retains the sort of vague directions' that Greg supposed 'an author might be expected to write'. These include directions for entries 'with others' (omitted from the plot); 'and others' (Jonas, soldiers, a guard and Christophoro the Governor of Tangier in the plot); 'Enter Stukley and the rest' (Stukeley, Jonas, Hercules and an Irish Bishop in the plot); and 'Manet Stukley and another', who is simply called 'The other' in speech prefixes ('manet Stu[kl]ey and Duke of Av[ero]' in the plot). Q also has several uses of the term 'traine' meaning unidentified followers, though in one case (Act 3, Scene 4 by Greg's count), a long list of characters is named in the plot, including Calipolis. This is the second entry in the plot for Muly Mahamet with his empress Calipolis in their chariot, and she is omitted from both corresponding entries in Q. The plot has numerous marginal reminders for music as 'sound' or 'sound sennett', most of them not in Q. The plot is generally more precise in requirements for properties and action than Q, as in noting a 'Chopping knife' needed for one of the Furies, whose weapon is mentioned in the text as a 'murderous iron'; in requiring 'raw flesh', where the text of Q has 'lyons flesh'; in calling for two to bring on 'a chair of state' in Act 3, not mentioned in Q; and also in noting 'boxes for Presents' to represent what are called in the text in Q 'tokens of their gratitude'. Apart from the full descriptions of the opening dumb-shows, which the plot lacks, there is one direction in Q calling for Muly's 'treasure' to be brought on stage (1.2). This is not noted in the plot, perhaps because, although it is mentioned in the text, there is no need for it to be displayed.

The plot includes both the names of the actors for each scene and the names of the major characters. It specifies 'sound' or music (fanfares of trumpets mostly?) in virtually every scene. It is also specific in noting what properties are needed, as in the dumb-show for Act 3, where scales, three vials of blood and 'a sheeps gather' are needed for the Furies. Beckerman (118) thought the differences between the plot and Q showed that Q's directions are 'imprecise', and literary rather than theatrical. The issue is complicated by the fact that while most directions in Q are printed in italic, some are in roman type, and Beckerman concurred with Greg in thinking that italic represents the vague directions an author might write, while the directions in roman type were added to shape the 'original copy into a prompt copy' and reflect 'the initial staging of the play' (121). There are fourteen places where directions in roman type are found, eight of them in Act 5, where the plot is lacking. The rest are in Acts 1 and 2. Eight of these directions begin with 'Alarum' or 'Sound an alarum'. The plot has 'sound' twelve times in marginal notes, and 'Alarum' once. The italic directions in the printed text include only two calls for sound, one for trumpets and drums, the other for trumpets. Beckerman made much of such differences, claiming that the directions in roman type 'deal with practical stage considerations', while the italic directions 'specify entries, often with the tag of an indefinite number of supernumeraries' (120).

In fact almost all the entries, italic and roman, have something to do with the entry of characters, and if the roman ones were added at some point, it was to make the printed text understandable. The stage directions in the printed text are such as a playwright who was used to working for the stage might have written. There are a few indications of an author imaging the action, as in the reference to 'lyons flesh', but the author presumably provided descriptive directions which were converted in the plot into notations of the order in which actors should appear, with a listing of properties and sound effects where required. If so, then the plot complemented the author's manuscript by providing a detailed mapping of entries with actors' names, a notation of properties required, and other practical indications of staging, as when the Furies 'lying behind the Curtaines' enter as from a cave in Act 2. It is not usually possible to separate authorial from theatrical directions in the way Beckerman claims. He is rehearsing a familiar received opinion that classifies dramatic documents in two ways, 'as documents designed to be working tools towards the production of the play and as documents designed to present a reading text for a different public' (Hammond, 72). It is more likely that in *The Battle of Alcazar* we have two different kinds of theatrical document. The author provided indications of the way he envisaged the action, and these were translated into production notes by the bookkeeper in the plot, who might expand, simplify or modify in other ways what the author had indicated, but without changing anything radically. He added to the number of actors mentioned in Q in what was one of the spectacular productions at the Rose; the plot contains the names of twenty-five actors, including eleven sharers, seven hired men, and seven or possibly eight boys, who might be used as mute pages to accompany a chariot (in 1.2) or to attend ambassadors (2.4); these pages are not mentioned in the printed text.

Three times in the first four acts Q has entries that call for a 'traine', twice for Abdelmelec, and once for the King of Portugal. This widely used term (140 examples, according to the *Dictionary*) does not appear in the plot, which lists the characters and actors required. So the second one at 3.4, if Greg's reconstruction can be trusted, demands a sennet and drum and colours to precede the Portuguese 'army', which includes the Duke of Avero, Stukely and others, who enter at one door, while at another door Muly Mahamet and Calipolis come on in their chariot with attendant moors on either side and young Mahamet. The entry in the *Dictionary* notes that '*train* can serve as a permissive term that leaves open the number of actors involved', as at *A Midsummer Night's Dream*, 2.1.59, and *2 Henry IV*, 5.5.4. When it indicates a retinue (rather than a garment) it could include important characters and must surely have served as a dramatist's shorthand that needed to be fleshed out with the names of the stage players added in the theatrical plot. The actors who formed the army, on the other hand, are not named in the plot, and presumably included anyone available.

Although dramatists might have individual quirks of wording, as Chapman alone uses 'gulf' to indicate a trapdoor, and Heywood alone uses 'fray' for a fight and 'fireball' for some kind of firework, the vocabulary of stage directions seems to have been in the main a shared one, and unusual terms are typically self-explanatory, even if we don't know how the players dealt with exceptional demands, such as that for 'A Crocodile sitting on a river's bank, and a little snake stinging it' (*Locrine*, lines 961–4). The occasional surprising phrase that seems to give us the author of a play in the act of writing, as in what seems to be Shakespeare's own wording in *Timon of Athens*, 1.2, 'Then comes, dropping after all, Apemantus, discontentedly, like himself', may prove not to be unique, as several characters in other plays appear discontentedly, and at least one other, Orlando in *2 Honest Whore*, 4.1.28, comes on 'like himself'. 'Like' is very common (300 examples), and here the term may be referring to what two lords said of the 'unpeaceable dog' Apemantus towards the end of the previous scene – 'He's opposite to humanity'.

It may be that a new author had to pick up some of the customary ways of presenting play-texts to a company. Marlowe, for instance, seems to have begun in *Tamburlaine* by simply naming the characters for a scene and rarely using the word 'Enter'; in his later plays he uses 'Enter' pretty consistently. In Part 1 of *Tamburlaine* many entries add 'with others' or 'with his followers' after the named characters; in Part 2, the word 'train' is used nine times, a term which seems to have been an accepted way for dramatists to indicate to the players that they wanted a show. The plot of *The Battle of Alcazar* shows that a 'train' could involve actions, the use of properties, and mutes not mentioned in the printed text. Each part of *Tamburlaine* is divided into five acts and scenes, and has some elaborate stage directions that might be authorial, such as that for soldiers to enter 'loden [= laden] with treasure' (1.2), or a direction such as, 'Tamburlaine goes to her,

& takes her away lovingly by the hand, looking wrathfully on Agidas, and says nothing'. In this last one, the adverbs are not so unusual, as the *Dictionary* shows, listing 'angrily', 'earnestly', 'strangely' and others found in a variety of plays;[8] but 'and says nothing' is superfluous, since no lines are assigned to him. In later plays Marlowe reduced and simplified his stage directions, which are much less descriptive, and more like a shorthand for players to expand. In *The Jew of Malta* there are act but no scene divisions, and not a single adverb; and directions may be very casual, as in 'Enter with a hammer above, very busy' (line 2281), where the name of Barabas is omitted, and no servants are mentioned, though he exchanges words with one in the scene that follows. *Edward II* has no act or scene divisions, and directions are limited in the main to entries, exits and indications in 'manet' or 'manent' that characters are to remain on stage. There are very few individual touches, the most unusual being 'Enter with Welsh hooks Rice ap Howell, a Mower, and the Earl of Leicester' (line 1912).[9]

A full accounting of Marlowe's stage directions would have to take into consideration the nature of the printed texts, and whether they can be identified as authorial or from prompt copy. However, stage directions relating to effects and to 'whatever the words leave out' may, as Antony Hammond argued, appear 'more extensive and complete' in authorial texts than in texts printed from prompt-books, but it does not follow that they show what was done on stage. At the Rose theatre the Admiral's men worked with a stable of dramatists, many of whom must have become acquainted with the way the theatre operated. Some, as perhaps Marlowe did, adapted to the ways of the players, and learned to streamline their directions. It would be wrong to generalize from the stage 'plot' of *The Battle of Alcazar*, but this shows that the bookkeeper and players interpreted the author's demands in their own way, and were concerned with practicalities. What authors describe may not have been what was done on stage; and the players, concerned with practical matters, may have used the plot rather than the prompt copy to specify how things were to be done, as, for example, in *The Battle of Alcazar*, 3.1, where one party enters at one door, the rest at another, but Q simply has

'Enter'. If relations between directions in printed texts and what the players did are complicated, there is yet another factor in the use of parts for players. Only one survives, that for Edward Alleyn in the role of Orlando in Robert Greene's *Orlando Furioso*, another Rose play.[10] The part abbreviates or omits many of the directions printed in Q, while adding some not in the printed version. A number are in Latin, e.g., 'pugnant' for 'They fight a good while', perhaps Alleyn showing off his knowledge, but a few, such as 'he walketh up & downe', and 'he whistles for him' indicate stage business and actions specific to the part of Orlando, of a kind not found in the plot of *The Battle of Alcazar*.

What does all this amount to? I have been focusing on what seem to have been working practices at the Rose in the 1590s. These practices may well have changed as time went by, and it may be that we should not lump together 'Elizabethan and Jacobean Stage Directions' as Antony Hammond did in his challenging essay. It would appear that at the Rose there were at least three documents involved in play production: the author's manuscript or a transcript, containing the author's ideas as perhaps modified by a bookkeeper; a stage plot, containing all the entries, with actors' names and notations for properties and effects; and actor's parts for some leading roles. The relationship between these seems to have been complex. It may be true, as William Long asserted, after studying manuscript playbooks, that 'nothing was done to an author's directions unless the players felt it to be necessary', but that does not mean that those directions were followed, for they may have been expanded or changed in a stage plot, the immediate working document for stage production; and stage business could have been added in an actor's part. The author's own directions might be very elaborate in imagining an action, as in Thomas Heywood's *The Brazen Age* (printed 1613, but performed at the Rose in 1595):

JASON

　　When setst thou ope
　The gates of hell to let thy devils out?
　Glad would I wrestle with thy fiery bulls.

OETES

Discover them.

*Two fiery Buls are discovered, the Fleece hanging over them, and the Dragon sleeping beneath them. Medea with strange fiery-workes, hangs in the Aire in the strange habite of a Conjuresse.*

Heywood wanted his *Ages* plays to be full of spectacle, but, lacking stage plots for them, we have no idea whether or how the players met his wishes. Henslowe's 1598 list of properties included a golden fleece,[11] but it would be interesting to know how the players dealt with the discovery of 'fiery bulls'. What the author desired may not be what the players did. What the players did we cannot know for sure in the absence of the plots and actors' parts that might have supplied this information.

There is also a problem in interpreting stage directions. There are two especially interesting ones in the plot for *The Battle of Alcazar*. At the end of Act 2 three Furies apparently bring on stage in turn three characters, Sebastian, Stukeley and Muly Mahamet, and simulate ripping out their vital organs. The marginal note specifies '3. violls of blood & a sheeps gather', or the heart, lungs and liver of a sheep. Does this mean that whenever this play was performed, the bookkeeper, Edward Alleyn, or someone sent one of the lads round to a nearby butcher to fetch what had been ordered in advance? Are we to imagine Alleyn saying, 'We'll really sock it to them today, plenty of blood and guts'? It would seem that here a 'real' property was used to simulate parts of the human body. But what was in the vials of 'blood' – required so often on the stage that there must have been a common substitute to represent this? While they were about it, the company probably also obtained from the butcher some 'raw flesh' for Muly Mahamet to stick on his sword in 2.3, where the stage direction in Q has 'lyons flesh'. The staging was evidently intended to be sensational.[12] What then of the direction at the beginning of Act 4, 'Dead mens heads & bon[es]' to be brought on in two dishes, with more blood? Many plays of the period have directions calling for severed heads, and Shakespeare was rather fond of them, so we must assume that the company had properties made to look like heads that could be stored and used repeatedly – a variety of heads are listed in Henslowe's inventory of 1598.[13] But were the bones also fetched from the butcher? It is not a simple matter to interpret the directions in the plot of this play.[14]

What I have been describing has implications for the editing of Shakespeare's plays. Editors tends to be cautious, as in the Arden edition, and treat directions found in the earliest printed texts with great respect, adding and changing as little as possible. George Walton Williams would encourage editors to emend and provide a correct direction where directions are absent or misleading in early printed texts. I would go further and suggest that editors should be encouraged to take more liberties in suggesting possible action. It could be useful for editors to use the *Dictionary* to distinguish for modern readers between directions that were in common use and part of an accepted theatrical vocabulary, and those that seem special to the author or play. If the actors adjusted the author's directions to suit their practices, as in substituting butcher's meat for lion's flesh, then editors should perhaps feel free to speculate on ways in which the directions found in printed texts might have been interpreted on stage. Since the 'plots' used on stage may have identified effects, properties and even characters not specified in the printed text, editors perhaps should also feel free to try to reconstruct what might have happened in action. Alleyn's part for Orlando has directions not found in the text of the play, so editors might go further and look constantly for possible stage business. Let me end with one small example. In editing *King Lear*, I based Lear's first entry in the opening scene on the Quarto and Folio texts: Q has 'Sound a Sennet. Enter one bearing a Coronet, then Lear, then the Dukes of Albany, and Cornwall, next Gonorill, Regan, Cordelia, with followers'. F is similar, but omits 'one bearing a Coronet'. Lear's entry is announced by Gloucester, 'The King is coming', and I now think that for a present-day reader it would be useful to expand the entry to 'Sennet [or flourish of trumpets introducing a formal processional entry]. Enter one bearing a coronet, then Lear [in majesty, crowned], then the Dukes of Albany and Cornwall, Goneril, Regan, Cordelia, and attendants'.

The crown is necessary to establish both the image of the king and the meaning of the lesser 'coronet', and the formal nature of the scene may not be obvious to laid-back readers of the twenty-first century.

## NOTES

1 *A Dictionary of Stage Directions in English Drama, 1580–1642*, compiled by Alan C. Dessen and Leslie Thomson (Cambridge, 1999), citing p. vii. Hereafter it is referred to as *Dictionary*.

2 Alan C. Dessen, *Recovering Shakespeare's Theatrical Vocabulary* (Cambridge, 1995), especially pp. 85–7.

3 Antony Hammond, 'Encounters of the Third Kind in Stage-Directions in Elizabethan and Jacobean Drama', *Studies in Philology*, LXXXIX (1992), 71–96, especially 71–2.

4 Linda McJannet, *The Voice of Elizabethan Stage Directions. The Evolution of a Theatrical Code* (Newark: University of Delaware Press; London: Associated University Presses, 1999), p. 21.

5 William B. Long, 'Stage Directions: A Misinterpreted Factor in Determining Textual Provenance', *Text*, 2 (1985), 121–37, citing 125.

6 Hammond, 'Encounters', 81.

7 Bernard Beckerman, 'Theatrical Plots and Elizabethan Stage Practice', in *Shakespeare and Dramatic Tradition. Essays in Honor of S. F. Johnson* (Newark: University of Delaware Press, 1989), pp. 109–23, citing p. 119.

8 Under 'look, looking', p. 136.

9 These 'hooks' are not indexed in the *Dictionary*.

10 Antony Hammond has tabulated the directions in the part against those in Q in an appendix to 'Encounters of the Third Kind in Stage-Directions in Elizabethan and Jacobean Drama', *Studies in Philology*, LXXXIX (1992), pp. 97–9.

11 *Henslowe's Diary*, ed. R.A. Foakes and R.T. Rickert (Cambridge, 1961), p. 319; and see E.L. Rhodes, *Henslowe's Rose* (Lexington, Kentucky, 1976), p. 118.

12 On the love of spectacle at the Rose, see Rhodes, *Henslowe's Rose*, pp. 116–23.

13 *Dictionary*, p. 112; *Henslowe's Diary*, pp. 319–20.

14 Neither 'bones' nor a 'sheep's gather' are indexed in the *Dictionary*.

# 10

# READING IN THE MOMENT: THEATRE PRACTICE AS A GUIDE TO TEXTUAL EDITING

*Lynette Hunter and Peter Lichtenfels*

We are interested in the extent to which theatre practice contributes to and interrelates with editorial practices. While our exploration is partly context-specific it also raises a number of general questions about editing, especially about the theory of copy-text.[1] The context for this essay is an edition of *Romeo and Juliet* for the Arden 3 series: one of us is a theatre director (Peter Lichtenfels) and one a bibliographer (Lynette Hunter). The bibliographic and textual context for the essay is bound to the editing history of *Romeo and Juliet* to which we have a specific remit to bring theatre practice.

The bibliographic context of the play materializes in the four editions published in quarto format before the Folio edition [F], with Quarto Four [Q4] possibly after. Quarto One [Q1] and Quarto Two [Q2] are quite different to each other, the former being roughly two-thirds the length of the latter. Q1 is plot-focused, based in romance, direct and with narrative point: for example, what does a young man do when feudal structures and late-medieval concepts of manliness disintegrate? Q2 adds material for actors to work on in terms of characterization, on rhetoric and figuration, on women, on the non-gentry characters, and is far more ambiguous about manliness, femininity and effeminateness, as well as more contradictory about the relation between capital and the law, the domestic, the civic and the state. Because we are interested in the social and political relations of the early modern period and how they have laid grounds for current liberal nation state democracies, our edition is based on Q2 and edited to offer a historically contextualized material object. It is not an 'authentic text', but a reconstructed text close to what was available to a sixteenth or early seventeenth century actor or reader, yet readable in the twenty-first century, and which actors, directors, readers and critics may engage with, adapt, cut and analyse for contemporary purposes.

The reconstructed text is difficult to see as a distinct material object outside of its apparatus and commentary because it often 'looks like' an authentic text which tries to duplicate exactly what the late sixteenth century had in its hands. The line 'O if I walke, shall I not be distraught' (4.3.49) is apparently the same, but for typography, in the Q2 edition and in that of the Arden 3. Yet the Arden has been thoroughly dismantled and rebuilt by editorial work informed by bibliographic, critical and theatre practices. At the same time, the Arden 3, in common with most editorial practices, also produces a text that does not 'look like' Q2 when we, as editors, consider the significance of the text to be curtailed. It is not necessary to deploy theatre practice in reconstructing a text, but what we have found difficult to articulate are the bases on which we have allowed theatre practice to inform our decisions about whether to keep or change the Q2 text, given that there is so little previous scholarly work that has wholeheartedly used the theatre.

Critics tend not to address the problem of whether to take Q1 or Q2 (or Q3 or Q4[2]). Bibliographers disagree about the status of Q1 and Q2: they do not know which was first, or the extent of influence of one on the other (both issues preoccupy them). Editors tend to go for Q2 because it is more complex, hence more satisfying for literary critics if not necessarily for cultural studies. And directors tend to opt for Q2 because most printed editions use it, but often cut it so that it resembles Q1. Editions make significant changes to Q2, as with any editing, but there is a particularly high variation because there are so many early texts and because of the popularity of the play on the stage. Despite the frequent 'failure' of stage performances, the play is often produced. Editions are at times influenced by a vague guideline called 'will it work in the theatre?', and take the theatre practice of cutting and adapting the text as a justification for a number of decisions. However, productions change texts in line with cultural pressures that are often economically and financially initiated, and to do with expected running time, rehearsal length, content and available actors. Hence this guideline is usually to do with cultural suppressions rather than engaged textual work. Just as frequently, a production will decide on a particular edition and simply reproduce, with cuts, many of the suggestions that appear in it.

The process of directing a play is completely different to the process of editing. The director is there to cohere the production company, and to structure the building blocks or the grammar of the production so that the actors can take responsibility for connecting, through the text, to themselves, to other actors, to the elements of the stage and to the audience. The director's primary task is to listen, and to ensure that all the elements in a production – from lighting to stage management to costumes – work on making it possible for the actor to continue to work out what is asked of them from moment to moment from the first rehearsal to the last performance. The actor will know the detail of their character better than anyone, including the director whose work is focused on finding and making possible the rhythms of the interaction of the production elements, not the rhythm of any one character. Unless there are specific elements such as swordfighting, blocking is not a director's function. As long as the situation is played, where the actors are on stage does not need to be predetermined and will be responsive to their training in breathing, movement and relaxation. The text is articulated through doing, not in advance. It has to speak to each audience and will change from one to another.

This is not to say that the insights of a director are impossible to bring to a critical edition, but precisely how to bring this experience to bear without replicating the reductiveness of the public stereotype of directing is difficult. This essay will focus on some elements of work that a director does with the actors, and on specific strategies for directing different kinds of texts. Having made the decision to reconstruct a material text historically contextualized by the late sixteenth century, we used a device from theatre practice to make one of our most important decisions. After a bibliographic study of the first four Quartos and the Folio, we decided to take Q1 and Q2 and put them into production as if they were new plays. This made possible an experience rarely realized on the modern stage: productions that used a text with little editorial input, except as a physical object, after 1623. Many subsequent editorial actions were informed by this experience, as we moved into more conventional editorial strategy. While there is an enormous amount of commentary that illuminated the text in ways the initial productions had not anticipated, there were also many instances where the social, cultural and political differences, the historical differences between an earlier edition and what it needed from its relationship with the text and our needs, became apparent.

The usual means for understanding the changes in a text is the collation. The bibliographer for our edition constructed a collation between the production of Q1 and those of Q2, completing it at the same chronological time as those latter performances. We were struck by the inexorable power of working on collation, during which one follows the historical logic of particular decisions, and how this generates a physical musculature of acceptance. 'Yes' the bibliographer would say, 'I understand that change, it's appropriate for the social context', and the new word or punctuation would sediment itself into understanding. Despite all the training in historical materialism and the theories of subjectivity and discourse, all the previously hard-won theoretical battles and risky writing, collation, like evolutionary theory, can trap one into progressivist concepts of literature and language. Even its visual format implies linearity.[3] When the bibliographer watched the final performances of Q2, she experienced considerable shock, as did many in the scholarly audience who were intensely familiar with the traditional editorial work.[4] One described the experience of hearing the word 'hour' instead of 'honour' at 1.3.68 and 69 as an awkward event, like recognizing a phantom limb after amputation, not getting the satisfaction of the expected completion to a body memory. Those who did not know the text apparently found the word acutely funny, going so suddenly from Juliet's momentous marriage 'hour' to the Nurse's sexual 'hour'.

At the same time, in retrospect, we would want to argue for the importance of collation as a strategy for foregrounding what is often implicit in editorial practice in general, that it precisely locates the historical specificity of decision-making. It makes us self-conscious about the ease with which audiences transform the past into what is appropriate for the present day, and it may be helpful to the actor who would like prompting to historical difference in order to work better on embodying current needs. But actors also work on language and text in ways less available to the literary critic: through their breath, their bodies, their physical interaction with other actors and the audience. The basis of this essay is to begin to try to articulate how some of those elements may guide editorial decisions, so that they may offer an alternative set of guidelines, not to replace traditional editing but to enhance it.

## ELEMENTS OF THEATRE PRACTICE IN TEXTUAL EDITING

The danger with the account here is that on the whole it deals with the strengths rather than the weaknesses of theatre practice[5] and with an artificial commitment not to cut the text. Q1 was workshopped with an undergraduate acting school yeargroup at Manchester Metropolitan University, and Q2 was produced with a mixed cast of undergraduates and graduates and semi-professionals in an MFA programme at the University of California, Davis.[6] In addition to semantics, rhetoric and gesture, the companies worked on punctuation, grammar and syntax, prose and verse layout, old and modern words, irregularly syllabic lines, act and scene division, stage directions, and various structural features. Some of these elements were later workshopped with the Globe Theatre (London) Winter Players. The result of the California productions, on which we will concentrate, was a reconstruction of Q2 that worked in theatre practice, and which included quite a bit that has been stripped away and forgotten by generations of editors, even if it also drew on and illuminated many of those decisions as well.

Take for example some of the structural features such as repetition which have worried modern editors. Nearly all of the major cruces of the Q2 text are concerned with repetition of material that generations of editors have explained away as having been 'lightly scored out' on the manuscript, an erasure carelessly ignored by the compositor. During the Friar's explanation to Juliet, Q2 includes the line 'Be borne to buriall in thy kindreds graue' (4.1.111). Presumably because of the word 'borne' being repeated in the fourth line, most editors excise this one. However, as Randall McLeod argues, the repetition could easily be part of the characterization of Friar Lawrence, who is elsewhere in the play quite wordy.[7] We would rephrase this to suggest that the repetition gives the actor something to work on in terms of breath and voice. In production the actor playing this part built a performance that led to the audience recognizing a sense of someone tending to think as he speaks, emphasizing the improvisatory quality of the Friar's plans for Juliet and Romeo and the unpredictableness of their actions. Similarly Romeo's fly encomium (3.3.40–4)[8] in Q2 has repetitions in lines 40 and 43 that prompt editors to rearrange the lines in various ways, often consulting Q1 or F. From the F text onward, which omits lines 43–4, editors have decided that these lines are problematic and partly redundant. However, the text constructs Romeo's part largely out of generic structures like the Petrarchan, or the Ovidian, or the neoplatonic, and here the 'fly' blazon, with a specific movement to disintegration in each one. An actor can work on the generic breakdown to find patterns of body movement, the repetition in this case providing the textual material to release the energy of disintegration.

Possibly the most substantial but least debated of the repetitions occurs at the end of the 'balcony' scene, 2.2.188–93, which concludes in Q2 with four lines before the penultimate couplet, similar to the opening four lines of 2.3. The repetition is not much debated, except in terms of whether to give the lines to Romeo or to the Friar (usually to the latter), and which lines to take or whether to take an amalgam of the two sets. Even R. McLeod notes that the repetition would not have been present in 'any production involving Shakespeare'.[9] McLeod argues for the inclusion of the lines anyway because they indicate the process of writing and revision the text has undergone, and their presence encourages the reader to read actively and think for themselves about the production of the text. It is an admirable position with which we would fully agree, but the fact is that the Q2 productions both used the repetition to good effect. The actors playing Romeo found the change of register from the preceding lyric into this Ovidian style required a complete change to their movement on stage. For the character of Romeo the lines indicate for the first time his recognition of the end of the night and the start of a day in a positive way. In contrast, the actor playing the Friar begins with this florid image that serves in practical terms as a way of thinking about waking up, and prompts him to think about whether the echo is a warning, a disturbance, or as an indication of how close the character is to Romeo. For the audience, the repetition implies an overlap of time that impels us from one scene to the other, constructing the illusion of haste that ominously emerges in 2.3.

The one repetition which the production could not handle positively occurs in 5.3 just before Romeo takes the poison. He is describing Juliet's body and begins a long passage of repetition with 'I will believe / Shall I believe' (5.3.102–3). In effect this causes little problem, and armed with the significant difference between 'will' and 'shall', the former indicating the simple future tense and the latter an sense of promise or command, the rephrasing can offer the actor more material for working on the growing desperation of the character. But the repetition of 'Depart againe, come lye thou in my arme. ... Thus with a kisse I die' (5.3.108) in various following lines, especially the concluding 'O true Appothecary: / Thy drugs are quicke. Thus with a kisse I die' (5.3.119–20), is difficult for an actor because death is an action that cannot be repeated. Quite apart from any critical sensibilities that may be offended by exact repetition, the theatre performance was not able to deal with the more pressing question of how to die the second time. It is of course possible to do so if the actor plays for comedy, but there is enormous resistance to maintaining the comic line of the play this far.

At another extreme of textual variance, the stage productions looked at punctuation as a guide to breath, voice and movement. Sometimes the Q2 punctuation was exceptionally helpful in understanding the dynamics of a scene. For example, 1.2.37–8 reads '... and to them say, / My house and welcome, on their pleasure stay.' while the Cambridge, Arden 2 and Oxford editions all read '... and to them say, / My house and welcome on their pleasure stay.' The latter editions signify by line 38 'My house and my welcome are waiting for them', but the comma after 'welcome' in Q2 indicates a different signification, 'They are welcome to my house. Wait to find out whether they can come.' Either reading makes sense, but the comma after 'welcome' changes the dynamic between CapF and Peter, making it far more practical as a command given to a servant.

Rhythm is also controlled by punctuation, and theatre productions tend to follow the rhythm built into the text they are using. Of course some changes from Q2 can be helpful. For example, 1.2.45 reads 'Tut man, one fire burnes out, an others burning,' yet as early as Q3, which often changes only grammar, spelling and what it perceives as punctuation 'errors', the comma after 'out' is deleted. Q1, Q4 and F follow this marking, and most editions since. The opening to ambiguity and double-meaning that the deletion makes possible is productive and enabling to the actor. In contrast we could turn to 2.4.154–61 during which the Nurse is angrily berating Peter and Romeo, the former for not defending her and the latter in anticipation of his manipulation of Juliet. The Q2 text inserts a colon after 'knave', 'worde', 'selfe', 'say' and 'yong', constructing a long hypotactic sentence out of the entire speech. The construction is exceptional in this play, and the actors working on this part found the colons controlled their breathing and led to the production of speech that kept finding dead ends or truncations, kept being frustrated from finding any completion. For the audience the speech began to signify the Nurse's confusion about her responsibility: she was supposed to set up a meeting for Juliet with Romeo, but after having seen the behaviour of the young men, here she was blustering around not quite being able to deliver the message, torn between the contradiction of being a servant and being a guardian. The Cambridge, Arden 2 and the Oxford editions substitute semicolons and full-stops for the colons, which for an actor will arrest the momentum of speaking. Yet there is a problem here because the colon is today not a frequently used punctuation mark, so it is difficult to decide how to render the pointing for a modern edition.

Other kinds of significance affected by punctuation can refer to the definition of a word. A contentious line by Juliet at 3.2.52 reads in Q2 'Briefe, sounds, determine my weale or wo.', a punctuation that in contrast to 1.2.45 is unchanged in Q3, and remains unchanged in Q4 and F. Most editions punctuate as 'Brief sounds determine my weale or wo.', implying that 'sounds' refers to the 'ay' and 'no' of the previous line, presumably because women of Juliet's social standing do not usually swear in Elizabethan plays (despite Queen Elizabeth I's reputation for doing so) and even more because editions have a hard time imagining Juliet as other than an innocent girl. But the punctuation in Q2 led the actors to read the line as signifying 'Be brief! zounds! determine my weal or woe.', in effect swearing at the Nurse for her lengthy prevarication which has tantalizingly suggested that Romeo may be in trouble, may even be dead. Juliet's line follows a speech (47–51) in which the text demonstrates a disarticulation of the self, a breakdown of sorts, which could easily leave the actor casting about for rhythm, stress and sense, making a swear word rather appropriate. 'Zounds' is a contraction of 'God's wounds', a word apparently so strong that the Folio editors twenty-odd years later would not set it.[10] But the Nurse's reply 'I saw the wound' indicates that she did probably hear this word, which is also spelt as 'sounds' elsewhere in the text (3.1.101).

A third area in which theatre practice can refresh editorial practice is in the handling of lines that are not syllabically consistent. This is a highly debatable element in Shakespearean study, because of the complexity of metrical understanding both today and in the late sixteenth century, and our lack of knowledge about verse-speaking in the early modern theatre. But acting craft today usually includes voice training in verse-speaking, and several techniques emphasize breaking down the text into syllabic units[11] and further into morphemic and phonetic elements. With syllables, an actor working on *Romeo and Juliet* is faced with considerable regularity: most verse lines are ten syllables long. The compositors working on Q2, Q3 and Q4 were clearly aware of the ten syllable convention, which anyway often marries up with the stresses in a line, and would change spelling to indicate whether or not to include say a spoken 'ed' ending by setting 'banished' instead of 'banisht'. But there are a number of instances where they do not regularize the syllable count, even though it would have been possible to do so. 1.2.14–15 reads in Q2 'Earth hath swallowed all my hopes but she, / Shees the hopefull Lady of my earth:', which remains unchanged in Q3 but is altered by Q4 to read 'The earth. ... / She is ...', presumably to conform to the ten syllable line. The actors working on the Q2 production, however, found the nine syllables of each line a provoking instability, a temporary wavering from the almost pedantically regular rhyming couplets CapF uses in this scene. For the audience the temporary difference seems to locate some loss of control, some disturbance in the presentation of character that could generate all manner of signification. Many recent editions recognize the potential and retain Q2, although Arden 2 changes 'She's' to 'She is'.

In contrast, at 3.2.77 Q2 reads 'Rauenous douefeatherd rauen, woluishrauening lamb,' which nearly all editors change to some shortened form such as 'Dove-feather'd raven, wolvish-ravening lamb' (Arden 2) or 'Dove-feathered raven, wolvish-ravening lamb' (Cambridge, Oxford). Q3 does not change the line except to hyphenate 'wolvish-ravening', and Q4, despite its concern to regularize 1.2.14–15, simply shifts the syntax to, 'Ravenous dove, feathred raven, wolvish ravening lamb', neither being concerned to change the syllable count. Actors working on the speech commented that the line's excess pinpoints the turnaround in the scene, from the rhythm of the initial distress and breakdown to the character's controlled logic and sudden mature hold on the situation. The line is not so much irregular as anarchically lengthened in the face of convention. Many other syllabically irregular lines, in comparison with the surrounding verse, make markedly different demands on the actor, whose work contributes to moments of extreme stress in performance.

If these examples indicate places where an edition might want to reconsider prevailing attitudes to what 'works on stage', an example of the way conventional theatre practice interacts uncritically with editing is in the relatively unaware attitude that productions take to their chosen texts. Scene 1.5 is a case in point: most editions refer to it as a 'ball scene', and most productions reproduce this setting. However, our production, working on Q2 as if it were a new text and therefore without this kind of editorial guidance, reinforced what the text actually tells us, that it is a 'supper' and that the young men gatecrash it just as it is finishing, yet the codes of hospitality demand that they be welcomed and a dance is started. Recent research has elaborated on the gatecrashing, demonstrating that the young men are likely to have been recognized as part of a group of 'amorous maskers', given special licence to disrupt and be entertained.[12]

Another instance of a place where the theatre productions frequently cut because they cannot understand the rationale is during Juliet's 'false death' scene in 4.5. The lamentation of the characters is repetitive and can initially feel redundant. Editions rarely cut it presumably because each lamentation is unique and they rarely comment on it as difficult for stage production. On stage the fact that the words are unique is not necessarily helpful, especially when the verse tells us little about action and is formulaic about character. Staging the scene in our productions led to the actors foregrounding the *commedia dell'arte* elements so that the scene becomes a burlesque, hovering on the line of mocking death at the same time as sharpening the sense of grief.

The scene provoked exceptionally strong reactions in the audience, with some objecting to the overt mockery but most overwhelmed with a sense of shocked nervous laughter. The scene can also be played with effect as a Senecan lamentation. We had the opportunity to work with the Globe Winter Players on 4.5 and the actors played the lines as if they were pieces of formal epideictic funeral rhetoric, each actor facing the audience and focalizing the grief of their character. Even more suggestive was an experiment indicated by Q1's stage direction 'All at once cry out and wring their hands'. For this work the Globe actors spoke at the same time first using the text of Q1, which is not as balanced in terms of lines or character as Q2, and which cuts the Nurse's part completely. This rendition of choral lament was untidy and difficult to orchestrate. However, when the actors turned to the same work with the text of Q2, the effect was rhythmically powerful, with words and sounds echoing from speech to speech, indicating that the whole lamentation could work as music rather than text.

## DISCUSSION ABOUT GUIDELINES

Recent editions pay lip service to traditional editorial guidelines, often saying that Q2 is their main text, or copy-text, but having few qualms about using Q1 where they prefer it and in fact ending up with a text more like Q4 with cuts. Editions of *Romeo and Juliet* rarely adhere to theories of copy-text, except very loosely, yet put nothing in their place. At the same time they accrete changes from other recent editions, or at times from earlier editions across the 400 years of Shakespeare edition history, to find a proof or source for a particular word or phrase that they like. This may be ameliorative with regard to recent editions, and arbitrary with regard to earlier editions. Either way, without explanation it is culturally passive, the result being a relativist text: one that does not provide a rationale for its choices, one that can give the reader, including the director and actor as readers, little guidance about how to engage with the text, and hence implicitly authoritative. For us this is a problem. Even if teachers are there to guide readers through an edition, the whole point of editing for us is not to make a text conform to what 'most of its readers' think it ought to be, but to encourage and engage the reader in the enjoyment, if hard work, of reading differently. Theatre productions are just as likely to read an edition with little interaction because they simply do not know how to engage.

Copy-text theory[13] was born of the 'New Bibliography' of the early twentieth century, and a recognition that the idea of a 'definitive text' based on an analysis of book production was self-defeating. The more we find out about the production and distribution of books, the more complex texts become, not less. The idea of copy-text attempted to anchor editorial decision in a set of common grounds that could at least be accepted as reasonable guidelines. But changes in reading practices mean that we can no longer distinguish between accidentals and substantives with the same confidence. Authorial authority is increasingly questionable, both in terms of theorizing about the status of the author as distinguished from the writer, and in terms of what historians have suggested about the probable interaction between writer, text and acting company. We have to have better reasons for using Q2 than copy-text theory, to provide more appropriate guidelines for reading the text today. As David Greetham has pointed out, neither psychologistic nor social textual critics address the problem of 'evidence',[14] probably because both still depend solely on the concept of subjectivity. Yet even those writers who do address this problem and distinguish as for example Tanselle does between document and work,[15] or as Shillingsburg between document, work and version,[16]do not offer an alternative concept for deriving one's source text. Greetham's own suggestion that textual editing is closely connected to psychoanalysis, while exceptionally generative, does not move beyond the discursive resistances to textual power. And as generative as it has been, McGann's concept of textual engagement as 'invariably multiple' cannot respond to the situated knowledges in which we all live,[17] for which interpretation is not only desire but need.

Producing the Q2 text taught us many things about the play that added valuable reasons to the decision to base our edition on this earlier printing, and which illuminated many of the issues that the play's text throws up. We would like to retain nearly all the repetitions of Q2 because, for different reasons, they worked in theatre practice. Similarly the punctuation of Q2, although not entirely helpful, was largely enabling: it constructed helpful ambiguities, encouraged the actors to work on breath rather than syntax alone, and indicated significance layered under contemporary assumptions; and the lineation of Q2 suggested many points of change in rhythm and meaning that were closed off by more recent editions. In addition, the productions of Q2 text helped to understand the text's scenic development in different ways that would have been outside the remit of conventional editing. And these are only a few of the elements that theatre practice can contribute. Among others are a better understanding of silences and absences, an awareness of how the actions prompt the words rather than the words the actions, and the aural play with etymological connections. Each element that guided us to a particular decision became apparent in rehearsal and/or performance, but in effect the actor or director is working as a reader, so all these elements can also inform readings by people working on text outside the theatre.[18]

Is our use of Q2 a return to an 'authentic text'? No. The work of theatre practice in producing a draft edition was not an attempt to restore the text but to reconstruct it, and reconstruction occurs in the present. We want to produce a text that gives readers and theatre people access to choices which have been stripped away and forgotten by generations of editors, on the basis that

(1) editions have removed or changed things because of the cultural needs of their historical position, which may not be appropriate to the readers or performers who will use this Arden 3 edition;

(2) theatre workers usually rewrite texts, and that if they do so from an already reduced version their choices and interpretations will be unnecessarily limited;

(3) readers need to be encouraged to do similar work on full texts but possibly for different reasons;

(4) traditional editorial practices can be evasive and implicitly authoritative, and editions sometimes justify cuts and changes because 'it wouldn't work on the stage' and theatre practitioners frequently go along with the changes, mainly because they don't have time to test them out.

There will however be many emendations and changes that are made because of an overlap: partly because of theatre practice and partly because of traditional editorial practice.

Is this a theatrical 'artefact'? It just happens that this production worked, but what basis does that give us for including or excluding or changing material? All editing has been the result of bibliographic or critical artefact. One needs good reasons, reasons that will be accepted as appropriate, for theatre practice as an editorial tool. Given that this is one of the first times a professional theatre director has been asked to co-edit a scholarly edition, we can only propose reasons that seem to be 'good' by analogy. There is a carefully prepared script that relates to bibliographic evidence. The work of actors and other theatre professionals on voice, movement and staging is taken account of in the script. And the critical reception and audience response has informed a number of decisions. However we also realize that one of the implications of bringing theatre practice to editing is to develop a new or different attitude to reading. Hence some 'good reasons' will only be testable after publication. Is this work a return to a 'definitive edition'? We were asked this question on a number of occasions and would firmly answer 'no'. Although there is a danger that copy-text could be replaced by copy-performance, or copy-production, just because these productions worked does not mean that we imagine that all subsequent productions should use all of Q2 as rendered in this edition. Theatre does not work that way, or at least engaged, responsive and responsible theatre does not. Our productions were editorial productions, produced for the specific reason of reconstructing the text. If another production gets the 'Depart again …' (5.3.108ff) speech to work in terms of voice and movement, staging and reception and response, then that might be a reason for including it. Of course if one thinks that the purpose of a production is to fix an interpretation, then there will be definitive editing from theatre practice, but that is not the purpose here. We would like to produce a printed text that offers the reader or theatre person more choice, and more possibility of engagement. If you like, the theatre director approaches textual editing as if the text were an element of the production process. Hence the main concern is to ensure the edition makes it possible for the actor to work on finding a rhythm from moment to moment each time the text is played.

These possibilities are the primary reasons for working on an alternative set of guidelines for editing which pays attention to theatre practice. Those familiar with the text will know how to engage, just as theatre people used to working on new texts will almost invariably reconstruct many elements in a script for their own purposes, so an edition like this will simply inform their decisions with detail of which they may not have been aware. But those unfamiliar with the text, which means most of its readers in the case of *Romeo and Juliet*, for although many know the story most encounter the text just once, are not used to the idea of choice. They do not get enough training in the craft of textual editing to understand how to use it; there is a problem in how to educate the reader into a more active engagement – with this play, an engagement with a text that nearly everyone thinks they already know. Readers not only have a right to know that some of the guidelines are different, but also that the difference in those guidelines highlights what is necessary to their engagement with the text. Indicating those differences is our most difficult task.

Producing the play for reasons of editing means working on exceptionally alien bits of the text and being committed to understandings that might be elusive, just as reading a critical edition is an act of reading committed to dealing with difference. Reading for difference takes resistant reading one stage further. Not only does one read in a 'writerly' way, resisting representation, but one also faces difference and negotiates the possibility that there are some things that will elude both understanding and resistance. Understanding is the ability to 'stand under', comprehend the grounds and uphold meaning in a way related to another representation of history or politics. Resistant reading challenges representation with its ability to make visible grounds in someone else's work, and to constitute significance that is denied by understanding. Reconstructive readings are specific to a cultural materiality; they depend on the ability to negotiate, to net together new grounds between oneself, one's context and the text, that will delineate the materiality of difference. Reconstructive readings build the supportive processes to validate actions that respond to the needs of a particular situation: they work moment to moment. Only when the grounds for negotiation are in place and value is recognized can resistant readings occur, and resistant readings are those that make us self-conscious/aware of the limits of understanding.

We are not going to jump out of the social and cultural envelope we are in, and many recent and not-so-recent editorial decisions and insights inform our own choices. However, *Romeo and Juliet* is a late sixteenth century text and part of the value of studying or reading it is to face difference, to develop a respect for history and culturally specific practices, to be better aware of those today. One of the aims of our editing is to reconstruct a text that has acted as a primary source text for other editions over the last 400 years, because we believe an awareness of the relations between them is part of modern history. Textual editors could take on the labour of enabling reconstructive readings more readily. Our edition wants to offer a text that not only raises the political and social and cultural questions which we want to address (and our current readers to address), but also encourages them to engage with these issues in their particular situation. This is a process enabled not only by critic (literary or intellectual and cultural transmission) and bibliographer (physical transmission), but also by theatre person (transmission on stage). This essay is an attempt to articulate how that might begin to happen.

## NOTES

1 Richard Proudfoot, our general editor, has been guiding us with exemplary attention to understanding of theatrical practice – although as they say any opinions voiced and any errors made are entirely our own responsibility.

2 See L. Hunter, 'Why was the editor of Q4 *Romeo and Juliet* so intelligent?' in M. Bell *et al* (eds), *Reconstructing the Book* (Aldershot: Ashgate, 2001), 9–21.

3 Computer hypertexts will help with this issue because they visualize in icons much of the combination of flexibility and cultural specificity built into editing apparatuses and commentary, and because contemporary readers are sophisticated in iconicity.

4 The productions were, in the later stages, watched by several Shakespearean scholars from the Universities of California system who were kind enough to offer their responses.

5 One weakness is the impossibility of all-male casting being particularly significant as an historical bridge, although the main productions in California did address gender issues in a different way.

6 The work on Q2 involved a rehearsal period of ten weeks, and two single-sex casts, one female and one male. The women's cast started off the performances, followed by the men's, and the final four days brought together the two casts in two mixed-cast performances each. The two casts did not rehearse together (except for the fight scenes, for safety reasons), nor did they watch each other's productions before going onstage in the final four days.

7 R. McLeod, 'The Marriage of good and bad quartos', *Shakespeare Quarterly* 33 (1982), 425.

8 S.A. Tomarken, 'Flea encomia and other mock eulogies of animals', *Fifteenth-Century Studies* 11 (1985), 137.

9 R. McLeod, 'The Marriage of good and bad quartos', as above, 427.

10 G. Taylor, 'Swounds Revisited: Theatrical, editorial, and literary expurgation', in G. Taylor and J. Jowett (eds), *Shakespeare Reshaped 1606–1623* (Oxford: The Clarendon Press, 1993), 51–106.

11 For detail on this technique, see Patsy Rodenburg, *The Need for Words* (London: Methuen, 1993), and Cicely Berry, *The Actor and the Text* (London: Virgin, 1987).

12 M. Twycross and S. Carpenter, *Masks and Masking in Medieval England* (Aldershot: Ashgate, 2001).

13 W.W. Greg, 'The Rationale of Copy-Text', *Studies in Bibliography* 3 (1950), 19–36.

14 D.C. Greetham, 'Textual Forensics', *PMLA* 111:1 (January 1996), 32–51.

15 G.T. Tanselle, 'External Fact as an Editorial Problem', *Studies in Bibliography* 32 (1979), 1–47.

16 P.L. Shillingsburg, *Scholarly Editing in the Computer Age* (University of Georgia Press, 1986), 47–50.

17 J.J. McGann, 'Literature, Meaning and the Discontinuity of Fact', *Modern Language Quarterly* 54 (1993), 167.

18 For an extended discussion of the analogous work carried out by both actors and readers, see W. Worthen, *Shakespeare and the Authority of Performance* (Cambridge: Cambridge University Press 1997), 21ff.

# 11

## ANNOTATING SILENCE[1]

*John Russell Brown*

In a book, Shakespeare's words say everything to a reader, arousing endless reactions, associations and visual images. But his texts can do more than that. In theatrical performance, with the help of actors and their many supporters, the plays take on a living presence and a spectator views a complex phenomenon, an imitation of the everyday world that transforms ordinary occurrences and sometimes transcends and intensifies ordinary experiences. The words are still there but as part of an event in which they take on meanings that a reader might never consider and, indeed, might judge to be impossible or plain wrong. Words are eaten up in performance, and digested with much added, subtracted, accentuated or ignored; they give rise to a happening on stage that, on every occasion, is unique and, to some degree, surprising.

The contrast between a play read and a play experienced has increasingly occupied critics and scholars so that editors of a Shakespeare text will today take as much care with stage directions as with dialogue and, in annotation, will often indicate what particular performers have contributed or what performances seem to be required by the text. Stage histories, photographs, drawings and extensive quotations are used to place the reader, as far as possible, in a similar relationship to the text as a member of an audience. Such a task is more easily contemplated than achieved since no-one can possibly annotate all that has, could, or should happen on stage: the possibilities are infinite, the effects fleeting. Editors can describe a moment in particular performances by quoting brief eyewitness accounts but this involves ruthlessly selecting from among available evidence and presenting it without reference to the moment's place in an entire performance and, usually, without regard for the cultural viewpoint and personal prejudice of the witnesses. Alternatively, an editor may describe an imaginary performance in terms of movements on stage and physical actions that seem to be called for by the words of the text, although such a speculative account can provide no more than a disembodied staging, more like a diagram than a theatrical happening, a map than a terrain. All these modes of annotation take a reader only a little distance towards a play's theatrical potential and deal with it in fragmentary and abbreviated form.

The fundamental difficulties facing an editor who wishes to pay attention to a play in performance have been studied in recent years with a new thoroughness. At the University of Stockholm, Willmar Sauter with his colleagues and students have recorded what members of audiences have to say about a great variety of performances, taking in opera, revues and circuses as well as texts by Shakespeare, Calderon and Molière. From this detailed and carefully sorted evidence one conclusion became increasingly obvious: for all classes and ages of audiences, except the very young:

> *How* something is performed is obviously more important than *what* is performed.... If the spectator is not pleased by the 'how' of the performance, the 'what' becomes secondary and at times even irrelevant. In other words, plot and characters, drama, and text are of little interest unless the overall presentation is satisfying.[2]

Once an audience's view is taken into account, a study of a play in performance involves both presentation and perception. To quote Sauter again:

> ... in the theatre the 'message' is not something which is neatly packed and distributed to an anonymous consumer; instead, the meaning of a performance is created by the performers and the spectators together, in a joint act of understanding.[3]

This study of what constitutes a theatrical event recognizes the crucial importance of actors and acting, very much as Elizabethan writers tell us that theatregoers would do. Sauter's *The Theatrical Event: dynamics of performance and perception* (2000) notes that, with regard to the multitude of audience responses that were collected, 'a spectator only shows interest in the content of a performance when s/he finds the quality of the acting sufficiently high,'[4] a conclusion that seems to presuppose a specialist audience capable of aesthetic and technical appreciation. But once a sensory response to acting is taken into account as fully as intellectual reactions to a spoken text, appreciation of theatre becomes at least partially instinctive, open to everyone in much the same way as life itself. A 'joint act of understanding' need not be verbalized, nor even recognized and still less defined. David Cole's *The Theatrical Event*, written in 1972 and based on first-hand experiences rather than audience questionnaires and statistics, is more radical in identifying the actor's presence before an audience, rather than performance, as the unique feature of theatre as an art and the controlling factor in an audience's response. Cole argued that theatre provides 'an opportunity to experience imaginative life as physical presence' and that the actor's body is the agent that makes this possible.[5] Similarly, in 1930, Max Hermann had argued that 'the shared experience of real bodies and real space' is the fundamental feature of theatre as an art form:

> it is the body performing in space which constitutes theatre – the actor's bodies moving in and through space and the spectators' bodies experiencing the spatial dimension of their common environment, the particular atmosphere of the space they share and their response to the bodily presence of the actors.[6]

These and other studies of what constitutes a theatrical event consider words as only one element of a play-text in performance and not the one that dominates an audience's responses. Any effect that the words of dialogue achieve in a theatre production depends on live actors present on a particular stage before an audience, together with the changing perception of those spectators during the time of performance.

With texts as verbally brilliant as Shakespeare's, critics will be reluctant to accept that the actors' presence is the dominating factor in an audience's reception of them. It is far simpler to treat the plays as any other piece of literature. It is in book form that they are 'widely acknowledged as the central achievement of English culture'[7] and they are frequently studied as such. Having set out a text, an editor will be concerned to annotate words and syntax, verbal borrowings and literary influences, historical allusions and social references. But the continued success of Shakespeare's texts in performance argues against such simplification. More than words and literary contexts are involved when a play holds the attention of audiences and, with these particular texts, this is true with actors of very different talents and skills, performing in a wide variety of theatres, languages and social conditions. The almost universal theatrical visibility of Shakespeare's plays can hardly be an accident and leads us to suppose that he imagined their texts in performance as he wrote and that he chose words that would encourage actors to play a highly significant part in determining their meanings in action before an audience.[8]

Taking this view, an editor who wishes to show what life a text may have in performance sets out on a task that can never be complete. The difficulties may best be illustrated when words are at their simplest because here the actors' presence in their roles is necessarily the principal means of holding attention and engaging the imagination of an audience. At moments of silence, reaction must be sustained entirely by the actors' performances and there are no words to annotate; such moments are often placed where they are crucial to the play's action so that special care is called for in annotation. It is not sufficient to describe how simple words have been or may be spoken or to note the gestures that have been used: an actor's state of mind and body, his wordless presence that continues in silence, will also affect an audience. To present the play as it takes shape and meaning on stage at these times, an editor would have to recount how the accumulated experience of the play will influence both the actors' performances and an audience's reception.

In his last speech when Richard the Third repeats his earlier words, 'A horse! A horse! My kingdom for a horse!' (*Richard III*, 5.1.13), what different gesture, timing or inflection does the actor use? Since the first time he had spoken them, has he become more desperate or more confident, more weary or more energized, more deranged and disfigured or more direct and honest? How can this cry be the culmination of his other expressions of need and intention? Having spoken these words, does Richard leave the stage to seek his own death or Richmond's? Then *how* does he play his part in the unscripted fight that must provide the end of his performance? Because the final impression made by this tragic hero does not depend on words at all, but on the actor's physical bearing in combat after sustaining the progress of the whole play, huge difficulties arise in attempting to annotate such a theatrical event.

Antony Hammond, the Arden Shakespeare's latest editor, discusses the sources of Richard's last words, but neither the reason for their repetition nor any effects they might have. With regard to the fight, he notes its importance and identifies a textual problem:

> This, the most physically exciting moment in the play, is badly served by the Q[uarto's] stage-directions. The minimum to make it actable has been added here, but the director ought to feel free to improvise to make this wordless encounter between Good and Evil as symbolically effective as possible.

While recognizing the physical nature of the fight, the editor assumes, without discussion, that it has a single moral effect. Several paintings and many photographs, together with verbal accounts of performance, show other dramatic possibilities here that present courage, endurance, defiance or triumph, even, expressed in an actor's very stance and individual features – not a depersonalized moral message such as a director might have controlled.

With less space for annotations in the much earlier New Penguin edition (1969), E.A.J. Honigmann also identifies the importance of the wordless moment and provides exactly the same moral interpretation, offering his own instruction to both director and actors:

> This duel, in which Good overcomes Evil, is the play's supreme confrontation. It passes without a word, perhaps to emphasize its symbolic and ritual implications. Richard should be given all the violent physical action, and Richmond must bear himself calmly, with complete self-assurance.

Again, no alternative effects or actual performances are considered but the editor's 'perhaps' alerts a reader to uncertainties in this climactic confrontation and the personal exposure it ensures.

John Jowett's annotations in the more recent Oxford edition (2000) are literary and historical, rather than theatrical. They note that Richard's call for a horse is 'famous' and echoes of it 'often parodical.' Three possible sources are identified and two mutually exclusive interpretations of the words offered: it is either a cry that the loss of his horse had lost him his kingdom or a call for a 'fresh horse to continue fighting at any cost.' Jowett notes that there is no historical evidence for the single combat but that a similar ending is found in *The True Tragedy of Richard the Third* published in 1594; he adds that this fight 'has often been impressive and sustained in the theatre' but says nothing about its possible effect. Annotations in Janis Lull's 1999 Cambridge edition are even less about the play in performance. They note how the call for a horse was to become 'famous' and identify a 'similar line in *The True Tragedy*'; they offer nothing concerning the final fight.

Some verbally simple and repetitive moments are so naturally phrased that a reader may not notice the accompanying need for action without some editorial comment. Lear's 'Never, never, never, never, never' is obviously remarkable but a reader might benefit from being told how very differently the sequence has been spoken, whispered and exclaimed, how hesitant or assured the actor has been. Intellectual issues are involved here, concerning fate, free will and comprehension, but the range of possible emotions is equally huge, from fear to tenderness, desperation, submission, endurance or anger. In his Introduction to the latest Arden edition, R.A. Foakes draws special attention to these words:

> one astonishing and heart-rending blank verse line brings [Lear] and the audience to face death not only as the loss of all that is worth cherishing, but as utter oblivion; there are no flights of angels to hint at some possible compensatory heaven, but only the crushing sense that a process which started with a refusal to speak more than the word 'nothing' finds its culmination in death and the bleakness of 'never'. (p. 78)

A reader has been given a sensitive and deeply considered reaction to the simple words that could not be contained within the customary bounds of annotation and yet more remains to add if the moment is to be presented as experienced in performance. In saying these words, what is the physical effect on the speaker and what are his feelings? Is he weeping? Does he gain strength or is he weakened by speaking? Does he seem to have lost his way or found it? Each different embodiment of this moment will have its own emotional charge and add to the effect of the spoken words.

*King Lear* has many repetitions awaiting an actor's performance. For Lear's last speech, textual variations, the unavoidable physicality of death and the presence of his dead daughter have ensured lively debate in critical accounts of the play and in annotations that try, in little space, to deal with the complexities of performance. The New Arden's annotation notes that Lear's final lines 'complicate the ending by their very ambiguity' and, from the final repetition of two simple words, 'Look there, look there!'; concludes that the hero 'dies with all his attention focused on Cordelia, not any longer on himself.' What the dying Lear has seen on the lips and to whom he speaks, and why and how he reiterates these few words, have to go without notice, although the dramatist's reliance on such elements of performance might be considered the most innovatory feature of this moment. While his words are few, simple and repetitive, Lear's very presence, whatever its nature at this stage of the play, is an unavoidable and eloquent element in any performance.

At such a moment, feeling and sensation are so deeply based and powerful that annotation can scarcely cope with even a single possibility. G.K. Hunter, in the much earlier New Penguin edition (1972), keeps a tight rein on commentary. In contrast to the

Arden interpretation, his Introduction explains that Lear's 'climactic fivefold' *never* expresses his 'rejection of a world full of unimportant somethings' (p. 26). His annotation of the final words states that 'Clearly Lear imagines he sees Cordelia coming to life again, and then briefly debates whether he 'dies of joy' or in 'a mere delirium.' Hunter adds that choice between these alternatives is 'not very important for the play as a whole' and that it 'would be difficult for any actor to project a precise interpretation.' The Oxford edition published in 2000, printing a text by Gary Taylor that follows the Quarto 'when it seems defensible' (p. 84), gives a much shorter version of the Lear's final moments but includes the non-verbal 'O, o, o, o.' of its copy-text. Stanley Wells, who provided the annotations for this edition, comments: 'Rosenberg, pp. 319–22, records a variety of ways in which actors have portrayed Lear's death.' That adds very little unless a reader has access to a library sufficiently stocked to have a copy of *The Masks of 'King Lear'* (1972); it seems that the annotator thought that how this tragic hero died was of little consequence or had found that adequate annotation was impracticable. While the end of Lear is verbally imprecise and capable of being spoken in many ways, the actor's presence, however it has changed in the course of the play, will sustain and shape an audience's experience of the emotionally charged and physically weak moment, leaving its members to reach for their own interpretations.

Perhaps an editor's main concern in annotating simple but physically and emotionally significant speeches should be to indicate a range of possibilities and give some impression of how, on one or two specific occasions, the play has been acted and received. Or questions might be raised. For example, what happens towards the end of *Twelfth Night* in the silence before or after the incomplete verse-line of Olivia's isolated 'Most wonderful!'? What physical signs of involvement does she show and how do other persons on stage react? Is it only wonder that 'enwraps' her now and is she sure that it is not 'madness' (4.3.3–4)? Does the performance express pleasure or confusion? A little later, when Sebastian replies to his sister's 'My father had a mole upon his brow' with the simple words, 'And so had mine', his actions and very presence in the silence that the incomplete verse-line indicates can say more than the words themselves about remembered intimacy or present amazement, pleasure, tenderness, confidence or impatience (5.1.221, 239). These matters are easily ignored by readers but, when simple words are placed so crucially, an actor's performance can modify reception of an entire play. Comedies almost invariably end with wordless moments, accompanied by kisses, laughter or dance, or with withdrawal to some other place for celebration, and how these shared and wordless actions are performed will bring the plot's uncertainties to whatever resolution enactment of the drama has achieved. Carrying a significantly different charge at each performance, they bring actors and spectators together in a common acceptance, according to their varying imaginations.

Even when simple words are clear enough in their principal meanings, annotation could usefully note how a change in an actor's bearing can speak independently or with additional force. In *The Merchant of Venice*, when Shylock has been thwarted in his revenge against Antonio, he speaks briefly – 'I am content' – and then, having said he is 'not well' and promising to sign away his wealth, he leaves the stage. As Gratiano taunts him, an audience's attention is drawn to his lone and silent departure and, in the words of Willmar Sauter, *how* he leaves, rather than *what* he has said, establishes the conclusion of his role; it will be expressed in his backbone, steps, hands, face, eyes and the way he draws breath (4.1.191–8). Malvolio has a somewhat similar exit in *Twelfth Night*. After 'I'll be revenged on the whole pack of you', he has to relinquish a central position and cross the stage in order to make his exit; an audience's attention is drawn to him and, then, Olivia and Orsino sympathize and send Fabian to follow and 'entreat him to a peace' (5.1.370–3). Stage presence and the timing of speech, influenced by what is *not* said, can sometimes influence the effect of unambiguous and simple words: for example, in *Henry the Fourth*, Prince Hal's 'I do, I will' to Falstaff when he is playing the king in a tavern; King Henry's 'O my son' speaking to Hal shortly before death; and Falstaff's 'Master Shallow, I owe you a thousand pound' after the newly crowned Henry the Fifth has rebuffed his approach (*Part One*, 2.4.464; *Part Two*, 4.5.178 and 5.4.73–4). All these words depend for their effect on an actor's performance.

Some simple words and silences are so contained within ongoing speech that they might escape a reader unless an editor draws attention to them. In *Hamlet*, for example, nothing in the text refers to the prince's silence through the first sixty-four lines of Act 1, scene 2; it will, however, be notable in performance because, like no one else, he is dressed in black and not appropriately for celebration of a marriage. Hamlet's interjections in his first scene with the Ghost are very explicit but so brief and occasional that his continuous involvement has to be sustained by physical bearing and unspoken reactions. For all his many words, Hamlet's presence, developing throughout an actor's progressive performance, will sometimes complicate an audience's response to unremarkable words. It gives substance to phrases such as 'But come' and 'Nay, come, let's go together' to his companions after the Ghost's departure (1.5.175, 198). Towards the end of the play, having said 'how ill all's here about my heart' he refuses to say more with 'it is no matter … It is but foolery, but it is such a kind of gaingiving as would perhaps trouble a woman' (5.2.208–12); these doubtful phrases are all the words to help an audience sound the depths of the thoughts and feelings that can be seen to possess his mind. Shortly afterwards, having wrestled verbally with thoughts of augury, providence and readiness for death, Hamlet breaks off from talk with Horatio still more secretively, saying only 'Let be' (5.2.220); the actor must in some way make this switch and these simple words seem credible. Hamlet's very last words – 'the rest is silence' – also break off from other concerns and disturb syntactical structures. In this final moment, whatever he feels but declines to put into words, whatever weight of consequence he bears within himself, will be apparent in the actor's entire being, and that can make the strongest impression on the audience that watches the hero die.[9] What that will be depends on how the actor has reached this moment through the course of the whole play and how each spectator is able to respond to it. Hamlet is borne from the stage by four captains so that his inert body continues to hold attention and speak silently for all that has happened.

The General Editors of the latest Ardens, by seeking to 'present the plays as texts for performances',[10] have taken on an endless task because, by the time he wrote *Hamlet*, Shakespeare had come to trust actors to express more than he wrote down for them to speak. He knew that they would 'tell all', as Professor Sauter would expect, no matter how 'brief' their words or how hidden their thoughts and instincts (3.2.136–49). Other persons in this tragedy besides the hero have 'that within that passes show', an inner mystery that words cannot 'denote truly' (1.2.77–86). Their presence also 'speaks' and what that presence communicates changes in the course of the play. Of the women this is especially true, perhaps because of a socially expected reticence or the limitations of the young male actors who acted these roles: repeatedly, with few words or none, their very presence on stage implies what is happening within them. At the close of the first of two scenes with her father, Ophelia says only 'I shall obey, my lord' and, at the close of the second, after being called three times to go with him to the King, she says nothing at all (1.3.136 and 2.1.120). In both cases, her father's, words make her the focus of attention and, as she walks five or more metres before reaching an exit on an Elizabethan stage, her physical bearing and movements, both in contrast to her father's, will necessarily express her thoughts and feelings; an audience's knowledge of her association with Hamlet will ensure that she is closely watched. Outspoken and good-humoured firmness with her brother and vivid fluency in her account of Hamlet's visit to her closet (1.3.46–51; 2.1.77–100) make the silence of her subsequent withdrawals the more noticeable and effective.

In Act 3 scene 1, when Hamlet castigates all women with increasing violence and sexual repulsion, Ophelia's brief and simple prayers on his behalf and her silence about her own feelings will draw at least some attention away from his stream of words so that an audience becomes increasingly aware of the suffering that she feels but of which she does not speak. After he has left the stage, her speech becomes sustained and explicit in soliloquy, only to be silenced again when she is joined by the king and her father. When Polonius tells her, in the middle of talking with the king, 'You need not tell us what Lord Hamlet said, / We heard it all', she says nothing at all, her silence being more remarkable after the preceeding soliloquy. Whether she weeps or shows little outward sign of emotion, an audience is likely to feel with her and be outraged by how she has been treated. If she leaves the stage taking her own time after the others have left, and perhaps in a different direction, she will gain total attention so that her silent bearing makes evident the effect of what has amounted to remorseless and unwarranted punishment.

In Ophelia's two mad scenes, unspoken thoughts and feelings force many changes of subject and mood that are otherwise inexplicable. The most affecting of all, because sustained for a long time, is likely to be her silence when she enters for the second time and is faced, unexpectedly, by her brother. Only he speaks and yet, even when he addresses her directly and lovingly, she does not acknowledge his presence but remains caught up in her own silently tortured and scarcely manageable consciousness. Having started to sing, as she had done in the earlier scene, she probably does speak to her brother to say farewell[11] but she does not leave now and what happens next is left very much for the actors to invent or improvise. She distributes herbs and flowers to those around her in such a way that no one thanks her for them and, when she again sings, Laertes speaks like a chorus, not attempting to communicate: 'Thought and affliction, passion, hell itself / She turns to favour and to prettiness' (4.5.185–6). With another abrupt change, she leaves praying for 'all Christian souls' (4.6.197) as if, for the moment, she has found some new purpose. Although she says nothing of this, some Ophelias will make their last exit as if fated to their death, others as if they seek release in suicide; Gertrude later announces her death without resolving this dramatic uncertainty (4.7.162–3).

An audience may sense Gertrude's significance in the tragedy from her first silent entry as the bride of Claudius, her second husband, and from her silence when Hamlet insists against her advice on continuing to mourn the death of his father. When Hamlet agrees to stay at court – 'I shall in all my best obey you, madam' (1.2.120) – Claudius cuts into their talk as if he wants to prevent further intimacy between mother and son. As soon as he is alone, Hamlet, in soliloquy, states clearly that Gertrude's second marriage is the motive for his intransigence and that he must 'hold [his] tongue' about the consequences (l.159), but it is only later that Gertrude speaks briefly of this as the cause of Hamlet's mad behaviour:

I doubt it is no other but the main,
His father's death and our o'er hasty marriage.

(2.2.56–7)

Throughout the entire play she speaks little compared with other persons and sometimes falls silent when further speech is to be expected: in doing so, she repeatedly draws an audience's attention to the physical expression of her silent thoughts.

In Act 3 scene 4, the only occasion when Gertrude is alone with Hamlet, their talk is at first forthright and adversarial, quickly angry and impatient of proprieties, but Gertrude again falls silent for long stretches of time after he has killed Polonius who has been hiding behind an arras; then it is her presence and silent, unspecified actions that will sustain her part in the on-going action. Although she had started by sharply interrogating Hamlet, she says little in response when he passionately attacks the sexuality, irrationality and shamelessness of her second marriage: the 'rank sweat of an enseamed bed' (1.92). Eventually, begging him to say no more, she admits that he has forced her to look into her 'very soul' and that his words have been 'like daggers' in her ears (ll.88–91, 94–6, 101). In performance her very presence must be dreadfully distraught since, when the Ghost appears to Hamlet to whet his 'almost blunted purpose', the sighs of her 'fighting soul' are so obvious that he orders his son to intervene (ll.110–15). This 'visitation' gone, Hamlet speaks more 'temperately' than before and Gertrude, though she has seen or heard nothing, is more submissive in speech: 'O Hamlet, thou has cleft my heart in twain ... What shall I do?' (ll.158, 182). Her words are still few and she listens in silence as her son speaks of 'rank corruption' in her soul and of 'the bloat king' with his stale endearments, 'reechy kisses' and 'paddling in [her] neck with his damned fingers' (ll.150, 183–7). She has nothing to say when Hamlet proposes to 'lug the guts [of Polonius] into the neighbour room' (1.214) and so dispose of his victim whom she will soon call the 'good old man' (4.1.11). Five times Hamlet says 'good night' to his mother and not once does she say a word in reply or acknowledgement, even though he has made his peace with her:

> Once more, good night,
> And when you are desirous to be blest,
> I'll blessing beg of you.
>
> (ll.172–4)

When Hamlet finally leaves '*tugging in Polonius*', as the Folio text has it, she still says nothing. The next scene starts with Claudius asking her to 'translate' her 'sighs [and] profound heaves' (4.1.1–2) so she has probably remained on stage, as the Arden and other editors suggest. She may look so shamed and broken in spirit that an audience will believe her to be incapable of doing anything at all and yet, after a silence indicated by an incomplete verse-line, her first words are to ask for privacy – 'Bestow this place on us a little while' (4.1.4) – and then to follow her son's instruction by telling Claudius that he is uncontrollably mad, not 'mad in craft' (4.1.5–12 and 3.4.189–90): unexpectedly, in her son's absence, she has regained control of herself.

In this scene, generally referred to as 'the closet scene', the extent to which Gertrude appears to suffer in love or sexual longing for her son, or to feel guilt or shame for what she has done, will depend on how the role has been cast and performed. It is her very presence, not the words she has been given to speak, that must sustain her speechless engagement throughout much of the encounter. She may seem more ignorant than weak-willed, respond more with tears that with signs of terror, draw physically closer to her son or further apart. Hamlet contributes many violent and searing words but the progress of the scene, its emotional charge and the nature of its culmination, will depend on the presence of both actors and their varying skills, resources and imaginations, and their instinctive reactions to each other; in their very different ways, the two contestants will be strongest when almost equally matched. Annotation of this centrally placed meeting of mother and son, by far the longest and, perhaps, the most passionate conflict in the tragedy, cannot give an adequate impression of the play in performance without taking into account the deep-seated qualities of the two individual actors and the silences of Gertrude.

In later scenes, Gertrude's power over both Claudius and Hamlet becomes more evident in performance. When her husband calls her three times to 'come away' and acknowledges the 'discord and dismay' in his soul (4.1.28, 38, 44–5), she makes no verbal response, but her resistance to his pressure, when she refuses to move, will be physically marked in an increasing separation between them that is entirely of her own choosing. After Ophelia's first mad scene, Claudius again asks for her sympathy:

> O Gertrude, Gertrude,
> When sorrows come, they come not single spies,
> But in battalions.

> (4.5.77–9)

Despite the silence indicated by his opening half-line, Gertrude again makes no verbal reply and may chose whether or not to respond in some other way. Later, however, at Ophelia's burial, when Hamlet fights with Laertes so that they have to be plucked apart, it is his mother, not Claudius or Horatio, who tries to reason with him and, eventually, brings him to admit, 'I loved Ophelia' (l.264). She is the one who calms him with a tender, maternal simile:

> This is mere madness,
> And thus awhile the fit will work on him.
> Anon, as patient as the female dove
> When that her golden couplets are disclos'd.
> His silence will sit drooping.

> (ll.229–33)

At once he is reasonable, able now to view events objectively and in their long gestation. Mother and son having, at last, been close and verbally intimate, the play's action moves forward towards its conclusion.

When a Shakespeare play is performed as part of a theatrical event, action and words seem to spring from unspoken thoughts and feelings in such a way that the persons of the play seem to be alive in their innermost beings. To present a Shakespeare text so that readers may become aware of this potential in performance, editorial annotations should indicate where, how and to what effect this comes about. As the researches of Willmar Sauter and earlier scholars have shown, any play communicates to an audience by acting and bodily presence of actors on stage, as well as by the words that are spoken; indeed, Sauter concludes that the quality of the acting will always make a greater and more lasting impression on audiences than any other element of a production. The annotations of an editor who wishes to 'present the plays as texts for performance', as the Arden General Editors enjoin, should therefore help a reader to recognize what actors can effect in performance, especially in silences when there are no words to communicate to an audience. Ideally, they would indicate what meanings and sensations physical enactment will add to the literary value of the entire text.

Annotation of what is unspoken in Shakespeare's plays calls for a close engagement with the texts as well as some evocation of theatrical performance. It is both an inviting and an endless task that has been tackled in a number of ways. Collecting descriptions of separable moments of a play in performance and quoting them in numerous short footnotes to the text, as Robert Hapgood has done in his *Hamlet* of 1999,[12] provides a wealth of relevant information but cannot easily show how individual performances develop in the course of the play or how one moment is influenced by others. Editors with little space for theatrical annotation can find more scope to consider individual performances in their Introductions, especially if they limit themselves to a few roles in no more than two or three productions. Extensive commentary on several different performances requires a book to itself rather than an edition and then an account of a play's continuous life and its emerging meanings and sensations is liable to overrun the capacity of a manageable book. A theatrical commentary brief enough to be printed on a page opposite the text of a play together with glossarial notes may be able to deal with particular cruxes in performance more fully than conventional footnotes; the limitation of space in this format can sometimes lead to sharper distinctions than more discursive commentaries occupying entire volumes.[13]

Not withstanding all the difficulties, the annotation of silences and what is unspoken is a crucial task for any editor who seeks to represent the play as it can find its life in performance. The minimum that might surely be done is to mark where the most significant silences occur and suggest a number of ways in which they might be played or describe how they have been played in one or two particular performances. Any one moment should be related to how performance has developed in the course of the action and, if individual actors are considered, the style, direction and cultural context of their performances should be described in an Introduction. To do all this an editor will be aided by first-hand and varied experience of the plays in a theatre and by published research in Performance Studies, Communication, Theatre History and Theatre Theory that has, in the last few decades, added much to knowledge of practical theatre and provided terms for describing performance. The annotation of silence calls for an editor's constant vigilance.

## NOTES

1 Where annotations are quoted in this article, line-references are to the latest Arden editions, as specified; line-references for other plays are to *The Arden Shakespeare Complete Works* (1998).

2 Willmar Sauter, *The Theatrical Event: Dynamics of Performance and Perception* (Iowa City; University of Iowa Press, 2000), p. 49.

3 Sauter, p. 2.

4 Sauter, p. 49.

5   *The Theatrical Event: A Mythos, A Vocabularly, A Perspective* (Middletown, Conn.; Wesleyan University Press, 1975), Introduction, p. x.

6   The translated quotation and the subsequent summing-up of Hermann's argument are taken from Erika Fischer-Lichte, 'From Text to Performance: The Rise of Theatre Studies as an Academic Discipline in Germany', *Theatre Research International*, vol. 24, No. 2, pp. 171–2.

7   Stephen Greenblatt, *Shakespearean Negotiations: The Circulation of Social Energy in Renaissance England* (Oxford; Oxford University Press, 1988), pp. 160–1.

8   This argument is elaborated and its consequences for study and criticism considered in John Russell Brown, *Shakespeare and the Theatrical Event* (London and New York; Palgrave, forthcoming 2002).

9   Hamlet's last words are followed in the Folio text with 'O,o,o,o.Dyes'. The Arden editor considers this an interpolation to indicate that, in early performances, the actor would die making an audible response. Later scholars have been more inclined to accept the four vowels as an authorial addition to an earlier version. George Hibbard in the Oxford edition of 1987 translated them into a stage-direction. '*He gives a long sigh and dies.*'

10   See George Walton Williams in this volume, p. 112.

11   So the Arden's annotation argues; in the Folio the words of farewell are printed as part of the song and in the second Quarto they are not distinguishable from it.

12   In the Cambridge University Press series, *Shakespeare in Production.*

13   See *The Applause Shakespeare* (New York; Applause Books, 1996 and on-going) of which the present writer is general editor and editor of some of the eleven volumes already published.

# PART IV

ANNOTATION AND
COLLATION

# 12

# THE SOCIAL FUNCTION
# OF ANNOTATION

## *G.K. Hunter*

Annotation has, in the simplest idea of its use, the function of explaining obscure references inside works whose general import is clear enough. At a more sophisticated level, as a response to some general ambiguity, it is concerned with questions more than answers, and operates as the interrogator of texts rather than the explainer. In this function it is concerned to create a space for new modes of understanding, allowing for differences between intention and effect or between one type of reception and another, so that alternative emphases and understandings can co-exist and illuminate one another. Texts which seem to have become canonical, and therefore fixed in their general significance, can, with a change of environment, still be opened up to a rereading and redefinition of the set of assumptions that accompanied them when they were created. In these terms the annotator can act as a necessary interpreter between one angle of vision and another, one culture and another.

Shakespeare's plays are prime examples of work in which there is enough uncertainty about original purpose ('what he intended'), enough overlap between alternative possibilities of meaning or effect to sustain a history of annotation. Elizabethan drama, like other popular arts, was designed to fit in with the society that sustained it, but its poetic language allows it to treat these local situations as part of a larger understanding, so that meanings are always open to alternative interpretations. The history of Shakespearean annotation is thus a history of the means by which the multiform indeterminacy of the original can be accommodated within the cultural expectations of one age after another.

The poetry of the Elizabethan stage was not written to be read, but understood as embedded in the performed action of the play. This means that its original perceived meaning depended on matter not made explicit in writing and so not directly available to later generations. The coherence of the theatrical experience in which the words were heard depended on the coherence of the acting company and the response of the audience – factors likely to change from night to night, so leaving open a gamut of different possibilities, each one able to claim authenticity.

Of course there is every reason to suppose that Shakespeare did write the words that the actors spoke in his plays, but it was in his own interest and that of the company in which he was a shareholder that the written texts of his plays should be perceived by the audience not as an individual's literary product but rather as one part of a corporate activity only properly realized when spoken on the stage; the written words disappeared into the new medium. The primary purpose of such a script was to provide a set of signals, like those in musical scores, to prompt performers, and so, through the medium of performance, to communicate meanings to an audience and stimulate individual (and various) responses. It is a situation in which the actors might be thought of as the first annotators: they determined, by voice, by gesture, by pause and speed of utterance, the focus of significance for the words they spoke, and different actors, or the same actors on different afternoons, no doubt changed the emphases they gave to their speeches, and so the range of meanings that audiences could take from them.

If the actors are thought of as annotators we are of course thinking of a very different kind of annotation from anything we usually understand by the term, coming out of an unstable and instinctive process; and the Elizabethan auditor could not be expected to carry away from the theatre experience anything more articulated than an overall sense of excitement rewarded, a comic or tragic process understood as completed, but never available again in exactly that form. The audience did not, so far as we know, go to a performance of a 'Shakespeare play' looking to enjoy and memorize its literary quality. There is no evidence that Shakespeare, though he was part of the team, took it upon himself to impose on the actors his own vision of how his words hung together; they were professionals who knew what the audience wanted and how to give it to them.

The texts of such Elizabethan plays as managed to reach print are not normally helpful in a search for an 'author's intention' or a 'true meaning' that annotation can try to pick out and point to as authentic. The early printed versions presumably represent some derivative from the 'book' that the dramatist presented to the company at the beginning of a project, when he read out his play to the actors and they began to respond in terms of how they could deal with it inside standard techniques and expectations. As in later stock companies, the performers could rely on conventional meanings for stage behaviour that allowed both actor and audience to understand what to expect. If a particular action created particular problems in staging, such snags could be ironed out in rehearsals without leaving any evidence of literary issues that annotation might fasten on.

The company kept this 'book' as its controlling document, marked with the censor's permission to perform it, but the printed texts that seem to emerge from this process are bare of interpretative information, and it seems likely that such matter was never written down. The stage directions in such printed texts normally describe only basic necessities – entrances and exits, the placing of properties and other simple movements ('he goes aloft' etc.), matters that the 'bookkeeper' or prompter needed to keep track of.

The company was anxious that access to the material of its plays should be restricted to those who paid to see them performed, in what they regarded as the authentic expression of the meaning. The Quarto versions of Shakespeare's plays – with the possible exception of *Troilus and Cressida* – which is specifically said to have been 'never clapperclawed with the palms of the vulgar' –

were all derived at some remove or another from acting texts; and so there was little room for lexical interpretations, let alone annotations, other than those that derive from the indeterminacies of acting.

The event that changed this situation and opened up a very different future for Shakespeare's plays did not occur till 1623, seven years after his death and thirteen years after his retirement to Stratford. In that year the company agreed to release their copyright and allow a printing of Shakespeare's collected plays, including ten plays never printed before, not in the penny-pinching quarto form that was standard for individual plays but in the majestic shape of a folio 'on good bible paper', as a contemporary complained. What this 'First Folio' provided was a conspectus of a literary career – though not in a chronological form – and a set of plays to be read as authorial creations rather than theatrical documents, now open to detailed criticism, interpretative questioning and relevant annotation of meanings. The Folios are of course free from any printed annotation, but the image of the author and his work presented in these documents gives Shakespeare a prestige that, in reading and speculating and rereading, might seem to justify the kind of annotation that is found in other classic texts. In his Folio representation Shakespeare took his place alongside Ben Jonson and Beaumont and Fletcher, whose Folio collections represent a claim that *some* Elizabethan/Jacobean works for the stage (now closed down by an act of parliament) can be read as literary texts. The passage of the Shakespeare copyright from the acting company to the printers allowed the plays to remain available to the public for the whole time the theatres were shut, and it is clear that they flourished as commercial properties even if not yet as national treasures. The book was popular enough to be reprinted in 1632, 1664 and 1685, with only minimal correction and some modernization of spelling and punctuation – compositors normally modernized their texts in these respects.

These reprintings, each one derived from its predecessor, carried Shakespeare's plays into a world in which, though the texts were hardly changed from 1623, the achievement had to be understood in completely different terms. After years of political and religious turmoil the country at last had space to think of itself as the possessor of a stable culture, linked to that of its continental neighbours by common standards of European culture, but independent of Europe in its vision of the 'free-born Englishman's' freedom to choose what he liked – a freedom that Shakespeare could be held to represent.

The acknowledged power of Shakespeare's poetry made him an important factor in this patriotic idea of separate English achievement and allowed him to appear as a vernacular classic who needed to be given the respect that belonged by right to a national figure. Jacob Tonson, the publisher of all the major writers of the late seventeenth century – Dryden, Addison, Steele, Tate, Congreve, Wycherley and Pope – obviously saw that there was a space for Shakespeare as another of his classic authors. He bought the copyright from the printers of the last Folio and commissioned Nicholas Rowe, dramatist and translator, to give the plays the proper classic treatment. In 1709 Rowe produced his first edition, and followed it up in 1714 by a second. Rowe was not himself an annotator, but by removing the disfiguring signs of the volume's origins in a hopelessly provincial, unfocused or 'Gothic' culture, he enabled the plays to show forth the classic quality that would support the dignity of annotation. He regularized spelling and punctuation, provided lists of characters and names of locations, plates or 'cuts' illustrating each play, and collected materials for a life of the poet.

There was of course some difficulty in this elevation of Shakespeare to classic status, which French critics did not fail to notice. Judgement of literary merit, it was agreed, depended on the fulfilment of neoclassical standards drawn from the theory and practice of ancient Greece and Rome. Classical literature provided the touchstones that would determine the validity of any claims for cultural importance. It offered the only acceptable models for a civilized society. Moreover, knowledge of the classics was supposed to provide a bulwark against inherited local backwardness, disruptive individualism and provincial vulgarity as well as grammatical and stylistic incoherence – elements that were frequently seen as the definitive characteristics of more primitive times, such as the Elizabethan age. If Shakespeare was to be allowed the status of a classic author, it was necessary that he should be defended in neoclassical terms.

If the definition of annotation offered at the beginning of this essay is accepted it will not be taken as surprising that the first systematic annotations of Shakespeare's texts should appear at the point when the claim that these were masterpieces was being argued in terms that the new society thought central to the idea of excellence – and these were the terms not of theatrical effectiveness but of neoclassical literature. Having begun, as Dr. Johnson remarks, 'to assume the dignity of an ancient and claim the privilege of an established fame and prescriptive veneration',[1] Shakespeare and his works had to be understood in terms that cut him off from the standards of his own profession and his own time – a time now generally agreed to have been without any proper understanding of classical social or literary values. But it was not enough just to claim that Shakespeare transcended the values of his own age; he had to be seen as embodying, in some way or another, the values of the age in which he had arrived. Only in these terms could his works be used as evidence of a well-established national culture able to compete with those of Italy and France.

To construct the terms of this claim was the business of a generation of scholars – Isaac Reed, George Steevens, Alexander Pope, Lewis Theobald, William Warburton, Samuel Johnson, Edward Capell, Edmond Malone and James Boswell – whose efforts to define by annotation the terms in which Shakespeare's works could be celebrated as classic texts fill the twenty-one volumes of *The Plays and Poems of William Shakespeare, with the Corrections and Illustrations of Various Commentators* (hereinafter '*Malone*').

The difficulty (or perhaps impossibility) of the task the neoclassical critics set themselves was what made these men the great annotators of the Shakespearean literary history. Driven by patriotic assurance that Shakespeare was a transcendent genius, 'our great dramatic bard, the pride and glory of his country ... whose renown [is] established on so solid a foundation as to bid defiance to the caprices of fashion and the canker of time'.[2] Such a foundation, it was assumed, could not exist outside the tradition of the classics.

This claim left behind it, of course, the question of how the details of the texts could be used to prove the neoclassical connection. These were works that showed few if any of the qualities that the age thought central to literary excellence. And how could these be considered as proof-texts of the national culture if they had been written not for an audience of well-educated gentlemen, but to persuade audiences of semi-literate apprentices and tradesmen, hooting and pushing without order and without reverence, to stand in the theatre and find amusement and understanding in what they heard?

Shakespeare had few or none of the qualities that were thought necessary for literary achievement in a neoclassical culture, having 'small Latin and less Greek', as Ben Jonson had pointed out; his education did not take him beyond grammar school; his friends and associates were no better placed in society than he was himself, and could not have provided models for his understanding of the great world of politics and passion that his poetry persuades us to enter.

To deal with this paradox requires an understanding of the unclassical process by which poetic speech creates character and character gives us access to meaning – a process too instinctive and too little under the control of accepted social norms to be representative of the nation's cultural achievement. In spite of this, however, by the middle of the eighteenth century Shakespeare had become a 'classic' in his own right, even if the cultural system had no consensual language to explain how that could be so. Dr Johnson made this very command of character the basis of his claims for Shakespeare's universality:

> Shakespeare is above all writers, at least above all modern writers, the poet of nature that holds up to his readers a faithful mirror of manners and of life. His characters are ... the genuine progeny of common humanity such as the world will always supply and observation will always find. His persons speak and act by the influence of those general passions and principles by which all minds are agitated.[3]

In these terms social distinction is abrogated; the truth of the imaginative creation is all that matters.

The moral high ground that Johnson occupies leaves little room, however, for the fact that characters in the theatre make their strongest impressions through their relation with current events and political excitements, effective on the stage because known in the street. It seems to follow that the flattening effect of the generalized understanding that parallels and annotation provide tended to set Shakespeare the poet against Shakespeare the dramatist in a dialectic that reflected the other larger eighteenth century dialectic between classical values and modern life, which annotators, if they were to deal with the realities of the texts, had to bring together as best they could.

Pope and Johnson find very similar ways to praise Shakespeare and at the same time preserve the primacy of classical standards by thinking of him as a figure like Homer, not simply as a representative of 'nature' but as an *original*. Pope tells us that, 'If ever there was an original it was Shakespeare. Homer himself drew not his art so immediately from the fountains of nature'.[4] The parallel with Homer allows the critics to make the point that a primitive and uncivil society could become the basis for a great poetry, able to bring a sense of fundamental human characteristics to the refinements of later ages. Such a view, however, evades the fact that Shakespeare did not write for the purified simplicity of a warrior society but for a lower-class urban proletariat – a society unlikely to be taken as representative of Nature, and all too close to the social experience of the eighteenth-century annotators.

In this dilemma an obvious resource was to stress the greatness of Shakespeare's poetry while playing down the social milieu in which the poetry had been brought to life. The theatre audience could be used to explain the presence of passages that did not fit in with the exalted image of the author, and Shakespeare the poet could be freed from the impropriety of writing everything that had come down under his name. The texts had come to the printers from the hands of the actors – two sets of despicable artisans, one after another, well positioned to corrupt the imagined poetic purity of the original. When the actors (or 'players') sold the texts to the printers, they no doubt, it was assumed, brought texts filled with their own ad libs, vulgarities and interpolations. The fact that Heminge and Condell proclaimed their responsibility for the printing of the First Folio – the document that Steevens calls 'the muddy reservoir that the errors of the printers all flowed into'[5] – made that prime source of readings particularly suspect. The nature of its origins allowed neoclassic readers and annotators to imagine that Shakespeare's original writings had once been free of vulgarisms, even if the true text was now lost beyond recovery – as were so many of the classic texts of Greece and Rome.

Using annotation to denigrate the players and the printers allowed critics, in fact, to free Shakespeare from responsibility for anything they did not like, and gave a license to editors to delete from the text anything that did not fit modern good taste. Pope, by making a distinction in print between 'shining' lines and 'bad' lines ('low' conversations, or workaday evocations of theatrical business, which he moved to the bottom of the page), turned a book of plays into a poetry book, and the work of annotation was transferred to the more powerful agency of print.

Warburton's annotations propose the even more radical idea of separating Shakespeare's thought (good) from its expression (bad). 'No one thought clearer or argued more closely than this bard', he argues, but 'when he came to draw out his contemplations into discourse, he took up, as he was hurried on by the torrent of his matter, with the first words that lay in his way'.[6] It was therefore the critic's business to find less random, more apposite words for Shakespeare's great thoughts so that in the privacy of reading the poet could be restored to the status of a true classic.

The dilemma of an acknowledged great poet whose poetry was a national glory but came out of conditions of social impropriety required the editors and annotators of the eighteenth century to explain away by any means at their disposal how the incompatibles in their judgment of Shakespeare could be reconciled. They could not hope to rewrite or translate whole texts into more acceptable words, for the power of the poetry lay precisely in its verbal felicity. They could only use their 'taste', their powers of literary discrimination, to pick out the 'obvious' corruptions that disfigured the text, and if they could not rewrite at least they could use their notes to indicate their participation in a shared patriotic effort to clear the national poet of the disgrace of supposing that he wrote all the matter that had come down from his own time, to the dismay of educated sensibilities.

Steevens's 'Advertisement' of 1793 tells us that, 'Every reimpression of our great dramatic master's works must be considered in some degree as experimental; for their corruptions and obscurities are still so numerous and the progress of fortunate conjecture so tardy and uncertain.'[7] This was a situation in which it had to be believed that there continued to be space, however difficult to define, for the 'improvements' that members of a self-consciously 'improved' society thought themselves properly equipped to discover.

In this work they were heartened by the achievements of classical scholarship. The classical models that ought to have sustained all subsequent writing had been submerged under the tides of war and invasion, the ignorant iconoclasm of barbarian tribes and religious zealots, and were reclaimed, insofar as they could be, only by the continuous effort of generations of Humanist scholars, whose emendations and annotations allowed readers to have a glimpse of what they had lost. Shakespeare, it was assumed, could be revalued as a great English classic if his texts were freed from the corruptions imposed by his milieu of boorish audiences, ignorant actors and incompetent printers; and it was the proper business of those attuned to classic taste to join in the common patriotic purpose of restoring Shakespeare's poetry to the classic forms that had been lost or effaced not only by the ignorance and vulgarity of his milieu but also by the turmoil of civil war, Puritan fanaticism and regicide. And if restoration was impossible it was the function of annotators to point out the unsatisfactoriness of what was left.

The parallel set up between the loss of classical literature and the corruption of Shakespeare's texts, so convenient for patriotic purposes, has perhaps its clearest expression in the advertisement to Bell's edition of Shakespeare's plays of 1754, where we are told that,

> Shakespeare's admirers, even the enthusiastic ones who worship him as *the god of their idolatry*, have never scrupled to admit that his most regular pieces produce some scenes and passage highly derogatory to his incomparable general merit; he frequently trifles, is now and then obscure, and sometimes to gratify a vitiated age, indelicate: but can any degree of critical taste, wish the preservation of dark spots, because they have grown upon dramatic sunshine? Is not the corrective hand frequently proved to be the kindest? Critics, like parents, should neither spare the rod, nor use it wantonly.
>
> There is no doubt but all our author's faults may justly be attributed to the loose, quibbling taste of his time ... Why then should not the noble monuments he has left us, of unrivalled ability, be restored to due proportion and natural luster, by sweeping off these cobwebs and that dust of depraved opinion which Shakespeare was unfortunately forced to throw on them; forced, we say, for it is no strain of imagination, to suppose that the Goths and Vandals of criticism, who frequented the theatre in his days, would, like those who over-ran the Roman Empire, have destroyed and consigned to barbarous oblivion the sublime beauties they could not relish.[8]

If the English Augustan age was to be able to rescue Shakespeare from the disadvantages imposed on him by his environment, it seemed, however, that the rescue would have to be carried out in radical terms, not only in the theatre, where the author is forced by the nature of his occupation into complicity with the 'Goths and Vandals' who provide his audiences, but in the larger terms of a general understanding of the ways in which a culture loses or recovers its capacity to maintain a continuity of civil existence.

Samuel Johnson saw that a failure to order the language was a basic part of this story. A failure to speak systematically produced a failure to think systematically and so an inability to live systematically. What Johnson does not say, but presumably has in mind, is that one great problem for English is that it is not Latin or Greek, not a language learned at school, not a 'dead language' with the rigidity of a stabilized form (and protected from innovation and degeneration by self-conscious policing action, agreed standards of correctness and an elaborate set of grammatical rules, without which good writing is impossible).

Johnson notes that Shakespeare was writing 'at a time when our poetical language was yet unformed, when the meaning of our phrases was yet in fluctuation, when words were adopted at pleasure from the neighbouring languages ... the reader is therefore embarrassed at once with dead and with foreign languages, with obsoleteness and innovation'.[9] Shakespeare was in particular peril since 'the nature of his work required the use of the common colloquial language and consequently admitted many phrases, allusive and elliptical and proverbial, such as we speak and hear every hour without observing them; and of which, being now familiar, we do not suspect that they can ever grow uncouth, or that, being now obvious they can ever seem remote.'[10]

Johnson's aim in his *Dictionary* is to stabilize the culture by 'fixing' the language, so that 'the atoms of our speech might obtain the firmness and immutability of the primogenial and constituent particles of matter'.[11] Only by observing these basic standards can the culture be rescued from 'the license and negligence with which many words have been hitherto used [which] has made our style capricious and indeterminate.' Johnson praised Shakespeare for his command of 'the diction of common life' but found the English of his time 'copious without order and energetic without rule'.[12]

> He sold [his works] not to be printed, but to be played. They were immediately copied for the actors ... vitiated by the blunders of the penman or changed by the affectation of the player; perhaps enlarged to introduce a jest or mutilated to shorten the representation and printed at last without the concurrence of the author.[13]

Johnson's aim was not only to 'fix' the language but to do so in terms of its 'elemental principles'[14] and he could not allow his admiration of Shakespeare to turn him into a model of linguistic propriety. He found his models of correct English instead in Bacon, Hooker, Milton and Boyle.[15] Shakespeare's power was over the diction of common life, and that did not provide a systematic basis for linguistic propriety. Shakespeare, 'the poet of nature', holds up to his readers (not 'his audiences' of course) a faithful mirror of manners and of life. ... His language is that of those who speak to be understood, [and] mixes comic and tragic', as in real life.[16]

The radical contradictions we find in Johnson and his contemporaries, between admiration for Shakespeare and the belief that his mode of writing was fatally flawed by ignorance and confusion, may be seen as a prime cause why this was the great period of annotation or 'illustration' in the history of Shakespeare's reputation. If annotation can be used to show that the flawed texts that came down to Nicholas Rowe from 'the players' have within them qualities of greatness, though overlaid by follies, then enlightened effort ought to be able to recover the real gold under the dross. It is the business of their annotations to find a way of describing poetic greatness inside a slovenly mode of expression.

The arguments used by those caught in this dilemma, as they try to take possession of Shakespeare as a national icon, are not primarily concerned with literary appreciation but with the more serious issue of English as a language able to bear the rigours of detailed annotation as used in classical scholarship. And it is the seriousness with which these inappropriate ideals were pursued that makes this the great age of Shakespearian annotation.

The attempt to find a language that would allow Shakespeare's plays to be assimilated to the standards of polite neoclassicism – his poems were too shut away in their conventions to have any impact – must be judged a failure in its own terms. The lack of precise focus in the language that Johnson deplored was also the comprehensiveness that allowed him not only to be read as a candidate for neoclassical honours, but also for the honors of any social ethos that developed. Shakespeare could not be saved in the guise of a neoclassical poet once the culture itself ceased to wish he could be, ceased to suppose that neoclassicism was not only the way of the present but also of the future. The plays, of course, continued to exercise their magical power over the reading public (not to mention the theatrical one, sustained by the current modes of action) but it became increasingly obvious that they were resistant to the overlay of systematic precision that Johnson for example sought to promote, and that of a 'stabilized' culture understood as a site of permanent values. As social values have been increasingly overtaken by personal values, annotation has had to accommodate interpretations that deal with the individual rather than the society, reinforced of course by the idea that this was what Shakespeare 'meant' or ought to have meant.

Nineteenth- and twentieth-century concerns with the autonomy of the individual moved the focus of judgment in Shakespeare's plays away from the figure of the author (and his intention) towards the dramatic characters themselves. One of the most interesting documents in this movement is the little considered edition of the plays by Charles and Mary Cowden Clarke (1864). Here the action is annotated not only in the usual terms of lexical definitions (most of these being dependent on the work of the eighteenth century), but also in terms of moralized emotional states and individual personal values found in the action (vindictiveness, feminine reticence, faithfulness, magnanimity, etc.). These are taken to define the status of the characters, in terms of the 'correct' feelings about social behaviour that sympathetic Victorian readers could endorse and attribute to Shakespeare. The physical conflicts of drama are transformed in a novelistic apprehension of the action into states of mind that can be evaluated outside the story. Thus the progression of the action in *King Lear* is apprehended less in the external terms of a political process than as a struggle of sensibilities. The annotation continually draws our attention to the moral categories that can be applied to characters and actions – a kind of judgment later periods have tended to find sentimental and simplifying. We hear of 'Cornwall's sneering mode', Regan's 'cool brutality', Cordelia's 'tender interest' in the fool (as found at 1.4.80). Where Dr. Johnson, with his tough-minded sense of the limits of doctrine, points to a failure of religious coherence ('our author by negligence gives his heathens the sentiments and practice of Christianity'), and a modern annotator (R.A. Foakes) speaks of 'moral incoherence', the Cowden Clarkes refer us to the sensibility with which the matter is handled. The author is seen less as a controlling intelligence than as a moral norm, showing 'the true Shakespearian magnanimity'. In 4.2.3, where Albany is reported as 'never a man so changed', and the modern annotator chooses to stay inside the fiction (referring to Albany's change as 'not unlike the change in Cordelia'), the Cowden Clarkes tell us of 'Shakespeare's subtle teaching on the subject of moral awakening'. In 2.2.360ff. where Foakes says that 'Lear's lines represent wishful thinking', the Cowden Clarkes offer us a whole symphony of emotions: 'ill-suppressed wrath, pathetic effect, indignant rage'.

The gap between what the Cowden Clarkes' annotations offer as a representation of what Shakespeare was trying to communicate is particularly obvious in a modern world in which the vocabulary they use can no longer be taken, any more than can the neoclassical strictures, as an objective expression of what is there for us in the play. The more reticent approach of the twentieth/twenty-first centuries is, we no doubt like to think, more objective, more scholarly, more fastened to the historical meanings of the words used. Modern editions and modern annotations of Shakespeare are primarily designed to describe a Shakespeare who, as a proper subject for school and university examinations, offers his readers a range of different meanings which the examinee can evaluate in terms of alternative cultural possibilities rather than set moral values. To some degree this represents a return to the openness of meaning that performance allows, and annotation can bring to our attention. But now this function is not seen as operating inside the set system of values that readers bring with them, whether in terms of social propriety (as with the neoclassicists), or emotional integrity (as with the Victorians). The modern space for theatrical indeterminacy is rather to be understood as a picture of the world that exists outside as well as inside the theatre, and that calls for pluralism as an appropriate response. The norms of an educated life that eighteenth-century culture found in Virgil and Horace can thus be deduced now from the pragmatism that allows Shakespeare's heroes (Hamlet no less than Falstaff or Cleopatra) to navigate a world of opposite demands. The application of scholarship to Shakespeare does not of course provide objective understanding, and modern annotation makes that point a central purpose. It is designed to uncover a liberating presence of puns and ambiguities, bawdry and non-judgmental social observation, so that Shakespeare can appear as a liberator from the presuppositions of the present – from the language of commercial efficiency and stern linguistic clarity.

The problem for annotators of Shakespeare, as translators into the latest idiom, cannot be expected to go away. The latest phase of Shakespeare's posthumous career – as the classic literary text that the culture sees as paradigmatic – allows the plays, as texts for examinations, to support the range of commentaries that have appeared and disappeared so regularly in the last fifty years. Once again, as in the age of Steevens and Malone, the format must offer a sense of finality or near finality in the interpretation supplied and the understanding achieved. Probably the most one can say, however, is that Shakespeare for exams has the entirely proper function of allowing those who best know how to translate innovation into tradition, turning the feelings of the present into the language and sensibilities of the past, to become the graduate guardians of the cultural heritage.

## NOTES

1 *Selections from Johnson on Shakespeare*, edited by B.H. Bronson (New Haven, 1986), 9–10.

2 Isaac Reed's 'Advertisement' in the 1823 edition of Malone, I.278.

3 Bronson, 10–1.

4 Maynard Mack, *Alexander Pope* (New Haven, Yale University Press, 1985).

5 Steevens's advertisement, in Malone (1793), 10ff.

6 Malone I, 52.

7 Steevens's advertisement in Malone (1793), I.34.

8 *Bell's Edition of Shakespeare's Plays* (1754), vol. I, sign. A3, 5–6.

9 Bronson, 3.

10 *Ibid.*

11  Samuel Johnson, 'The Plan of an English Dictionary', *Works* XI, 210.

12  Samuel Johnson, 'Preface to the English Dictionary', *Works* XI, 224.

13  Bronson, 1–2.

14  *Works* XI, 254.

15  *Works* XI, 260.

16  Bronson, 10ff.

# 13

# THE CHARACTER OF A FOOTNOTE ... OR, ANNOTATION REVISITED

*Helen Wilcox*

One of the most fascinating aspects of working with English literary texts written in the sixteenth and seventeenth centuries is that they are never as far as one might expect from the experience of their twentieth- and twenty-first-century readers. Among the ranks of 'Characters' to be found in those splendid early modern collections of short essays identifying the nature of human types, for example, an imaginative modern reader might well discern the features of familiar personalities from many areas of our contemporary life.[1] Indeed, it is quite possible to find aspects of the modern editor and annotator tantalizingly foreshadowed in a Renaissance personality sketch. I would suggest, for instance, that recent generations of editors, particularly those working on the Arden Shakespeare series, display a number of character traits which are shared by some well-known early modern types, including melancholics, wives, pedants and trimmers.

The editor is, after all, chronically *melancholic*, marked by bouts of despair at the enormity of the Shakespearean editing project and its demands in the fields of textual scholarship, historical knowledge, theatrical experience, critical integrity, creative insight and patience. Editors know, too, that their relationship to the text is very much that of a Renaissance *wife* to her husband: devotedly secondary. Just as John Florio commented that translations were 'defective', reproducing rather than producing, and therefore 'reputed femalls',[2] so the modern editor is also aware of being in that second place, restlessly humble with respect to the primary text. (Is this, perhaps, also a contributory factor to the melancholic tendencies outlined above?) Editors are also constantly vulnerable to the *pedant*'s instinct which, alas, too often urges painstaking accuracy and long-windedness at the expense of a deeper wisdom. As Nashe wrote in 1596, a 'precious' pedant will find 'matter inough to dilate a whole daye of the first inuention of *Fy, fa, fum*'.[3] And the *trimmer*? Yes, the editor, like Halifax's 'trimmer' as characterized in the Restoration period, is ultimately required to find compromises and practical solutions, anxiously wishing to be 'in the right', rejecting 'the oppressions of wrangling sophistry on the one hand' and 'the short dictates of mistaken authority on the other'.[4]

As this short essay is in honour of a distinguished editor whose authority is neither wrangling nor mistaken, it would be presumptuous to explore this particular character any further here. Indeed, editors, like the 'Truth' which they and Halifax's 'trimmer' equally seek to uphold, have 'in all ages ... been scurvily used'[5] and it is not my purpose to add to that history of misrepresentation. Rather, it is one particular aspect of the editor's task – annotation – that will be the focus of discussion for the next few pages. The preparing of footnotes is a major aspect of the editor's work, particularly in a series such as the Arden Shakespeare, and yet this part of the process is often relegated to the category of 'harmless drudgery',[6] overshadowed by the grand debates about textual decisions, on the one hand, and lively discussions concerning theatrical practice on the other. But somewhere in the middle, quietly consulted by researchers, teachers, students, directors and actors alike, is the lowly footnote. To continue to put the matter in appropriately personified form, the question being considered here is: what is the character of a footnote?

At first glance, the footnote seems a modest type, shyly self-effacing, hovering at the bottom of the page in smaller print than the rest of the text. Despite the fact that there can be unexpected hierarchies among footnotes – in the third series of the Arden

Shakespeare, for example, the notes on textual variants have been placed even lower and in even smaller (italic) print than the rest of the notes – there remains a general air of bashfulness about this character. To have been mocked by Pope in the pages of *The Dunciad* and damned by Samuel Johnson as a 'necessary evil'[7] is a history which it is hard to shake off. The resultant self-denigrating quality is confirmed by the apparent unwillingness of the footnote to make its presence felt or to interrupt the flow of reading of the original text that it is glossing, remembering Johnson's warning that the mind would thereby be 'refrigerated by interruption'.[8] It is quite possible – and no doubt properly so – to read the entire original work without looking once at the annotation. The footnote can, thus, remain a silent witness of the reading process. Its style, too, is rather plain and low-key, using brief and sometimes grammatically incomplete sentences rather than grand or polished rhetoric. Here we find none of the confident sweep of introductory essay or full-blown appendices, but rather the truncated manner of an editorial telegram, discreetly passing on information about sources, proverbial sayings or the quality of wool stockings.[9]

But if we look a little more closely, we may discern other sides to this personality. Despite its low, Hermia-like physical stature,[10] the footnote can walk tall in the knowledge that it is of vital importance to the proper interpretation of the text it serves. Indeed, 'serves' is perhaps not the right word, since the vast range of knowledge assembled in the annotation suggests that the footnote is really *the* authority – not a 'mistaken' one, but genuinely in charge. The original text may deal in flights of fancy – indeed, is expected to do so in the case of an imaginative work – while the footnote presents truths, dry and humble in appearance yet unlocking secrets of which often the reader, and sometimes even the original author, was unaware. There is, therefore, a quiet confidence about the footnote which, if not kept under control, can border on arrogance. The tensions between text and annotation can become quite severe, particularly when the footnote takes on a rebellious or critical character. And the more that texts are seen as products of a cultural-historical moment, the more dependent on annotation the reading becomes. In some sense the footnote is entering into its heyday, as increasingly the original work and its annotation – or text and supplied context – cannot function in the modern reader's world without one another.

It could, therefore, be claimed that the footnote is a much more interesting character than perhaps it at first appears. It has a paradoxical nature: modest yet learned, lowly yet powerful, in a supporting role and yet possibly having the ultimate authority in the business of reading and interpreting the established text. (There are shades here of the Renaissance wifely function earlier identified with editing in general.) A further paradox of the footnote is that it seems minor when read in isolation and yet it cumulatively achieves an important status in an edition. It is not in itself a narrative – as far as I am aware, no-one ever reads the notes one after the other in an uninterrupted sequence – and yet the commentary still has a story to tell. The character of the footnote is also perceived in several contradictory ways when it comes to its function in an edition. Does it, for example, encumber or clarify the text? Does it function to bring the original text closer to the modern reader/performer, or does the crowd of footnotes (for which the collective noun is commentary) inevitably increase the distance between the edition and its user?

To understand the footnote and appreciate its function(s) in a Shakespearean edition, we need to identify some sub-types of this perplexing character, beginning with the first two, which are most closely related to the text, and moving gradually outwards to those pursuing a potentially more independent life. The first sub-type is the *textual* note, identifying variants, cruces and other issues in the establishing of the text which is now before the reader's eyes. This type of note, particularly when kept quite separate from any interpretative discussion, is characterized by extreme brevity and clarity of factual information. Its nature can be somewhat deceptive, however, since it, too, requires further annotation and explication; to be understood properly it must be read in close conjunction with a list of abbreviations (spanning in code the entire textual life of a Shakespearean play from 'Q1' to 'Oxf'[11]). The second sub-type of footnote is the *etymological* note, clarifying the meaning of an individual word or phrase by glossing the history of its evolution and use. This type is frequently to be seen in the company of the *OED* and is again characterized by a dispassionate and referential manner.

Far more colourful, though not necessarily thereby more worthy, is the *intertextual* note, which points out connections between the original text being annotated and a range of other texts which may clarify it. Although the most immediate link may well be with the direct source(s) which lie behind the play or particular passage, equally important to this type of note are the cross-references to relevant passages within the Shakespeare canon or beyond it in early modern literature. Consequently, there is the potential here for fascinating and enlightening parallels to be drawn, though equally a tendency to expansiveness which can overwhelm the reader. A close relative of this sub-type, sharing the same positive and negative characteristics, is the *contextual* note, placing the passage in question firmly in its historical (social, political, cultural) environment. This note can be crucial in the successful interpretation of the play, but can be a domineering type if left unchecked.

Moving away from the text in its immediate linguistic, literary and historical setting, we meet two sub-types of the footnote which bring with them all the experience and authority of other worlds. The first of these is the *dramatic* note, a term which identifies its connection with the realm of the theatre but could also be used to define its character. This type is increasingly present in the Arden 3 Shakespeare editions, perhaps to the discomfort of the above-mentioned bookish footnote types more at home in a library than a theatre. However, commentary on the significance of a word or phrase for the interpretation of a character, on the hints given in the text for action during the speech, or on the complexities of staging a particular scene, are indeed vital for an edition of a play which is to be translated into performance. This knowledge of its unique position gives this particular type of note a kind of flamboyant, breezy authority.

The only major challenge to its position comes from the last sub-type, the *critical* footnote, a heavy-weight character which intervenes in the interpretative process with insights from the critical debate about the line(s) in question – which in the case of Shakespeare is an almost limitless source of ideas and information. While footnotes have traditionally prided themselves on a scholarly neutrality, these last two types are the most daring and outspoken. Not only do they bring to bear upon the text the perspective of two worlds which are very distinct from it – theatre and academia; they are also willing to take sides in issues of performance and interpretation, or at least to give clear indications of the potential for taking the wrong side.

There are doubtless many more sub-types (or even sub-sub-types) of the footnote, but these six – textual, etymological, intertextual, contextual, dramatic and critical – should satisfy all but the most scholastic interpreters of character. (In other words, the sub-categories here are insufficient for a Robert Burton, with his forty-one sub-causes of melancholy, but will probably suffice for the rest of us.[12]) In order to bring these annotating types alive, however, and put flesh on the composite character of the footnote, a test case is in order. For this I have chosen the second part of the first scene of *All's Well that Ends Well* – the encounter sometimes known as the virginity scene – in which the heroine, Helena, is engaged by the disreputable Parolles in a spirited and witty exchange. This 'notorious liar' with a 'stain of soldier' in him[13] begins by asking Helena, who is in fact lamenting the departure of her beloved Bertram for the French court, if she is 'meditating on virginity' (1.1.108). Since in some sense she is, Helena introduces a mock-military discussion about virginity and its 'enemy', men, which runs for some fifty lines of prose. It appears to end when Parolles asks her, 'Will you anything with it?', to which she ambiguously replies, 'Not my virginity; yet …' (1.1.161).

In this short section of the opening scene, all six sub-types of footnote are required in order to elucidate the text, and no doubt they are to be found jostling for position at the bottom of the page. The most significant moment for the *textual* note is Helena's closing remark, 'Not my virginity; yet …' in answer to Parolles's question as to whether she will do anything with her virginity. The Folio (the earliest text of this play) gives no punctuation between 'virginity' and 'yet', whereas a number of modern editions, including Arden 2 (cited here), introduce some punctuation in order to clarify the meaning. The textual note must record these variants, and its first cousin, the textual commentary, must explain the background to the differences (possibly a corruption in the original on which the Folio was based, since the line itself is incomplete) and the consequences of the editorial choice. The absence of punctuation, for example, allows 'yet' to mean 'thus far', highlighting Helena's awareness that, so far, she has been unsuccessful in the pursuit of Bertram and now he has gone away she has no plans (or hopes) to give up her virginity. By contrast, the introduction of a break (with a comma or semi-colon) between 'virginity' and 'yet' forces an anticipated connection with the following line (in which Helena thinks of Bertram having many admirers at the French court) by inviting us to understand 'yet' as 'but on the other hand' or 'now I come to think about it …'.

This brief line, 'Not my virginity [;] yet', contains the key noun for the entire 'skirmish of wit'[14] between Helena and Parolles, demanding considerable attention from the footnotes. An *etymological* note must consider the original meanings of 'virginity' as well as its developing overtones as the scene progresses. Virginity, literally 'the condition of being or remaining in a state of chastity' (*OED* 1), has an intriguing range of meanings and associations stemming from the word 'virgin'. The primary significance of this virginal state, according to the *OED*'s hierarchy of meanings, is religious, linking chastity directly with holiness and martyrdom (*OED* 'virgin' 1). Since Helena later experiences a kind of social martyrdom in the play, sacrificing her chaste self to Bertram's rejection as well as later adopting the disguise of a devout pilgrim, these overtones of the term 'virginity' are not without significance to the action. However, more immediately appropriate to Parolles's banter are the more secular and physical meanings of 'virgin': a pure maiden (*OED* 2a) and an unmarried woman (*OED* 3). It is in these senses, implying a refusal of men's desires, that Parolles sees virginity as 'too cold a companion' and, worse still, 'peevish, proud, idle, made of self-love' (1.1.129–30, 141–2). Indeed, the term 'virginity' becomes increasingly negative as the scene progresses, since it is said to be a 'commodity' which 'will lose the gloss with lying' (1.1.149), thereby coming closer to the pejorative definition of a virgin as an 'old maid' (*OED* 2b). Parolles's likening of 'your old virginity' to 'one of our French wither'd pears' (1.1.156–7) is also no coincidence, since the *OED*'s ninth definition of a virgin is 'a kind of pear'. The shifting definitions of the word 'virginity' during the scene, which the notes must track, is highlighted by the problems of translation. The Shakespearean translator Burgersdijk found that one Dutch word was not sufficient for the multiple uses of 'virginity' in the scene, using 'maidenness' (*maagdelijkheid*) in the early stages but changing to 'unmarried state' (*jufferschap*) by line 161.[15]

The material for the first two sub-types of note, textual and etymological, has already begun to explicate the nature and complexity of this exchange between Helena and Parolles. Our third type, the *intertextual* footnote, also has its work cut out with this scene. Shakespeare's major source for *All's Well*, William Painter's 'Giletta of Narbona' from *The Palace of Pleasure*, cannot be directly invoked since Parolles was entirely the playwright's own addition – though the absence of immediate sources is often in itself worthy of mention. There were, however, many other authors whose texts were influential in the humanist debate about virginity, including Erasmus, from whom Shakespeare is likely to have borrowed the paradox expressed by Parolles as 'there was never virgin got till virginity was first lost' (1.1.126–7).[16] This conundrum sets sexual desire and the need for procreation against the Christian tradition inherited from the teachings of St Paul, whose emphasis on chastity was succinctly summed up by George Herbert: 'virginity is a higher state then Matrimony'.[17] The tension and wit in the scene turn on the opposition between these two groups of sources, asserting the preservation of virginity on the one hand and, on the other, the need to 'blow up' virginity (1.1.117) in order to affirm life.

The intertextual annotation of the word 'virginity' must go further than reference to Shakespeare's sources, since it can be most enlightening to note parallels with other texts which cannot be claimed as direct echoes, whether from within Shakespeare's own oeuvre or in the work of his contemporaries. It is fascinating (and perhaps significant) to learn, for instance, that 'virginity' is used more often in *AW* than in any other play by Shakespeare: eighteen times (sixteen in this scene) as opposed to three, for example, in *Pericles*, a play notorious for the attempt to 'crack the glass' of Marina's virginity (4.6.142). Interestingly, one of Shakespeare's other uses of the word is to be found describing the 'rich worth' of Shakespeare's other Helena, in *A Midsummer Night's Dream* at 2.1.219. Further early modern parallels also illuminate the paradoxical values associated with virginity. It is, perhaps not surprisingly, harshly termed a false 'idol' in Marlowe's erotic epyllion *Hero and Leander*, but in the context of praise of the dead it is seen as the ultimate spiritual innocence in Donne's 'Elegie on the Lady *Marckham*'.[18]

The differences between the characters of intertextual and *contextual* notes are very slight, as the above intertextual examples make clear. Most of our evidence for historical contexts is, in fact, also textual, though the emphasis in the contextual element of the footnote is more on society and ideology than on other literary uses of a word such as virginity. For example, a contextual annotation of virginity will consider the importance of the concept in early modern England, particularly in its impact on the roles and expectations of young women. At various points in the annotation of this scene, the shifting uses of 'virginity' must be contextualized by drawing on its associations with the Virgin Mary and Elizabeth I, the Virgin Queen,[19] as well as the discussion of virginity in legal documents concerning marriage and dowries, and in conduct books such as Edmund Tilney's *The Flower of Friendshippe*.[20] Even though he was defending marriage, Tilney first had to admit that his arguments were 'setting virginitie aside, as the purest estate'.[21]

Setting the ideological context aside for a moment, what might a *dramatic* aspect in the footnotes add to our understanding of this debate between Parolles and Helena on the question of virginity? The scene is not difficult to perform, and it does not contain any confusions concerning lines mistakenly assigned to the wrong speakers, or hints of uncertain locations, or complex interactions between characters. And yet there is always something useful to be contributed by an editorial consciousness of performance, whether historical or current. The fact that Parolles and Helena are alone together on the stage so near to the beginning of the play is an important indication of their parallel roles during the drama. Both follow Bertram – for quite different reasons – and socially they are the two outsiders in the play. This was emphasized in a recent production by giving them both idiosyncratic costumes which set them apart from the rest of the company, who wore more courtly dress.[22] At the climax of the play's events, Helena tricks Bertram by substituting herself for Diana in bed with him – losing her virginity at last – while at the very same time Bertram has arranged the tricking of Parolles in the affair of the stolen drum. Helena becomes pregnant as a result of her experience; in the terms of Parolles's earlier discussion, her virginity has been able to 'make itself two, which is a goodly increase' (1.1.145). Parolles, by contrast, learns from his less pleasant experience that 'every braggart shall be found an ass' (4.3.325). The connections and oppositions between the two characters, which are established in the opening scene, are fundamental to the structure of the play and can be developed as such visually in costume and staging patterns.

The virginity scene also establishes the characterization of Helena and Parolles. Does the actress playing Helena, for instance, show her character's quick wit and self-confidence in this scene, or does she allow its bawdy conversation to appear to go against the grain of her upbringing? When she answers Parolles with 'Not my virginity [;] yet', is she firmly dismissive of his idea that she might relinquish her chastity, or meditative in reflection on her state, or does the 'yet' awaken all kinds of possibilities, exciting and disturbing, in her mind? The notes, in offering the textual and contextual evidence with performance clearly in mind, enable the dramatic interpretation to take place.

The final sub-type of the footnote, the *critical* or interpretative note, undoubtedly lurks within all the other types, since editing always involves choice, and choice has the impact of interpretation. After all, editors are reasonable characters, and, as Milton knew, 'reason is but choosing'.[23] The editor's choice, at the stage of establishing the text itself as well as in all aspects of the commentary, determines the critical emphases of the edition. But the critical footnote can specifically supply information on the interpretative choices of others, whether preceding editors or critics. With reference to the virginity scene, for example, the focus of critical discussion has shifted from questioning whether Shakespeare could have been the author of such a sexually charged scene, via commentary on the metaphors of siege warfare in the witty dialogue, to exploration of the scene's significance in early modern ideas of gender.[24] All these aspects of the critical reception of the scene, as well as discussion of critical intervention at the more detailed level, form the last element of the annotation.

The character of the footnote is thus composed of at least six sub-types, overlapping and interlinked but each nonetheless having a significant role to play in rendering the commentary as complete and informative as possible. Has this character been fundamentally the same since the days of the earliest Shakespeare editors, or is it possible to discern significant changes over the centuries? There is a measure of continuity, I would suggest, in the desire for the footnote to appear factual in its approach, soundly based on painstaking research supplying reliable evidence, even while the materials assembled actually reflect the sympathies, the learning and the priorities of the individual editor. There is a reassuring stability in this paradoxical process. In two major ways, however, the character of the footnote has changed radically over the centuries: in the nature of its author and the kinds of audience it addresses. The early Shakespearean editors were eccentric individuals, highly learned but often idiosyncratic in their approach to the editorial task. Their annotation was mainly textual and relatively sparse, though the notes enabled what Theobald called 'an Inquiry into the Beauties and Defects of Composition'[25] with an assumption of personal judgements. The modern Shakespearean editor, by contrast, tends to be a member of a team with carefully drawn-up editorial guidelines to ensure that the publisher's series is consistent and its house style recognizable. There is still room for a measure of individuality, but the editorial process, footnotes included, has become institutionalized to a large degree.

This newly streamlined, and more impersonal, editorial process is closely linked with the second change, namely the new audience for which Shakespearean editions are prepared. In the eighteenth and nineteenth centuries, Shakespearean texts were published for a much narrower market, and there was a sense in which the editors were addressing each other. As Mary Cowden Clarke wrote, footnotes were 'mere vehicles for abuse, spite and arrogance',[26] the first two of those features being mainly aimed at fellow editors. Nowadays the anticipated readership of an Arden edition includes senior school pupils, students, teachers, scholars, directors and actors, many of whom will not have English as their first language and most of whom will not have read the works, including the Bible and the classics, to which many footnotes refer. The nature of annotation has been transformed by this worldwide readership and the changing nature of general knowledge. There is greater need for notes which define, translate, contextualize and explain what previously might have been taken for granted. Though some may lament this need, it has no doubt led to a sharpening up of the footnote. No longer is there scope for the kind of note which took one look at Parolles's jokes, such as 'Virginity being blown down man will quicklier be blown up' (1.1.121–2) and fobbed the reader off with a phrase such as 'bawdy quibble' – managing to be both coy and unhelpful – or referred to an ancient source which was quoted minimally, out of context and in the original Latin. The new editorial style has outlawed obfuscation, so that, as it was put recently by Donald Reiman, 'the reader need not consult a library to understand a note'.[27] The note has begun to shake off its dowdy image, though it will continue to be a supporting actor rather than a star.

Before we end this exploration of the character of the footnote, one more question needs to be asked: is the *Shakespearean* note a special kind of character, decidedly different from the ordinary footnote? Perhaps to the disappointment of the Shakespearean note – or its group identity as the commentary – I would suggest that there is no fundamental difference between it and the annotation of other comparable works, except perhaps in the enormous range of critical material available for consultation and reference. The danger of over-extensive notes is, therefore, greater in the case of Shakespeare, but the range of sub-types of notes remains the same as for the editing of any other play from the early modern period. It could be claimed that the annotation of non-dramatic texts involves a narrower editorial scope, since the dramatic note and the whole context of performance are not relevant. However, not only are all the other types of notes – textual, etymological, intertextual, contextual and critical – required in at least as intensive a manner for an edition of, say, Renaissance lyric poetry; there is also another category of annotation which may be seen as equivalent to the dramatic note, and that is the note considering the processes of manuscript circulation, the nature of the readership and the importance of musical performance. The realization that social and cultural settings are as relevant to poetry as to drama in this period means that the principles of editing non-dramatic and dramatic texts have become almost identical.

If there is any significant difference between groups of edited texts, then perhaps the distinctions are based more on relationship to the canon than on genre. The widest gap, in my experience, is between the editing of canonical and non-canonical texts. In the case of the well-known text, such as a Shakespeare play or the poems of George Herbert, editing is a process of slightly altering the focus but essentially adding to the immense heritage of ideas and comment from the interpretative community. The footnotes in these cases are the latest butlers seeing to the smooth running of a house which has been standing, with occasional alterations and rebuilding programmes, for centuries. However, the notes to a little-known text, such as a newly discovered manuscript by an early modern woman writer, have a more challenging job, comparable to opening up a modest country house to the public for the first time. The building must be cleaned and renovated, the histories of the architect, the owners, the household and its occupants all have to be reconstructed and presented, and the needs of the modern visitors to the house must also be taken into account. Indeed, these notes will be so busy that it may be difficult for them to keep the proper perspective on their text and avoid dominating the first readings of the original work itself. Where the discourse of the text has still to be heard for the first time, it is especially important for the notes to rediscover their modesty and keep their own characteristic voices 'soft, gentle and low'.[28]

## NOTES

Place of publication is London unless otherwise stated.

1 See, among others, Joseph Hall, *Characters of Virtues and Vices* (1608), Sir Thomas Overbury, *Characters* (1614) and John Earle, *Microcosmography* (1623).

2 John Florio, preface to his translation of Montaigne's *Essayes* (1603), A2r.

3 Thomas Nashe, *Have With You to Saffron Walden* (1596), 43.

4 'The Character of a Trimmer' (1684), *The Complete Works of Lord Halifax*, ed. J.P. Kenyon (Oxford, 1969), 101.

5 *Ibid.*

6 Samuel Johnson's (implied) teasing definition of lexicography in his *Dictionary of the English Language* (1755).

7 See the splendid satire of annotation in *The Dunciad Variorum* (1729), and Johnson's Preface to *The Plays of William Shakespeare* (1765): 'Notes are often necessary, but they are necessary evils' (Johnson, *Selected Poetry and Prose*, ed. Frank Brady and W.K. Wimsatt (Berkeley, 1977), 335).

8 Johnson, Preface, 335.

9 For full details of this last subject see R.A. Foakes's Arden 3 edition of *King Lear*, note to 2.2.16, 'worsted-stocking knave'.

10 Hermia's description of herself as 'so dwarfish and so low' (*MND* 3.2.295) seems particularly apt for the footnote.

11  The earliest possible text of a Shakespearean play (though by no means in existence for them all) is the first quarto, Q1, and one of the most recent modern editions is the (Oxf.) *Complete Works*, ed. Stanley Wells and Gary Taylor (Oxford, 1986 and 1988).

12  See Robert Burton, *The Anatomy of Melancholy*, ed. Thomas C. Faulkner, Nicolas K. Kiessling and Rhonda L. Blair (Oxford, 1989).

13  *All's Well that Ends Well*, ed. G.K. Hunter (1959), 1.1.98, 109.

14  The phrase used by Leonato to describe the banter of Beatrice and Benedick, *MA* 1.1.60.

15  L.A.J. Burgersdijk, *De Werken van William Shakespeare* (Leiden, 1888), II, 201–2.

16  There are several echoes of Erasmus's *Colloquies* (1516), particularly the colloquy 'Proci et Puellae'.

17  George Herbert, *A Priest to the Temple, Works*, ed. F.E. Hutchinson (Oxford, 1941), 236.

18  Christopher Marlowe, *Hero and Leander, Complete Poems and Translations*, ed. Stephen Orgel (Harmondsworth, 1971), Sestiad I, l.269; John Donne, 'Elegie on the Lady *Marckham*', *Complete English Poems*, ed. C.A. Patrides (1985), l.38.

19  See, for example, Helen Hackett, *Virgin Mother, Maiden Queen* (Basingstoke, 1995).

20  Edmund Tilney, *The Flower of Friendship: A Renaissance Dialogue Contesting Marriage*, ed. Valerie Wayne (Ithaca, 1992); see also T.E., *The Lawes Resolutions of Womens Rights* (1632).

21  Tilney, *Flower*, 105.

22  The New Shakespeare Company, Regent's Park Open Air Theatre, summer 1997, directed by Helena Kaut-Howson and designed by Claire Lyth, with Isabel Pollen as Helena and Nigel Planer as Parolles.

23  John Milton, *Areopagitica* (1644), *Selected Prose*, ed. C.A. Patrides (Harmondsworth, 1974), 220.

24  Burgersdijk, for instance, doubted whether he should include the dialogue in his translation (*Werken*, 235); R.B. Parker, 'War and Sex in *All's Well That Ends Well*', *SS* 37 (1984), 99–113; Susan Snyder, '*All's Well That Ends Well* and Shakespeare's Helens: Text and Subtext, Subject and Object', *ELR* 18 (1988), 66–77.

25  Lewis Theobald, preface to the 1733 *Works*, xl.

26  Mary Cowden Clarke, *Shakespeare's Works* (London and New York, 1860), vii.

27  In *Scholarly Editing: A Guide to Research*, ed. D.C. Greetham (New York, 1995), 322.

28  *King Lear*, 5.3.270–1.

# 14

## TO BE OR NOT TO BE

*E.A.J. Honigmann*

'The likening of death to a sleep ... was a Renaissance commonplace descending from such works as Cicero's *Tusculan Disputations*', according to Harold Jenkins's monumental edition of *Hamlet* (The Arden Shakespeare, 1982, p. 489). It has not been noticed, I believe, that Cicero's text probably inspired other words and thoughts in 'To be or not to be'. 'All men are anxious ... about what will happen after death' (XIV: I quote from Book 1 of the *Tusculan Disputations*, ed. J.B. King, 1927, in the Loeb Classical Library); 'if sensation is obliterated and death resembles the sleep which sometimes brings the calmest rest, untroubled even by the appearance of dreams, good gods, what gain it is to die!' (XLI). Compare

> 'tis a consummation
> Devoutly to be wish'd. To die, to sleep;
> To sleep, perchance to dream ...

Again 'who would be such a madman as to pass his life continually in toil and peril?' (XV) seems to anticipate 'For who would bear the whips and scorns of time?' But the best reason for thinking that the above and other extracts from Cicero-influenced Shakespeare's soliloquy is this: Shakespeare seems to have borrowed from Cicero the actual words of his opening line. 'Quasi non necesse sit, quidquid isto modo pronunties, id *aut esse aut non esse*' (VII: 'As if anything stated in a proposition of such a kind must not necessarily either be or not be'). While the sentence structure is different, here we have [to] be or not [to] be' in a similar context, Cicero's subject being the wretchedness of life and the fear of death.

Does Cicero's philosophical disputation help us with a question that has divided critics for almost three centuries? – 'whether Hamlet is discussing his individual dilemma or whether, as Kittredge insists, "the whole course of his argument is general, not personal"' (Arden ed., p. 485). Cicero's quasi-dialogue, as it has been called, is both general and personal, rather than either one or the other. It is true that the first ten lines, excluding personal pronouns, may appear to be general when taken on their own. But, as I argued elsewhere (*Shakespearian Tragedy and the Mixed Response*, Newcastle upon Tyne, 1971, p. 9), 'placed in its context in the whole play's process', the soliloquy resumes a topic that is already powerfully established. 'O that this too too sullied flesh would melt' and 'You cannot, sir, take from me anything that I will not more willingly part withal – except my life, except my life, except my life'. Such earlier passages determine our immediate impression that in 'To be or not to be' Hamlet again has in mind his own death, though he does not actually say so. While his argument may be general, we cannot miss its continuation of his previous thinking and its relevance to his personal situation.

# 15

## RICHLY NOTED: A CASE FOR COLLATION INFLATION

### *Eric Rasmussen*

Let's face it, textual collations – memorably characterized by Thomas Berger as the 'band of terror', by Edmund Wilson as the 'barbed wire' between the text and the explanatory notes, and (more sympathetically) by Richard Proudfoot as 'the filling of the sandwich' – are often incomprehensible to the average reader (see Marcus, 72, Proudfoot, 4). Virtually no-one would wish these collations to be longer than they are. Even some editors do not see the value of collating previous editions.[1] Bibliographical collation may be a dying art. However, this essay comes not to bury collation but to praise it. I shall argue that in modern critical editions the 'band of terror' is, in fact, not terrifying enough – or, to borrow Proudfoot's metaphor, that the filling of the sandwich often makes for a rather meagre repast. Indeed, instead of cutting back on collations, perhaps we should actually be encouraging editors and students of Shakespeare to assemble and analyse them more thoroughly.

Although every eighteenth-century edition of Shakespeare advertised its text as the result of textual collation, the practice of printing lists of the variant readings was slow to evolve. The title-page of Alexander Pope's 1723 edition presented '*The Works of Shakespeare* ... Collated and Corrected by the former Editions', but Lewis Theobald charged that Pope had only 'pretended to have collated' the old texts. Theobald's own '*Works of Shakespeare* ... Collated with the Oldest Copies and Corrected' (1733) inaugurated a tradition in which Shakespeare's editors justify the need for new editions by pointing to the failings of their predecessors.

In 1773, Charles Jennens archly implied that previous editors had not actually undertaken the collations they claimed: 'if they do collate', Jennens asked, 'why do they not publish their collations, so that their readers may be in possession of them?' Jennens maintained that an editor does not have the right 'to give his own conjectural interpolation, without producing the readings of the several editions' such that

> the public may be indulged in their conjectures, as well as himself. In this view, some readings that at present appear insignificant, may hereafter be assistant to the critical conjecturer when any new difficulties may start; and on this account an editor may not, with safety, omit any various reading, though ever so trifling; because he knows not what may, or what may not, become of use.
>
> (Jennens, xi)

Jennens edited five Shakespearean tragedies, published each in a separate volume, and provided, at the foot of each page, a collation of all variant readings from all previous editions. Jennens's play-per-volume format, with a list of textual variants on each page, set a precedent for modern critical editions of Shakespeare – a claim to fame that perhaps does not eclipse his earlier achievement in writing the libretto for Handel's *Messiah* (see Kliman).

Edmond Malone's edition of 1790, modifying the standard 'collated and corrected' title-page claim, advertised its text as 'collated *verbatim* with the most authentick copies'. Using a marked-up copy of the Johnson and Steevens edition of 1785 as the basis for his own edition, Malone claimed to have had this copy-text read aloud to him while he read along in the First Folio:

> By this laborious process, many innovations, transpositions, &c. have been detected. ... Wherever any deviation is made from the authentick copies ... the reader is apprized by a note; and every emendation that has been adopted, is ascribed to its proper author. When it is considered that it was often necessary to consult six or seven volumes, in order to ascertain by which of the preceding editors ... each emendation was made, it will easily be believed, that this was not

effected without much trouble ... it is a laborious and a difficult task:
and the due execution of this it is, which can alone entitle an editor of
Shakespeare to the favour of the publick.

(Malone, xliv–li)

Whereas previous editors had collated early texts in order to
provide a stockpile of viable variant readings from which to choose,
Malone viewed collation not as a preliminary step to preparing
his edited text, but as a means of checking that text for accuracy.
The collation with the First Folio enabled Malone to weed out
unintended errors from the Johnson–Steevens text; just as
importantly, it helped him identify intended emendations, many
of which were unattributed. Malone then turned to other editions
in order to locate the first occurrence of each emendation so that
he could give proper credit to its originator.

For both Jennens and Malone, textual notes served as
important reminders that a portion of the text was not fixed
but editorially constructed. For Jennens, the full listing of possible
readings proposed by previous editors invited serious readers
to join in the process, to bring their own critical faculties to bear
in evaluating the various conjectures. For Malone, on the other
hand, it was sufficient simply to list the emendation and its
source. Given that literally hundreds of editions of Shakespeare
have appeared in the last two centuries, today's editors may smile
wistfully at Malone's complaint about the labour involved in
having to consult 'six or seven' previous editions. Compiling a
full historical collation is now a monumental task. Consequently,
relatively few editors have followed Jennens's lead in attempting
to collate all previous editions. Most editors follow Malone's
practice: rather than compiling a list of all variant readings, they
undertake a scaled-down collation in order to identify the source
of every reading in their edited text that departs from the basic
folio or quarto copy-text.

As it happens, I am now at work (with colleagues Bernice
W. Kliman, Hardin Aasand and Nick Clary) on a full historical
collation for the New Variorum edition of *Hamlet*. I have also just
completed a more limited collation of thirty editions of *King Henry*

*VI Part Three* in the course of preparing an edition of that play, in collaboration with John D. Cox, for the Arden 3 series. One of the hallmarks of the Arden Shakespeare are the textual notes; these collations, designed to let readers know where the edited text departs from the early edition on which it is based, standardly record both the rejected reading of the early edition and the source of the emended reading that has been adopted, and occasionally list a handful of other proposed emendations. As Paul Werstine has observed, if critical editions were to record all substantive variants, or even just those from the most prominent eighteenth-century editions, it 'would swell a historical collation with many readings no modern editor could consider seriously' (99). Fredson Bowers concluded that the custom of crediting the source of an emendation is sufficient in that it 'establishes historically the precise details of the refinement of the textual tradition' (237).

There are certain instances, however, in which one wishes that the Arden 3 series convention might be expanded to accommodate the fullness of a variorum collation. For example, when an eyewitness to the Duke of York's murder arrives in the second act of the play, bringing the news to York's sons, the Folio reads '*Enter one blowing*' (TLN, 697; 2.1.42.1). This stage direction has since gone through a number of permutations:

| | |
|---|---|
| First Folio (1623) | *Enter one blowing* |
| Rowe (1709) | *Enter a Messenger* |
| Cam$^1$ (1952) | *Enter one, blowing a horn* |
| Pelican$^1$ (1967) | *Enter one [Messenger] blowing [a horn]* |
| Cam$^2$ (1993) | *Enter [a Messenger] blowing [a horn]* |
| Pelican$^2$ (2000) | *Enter one blowing a horn* |

Nicholas Rowe's edition in 1709 specified that the '*one*' is a '*Messenger*' (a reading that, coincidentally, also appears in the Q3 reprint of 1619) and deleted the final verb. Every subsequent eighteenth- and nineteenth-century edition reproduced Rowe's emended direction, '*Enter a Messenger*'. In 1952, John Dover Wilson's Cambridge edition restored the '*one*' and the verb '*blowing*', and further specified that '*a horn*' was to be blown; a textual note recorded this emendation, provided the original

Folio reading, and explained that 'The blowing of a horn denoted one riding post'; this note has since become a standard gloss on the stage direction. The editors of the original Pelican edition (1967), Robert Kean Turner and George Walton Williams, retained Rowe's '*Messenger*' as well as Dover Wilson's '*horn*', but employed square brackets in order to mark these as editorial additions.[2] Michael Hattaway's New Cambridge edition (1993) deleted the superfluous '*one*', retained the bracketed '*Messenger*' and the '*horn*', and provided a collation note identifying the source for '*Messenger*' as Q3 and for the '*horn*' as simply '*Eds*', thereby classifying it as one of those 'insignificant and obvious editorial practices ... which do not need to be ascribed to one originator' (Cam[2], 62). Finally, William Montgomery's New Pelican edition (2000) restored the Folio's '*one*' but removed the brackets around '*a horn*'. Montgomery did not provide a textual note recording these changes, so there is nothing to alert readers that the horn is an editorial invention.[3]

The problem is that the fellow who enters here is probably not blowing a horn, he may simply be out of breath. A similar stage direction appears in the anonymous play *The Honest Lawyer* (1615). The direction reads, '*Enter Nice blowing*' and the entering character says, 'I have lost my wind' (sig. F1v). Shakespeare uses the word in this sense in *The Merry Wives of Windsor* where Mistress Page appears at the door 'sweating, and blowing, and looking wildly' (3.3.80). In his note to the stage direction in our Arden 3 edition, John Cox points to instances in Shakespeare's chronicle sources for this battle where 'blowing' means 'panting heavily'. To transform an eyewitness who is out of breath into a professional post-rider blowing a horn strikes us as an untenable editorial leap of faith. We break ranks with recent editorial tradition and do not provide the messenger with a horn, but this textual decision is not reflected in the collations in our edition since those notes, of course, only record divergences from the original text.

Like our eighteenth-century predecessors, John Cox and I present our edition as the result of a careful textual collation. Moreover, we believe that our edited text is superior in certain respects to other recent editions. Although the principles of economy which lie behind textual notes that merely list an emendation and its source are understandable, I would suggest that in the instance of the Messenger's entrance direction, and others like it, such a note does a disservice to the details of the refinement of the textual tradition, whereas a full collation listing the multiple versions of this stage direction throughout history has an infinitely more interesting story to tell about Shakespeare's editors blowing their own horns.

I realize, of course, that those of us who devote enormous amounts of time and energy to compiling full records of four centuries of variant readings have a vested interest in convincing ourselves – if no one else – that the fruits of our considerable labour will actually be of use. I recently suggested to a gathering of feminist critics that they might find some surprising food for thought in the collations in the forthcoming New Variorum edition of *Hamlet*. They were somewhat skeptical at first, but soon found themselves engaged by the record of a small but significant textual variant in the Dumb Show that opens the play-within-the-play. The Q2 text calls for a mutual embrace between the Player King and Player Queen: '*the Queene embracing him, and he her*'. The Folio text, however, calls for a decidedly one-sided embrace followed by supplication: '*the Queene embracing him. She kneeles, and makes shew of Protestation vnto him*'. The historical collation reveals that Victorian editors tended to adopt the patriarchal Folio reading, whereas the perhaps more enlightened editors in the twentieth century favoured the Quarto. Clearly, there is some fascinating material for cultural analysis to be gleaned from what might seem to be an unpromising record of textual variants. And one suspects that Shakespearean scholarship will be enriched in untold ways if and when critical readers begin to turn their talents to this long-neglected 'band of terror'.[4]

## REFERENCES

Bowers   Fredson Bowers, 'The Historical Collation in an Old-Spelling Shakespeare edition: Another view', *Studies in Bibliography*, 35 (1982), 234–58.

Cam[1]   *The Third Part of King Henry VI*, ed. John Dover Wilson (Cambridge, 1952).

Cam[2]   *The Third Part of King Henry VI*, ed. Michael Hattaway (Cambridge, 1993).

Duncan-Jones   *Shakespeare's Sonnets*, ed. Katherine Duncan-Jones (1997).

Jennens   *Hamlet, Prince of Denmark. A Tragedy. By William Shakespeare. Collated with the Old and Modern Editions*, ed. Charles Jennens (1773).

Johnson   *The Plays of William Shakespeare*, ed. Samuel Johnson, 8 vols (1765).

Kliman   Bernice W. Kliman, 'Charles Jennens' Shakespeare and His Eighteenth-Century Competitors', *Cahiers Elisabethains: Late Medieval and Renaissance Studies,* 58 (2000), 59–71.

Malone   *The Plays and Poems of William Shakespeare*, ed. Edmond Malone, 10 vols (1790).

Marcus   Leah S. Marcus, *Unediting the Renaissance: Shakespeare, Marlowe, Milton* (1996).

McKerrow   R.B. McKerrow, *Prolegomena for the Oxford Shakespeare* (Oxford, 1939).

Pelican[1]   *The Second and Third Parts of King Henry the Sixth*, ed. Robert K. Turner and George Walton Williams (1967).

Pelican[2]   *The Third Part of Henry the Sixth*, ed. William Montgomery (2000).

Pope   *The Works of Shakespear,* ed. Alexander Pope, 6 vols (1723–5).

Proudfoot   Richard Proudfoot, *Shakespeare: Text, Stage, and Canon* (2001).

Rasmussen   Eric Rasmussen, 'The Year's Contributions to Shakespeare Studies: Editions and Textual Studies', *Shakespeare Survey 52* (1999), 302–25.

Rowe   *The Works of Mr William Shakespeare,* ed. Nicholas Rowe, 6 vols (1709).

Theobald   *The Works of Shakespeare*, ed. Lewis Theobald, 7 vols (1733).

Wells   Stanley Wells, *Re-editing Shakespeare for the Modern Reader* (Oxford, 1984).

Werstine   Paul Werstine, 'Modern Editions and Historical Collation in Old-Spelling Editions of Shakespeare', *Analytical and Enumerative Bibliography,* 4 (1980), 95–106.

## Notes

1 The recent Arden 3 edition of *Shakespeare's Sonnets* announced a 'divergence' from the normal editorial practice in that, instead of collating all of the significant early editions of the *Sonnets*, the editor chose to collate only Malone's and Capell's (Duncan-Jones 103). For my analysis of the implications of this decision, see Rasmussen (302–4).

2 The use of square brackets to indicate editorially-added stage directions is a convention of comparatively recent origin. In the *Prolegomena for the Oxford Shakespeare* (1939), R.B. McKerrow explained that in the edition he envisioned (but would not live to complete), when it was 'absolutely necessary' to flesh out stage directions that were inadequate in the original texts, square brackets would be used to flag the added material. Doing so, McKerrow argued, would alleviate the need to list these changes in the textual apparatus: 'If it is understood that a bracketed name or direction is not in the copy-text, this will in practice often save much space in the collation notes' (51).

3 McKerrow's ultimate successor as general editor of the Oxford Shakespeare, Stanley Wells, found square brackets 'an irritating distraction' and declared, in his own statement of editorial procedures, that 'we shall not print square brackets to signal alterations or additions to directions when we believe that they are indisputable' (Wells, 78). Montgomery, one of the associate editors of the Oxford Shakespeare, carried on the practice in the New Pelican, explaining that his edition 'silently ... expands stage directions where this appears necessary' (Pelican[2] xliii).

4 My thanks to Arthur Evenchik, John D. Cox, and the members of the session on 'The End(s) of Editing' at the 2001 meeting of the International Association of University Professors of English for much valued help during the composition of this essay.

# PART V

## THE PLAYWRIGHT AND OTHERS

# 16

## SOURCES AND CRUCES

*John J.M. Tobin*

Multiplicity is so valued by critics – two *Lears*, three *Hamlets*, and in so many plays so many useful variants, all providing grounds for often interesting, even exciting speculations – that we forget that however full the qualifying commentary, the footnotes, and the *Arden* long notes can be, as devices to expatiate upon rich possibilities, editors do feel obliged to choose, on the basis of principle, one reading over another in a particular line. Of course, there are contrasting views that Shakespeare should not be edited at all or, as is said, remain unedited. See, for example, the often brilliant insights of Randall McLeod and Leah Marcus, but for those who do not deny the collaborative nature of the drama and the many clear instances of revision and who note the limitations of the old Greg-associated model of tracing print versions back to authorial manuscript origins, there is still the pressing need to choose one reading over another or others in the instances of variants or of unclear single terms which allow for several possible readings. As a wise man once wrote, one must 'beware of the practical editor's envy of the theorist's freedom of speculation.'[1]

For those who are innocent of theory-envy and still harbor a lingering enthusiasm for both origins and authorial intentions, and who do feel the pressure of choosing one word over another, let me suggest that Shakespeare's known sources often provide answers to certain textual problems or cruces. 'Crux' in the *Oxford English Dictionary* is defined, '3. Fig. A difficulty which it torments or troubles one greatly to interpret or explain, a thing that puzzles the ingenuity; as a "textual crux".' Let me also appeal to the words of another 'Mr. W.S.', an actor and gentleman (without a coat of arms), a man whose own procedure parallels that of Shakespeare in the latter's recidivistic borrowing of materials from several quite identifiable texts belonging to other writers, with Shakespeare himself, as John Pitcher will elegantly describe him in the final essay of this volume, as his own Autolycus. I refer, of course, to Willie Sutton (1901–80), the once-notorious American bankrobber (a kind of armed plagiarist), given the sobriquet 'The Actor' for his use of disguises, and generally described as 'gentlemanly' because of his politeness to the victims during the robberies. It was Willie Sutton who unwittingly described Shakespeare's interest in returning to certain proven malleable sources when he answered the question why he robbed banks not with a response one might have anticipated, that is, why robbery and not honest labour, but with one which distinguished between banks and less valuable targets, like gas stations or grocery stores, '*because that's where the money is*.'[2] In the case of Shakespeare, one of the chief branch banks of his many sources returned to again and again for unacknowledged (but then quite legal) borrowings is the work of Thomas Nashe.

If we consider the kinds of cruces editors are faced with and then return in the footsteps of Shakespeare to his Nashean vaults, we can test the validity of this principle of editorial choice, one which works with reference to other writers whose books Shakespeare returned to just (or almost) as often, e.g., Holinshed, North's Plutarch, Adlington's Apuleius, Florio's Montaigne, Spenser and still others. Probability is increased when the parallels are not only from the works of the same author but sometimes the same work previously used, sometimes the same section of that work, and even sometimes, the very same page. Here let us focus on Nashe and four cruces in the Bradleian tragedies, plays written after the death of Nashe and therefore free from any possibility of Nashe's being the borrower from Shakespeare. Again, we are, of course, arguing for increased probability in the selection of one instance over another, basing our judgement on the commonsensical view that while Shakespeare's genius could modify, change, add, subtract, as well as interweave and even fuse his source materials, the elements from those source materials which are so transformed are still discernible in the newly created passage. Indeed, while there's no doubt that Shakespeare could have invented his works without reference to previous texts of his own and others, such was not his preferred practice. As Geoffrey Bullough succinctly expressed it: 'Of course Shakespeare could have invented everything, but he never liked to do that, preferring always to remake suitable existing material.'[3]

Some readings involve a choice (1) between clear meaning and nonsense, some (2) between a clearly more vivid expression as opposed to one bland yet still meaningful, and some (3) between two quite interestingly meaningful options. Among the first is '*tyke* or *trundle tail*' in Quarto *King Lear* (3.6.67) versus Folio *Lear*'s '*tight* or *troundle-tail*'; from the second we can instance Folio *Hamlet*'s '*hire and salary*' (3.3.79) as opposed to the Q2 bland expression '*base and silly*' or Q1's '*a benefit*'; and from the third category, Quarto *Othello*'s '*Indian*' (5.2.345) as over against Folio *Othello*'s (but not F2 which has '*Indian*') '*Iudean*'. To complete the quartet of Bradleian tragedies as texts illustrative of cruces that can be resolved by appeal to recognized sources, we can consider *Macbeth* 1.7.6 and Theobald's brilliant emendation '*shoal*' for Folio '*Schoole*,' an emendation that has rightly held sway with only one or two exceptions. This crux seems to belong to category three, depending upon the vividness or blandness one attaches to '*Schoole*.'[4]

In the small world of the Elizabethan theatre, Nashe and Shakespeare, one speculates, had some mutual admiration, after the initial awkwardness of Nashe's 'Greeneian' hostility to upstart (non-academically credentialed) writers. This reciprocal admiration, perhaps based in part on recognition of each other's differing but not unrelated verbal talents and in part on the shared opposition to the Puritans (e.g., Nashe's work in the anti-Marprelate pamphlets and his caricaturing of Gabriel Harvey and Shakespeare's Malvolio, the latter itself a sign of his own sensitivity to the growing opposition in London and Stratford to 'his own profession.')[5]

At all events, this relationship allowed Shakespeare to profit enormously from his recognition of Nashe's vivid, useful prose (and in the case of *Summer's Last Will and Testament,* verse) and its ready availability.

Nashe's pamphlets have a dramatic aspect and his language itself is famously lively in both turn of phrase and image. Much of the sense data missing from Shakespeare's prose sources and hints as to gesture and attitudes are to be found in Nashe's writings, and were so found by Shakespeare. And much of the business of the dramatist craftsman of the sixteenth century is present in Nashe – wills, pretended letters, appeals for justice by kneeling suppliants, mutual holding of a transferred crown, ambitious malcontents, a predatory Jew, a doltish Ajax, thrasonical soldiers, jokes in Latin, jokes on vocations, dreams and nightmares which anticipate events, faces with bulbous noses, faces with warts, inarticulate doctors with urinal cases, biblical analogies to sparrows and to camels in the eye of a needle, threatened rapes and actual murders, modest lovers defeated by language, croaking ravens, cannibalism, fops, pedants, mock addresses, dancing hypocrisy, disguise, Puritan hypocrisy, and still more disguises. And if these treasures from Nashe were not enough, Shakespeare, in looking through Harvey's side of their notorious flyting, found serviceable expressions of injured merit and threats of imminent revenge.

Shakespeare is interested as ever in Nashe as a jester and satirist, but, in addition, he makes use of Nashe the social critic and moralist as well, especially in the anti-Puritanism of *As You Like It* and *Twelfth Night,* and the reflection on pride and humility in *Richard II,* prodigality in *1 Henry IV,* and hypocrisy in *As You Like It.* And in Nashe the storyteller, from the adventures of Jack Wilton through the mock-narrative of the life of Harvey in *Have With You to Saffron Walden* to the vignettes of the mock-encomium of *Lenten Stuffe,* Shakespeare finds such anecdotes as those of narcissism, entrapment by forged letter into incarceration, and transvestite disguise. For his 'mirror scene' and his scene with a mirror in *Richard II* he finds a looking glass for both prognostication and reflection, as well as the motif of the deed done, but the doing denied, and the identification of royal moralist with Christ. Needing vivid signs of appetite, he finds in Nashean physicality bread and salt, salt butter, toasted cheese, metheglin, capons, cakes and ale. Seeking to dress his characters suitably, he discovers in Nashe a variety of clothing items and related adornments, including purses, buckram, hotspurs, daggers, kerchief, napkin and thrumd hat. To the Nashean crocodile and alligator he adds the Nashean ass, camel, bell-wether and borrowed horses. Proper names from the august Galen and Hippocrates to the vulgar Gillian of Brantford are found along with things that can be made into people as the Pantheon turns into Panthino, as the weapon pistol becomes Pistol and the jeweller's tool, the touchstone, becomes our Touchstone. Urinals and dice, stolen titles and stolen virtue, objects and abstractions are found along with acts and gestures, false gallops, pressing to death, making a pish, cogging, stroking a beard and cutting flesh. Tongue-in-cheek puns, puns on tongs and tongues, cheeke and Cheke, and even the origin of a sweaty metamorphosis do but scratch the surface of Shakespeare's co-opting delight in Nashe's brilliant vocabulary.

It has been quite rightly said by Park Honan that:

> For all his originality, the dramatist had an idiosyncrasy which might be ascribed to modesty, to caution, or perhaps to his having been a hireling and then a major actor. He often looked for the grain of sand, or the phrase, the simple authentic remark or known situation uninvented by himself on which his imagination could set to work.[6]

Nashe's writings were a treasury of such grains, phrases and known situations – and rhetorical structures. Of course, we are all sensitive to the fact that as students of Shakespeare's sources and influences as indicators of his habits of mind, we are not limited to point by point verbal parallelism, interested as we are in larger cultural atmospheric forces which need not have come to Shakespeare in the form of books, or if present in the literary milieu, nor necessarily in books that Shakespeare had read. Yet, if we are still listening to, and for, the resonance of verbal echoes, we know that it is not a matter of mere parallelism of common terms, nor only rare or unique terms in the Shakespearean vocabulary, nor even sometimes proper names that have a necessary presence in Nashe's historical allusions and only an elective presence in Shakespeare's imaginative dramas, or even of clusters of such terms, or of syntax, but of rhetorical structures like an oration or last will and testament or a joke with its narrator, audience and victim. And when we see repeated borrowings of a particular source we should perhaps note that Shakespeare's personal concerns and the materials of his chosen sources (themselves partly the result of those personal concerns) overlap. For example, the fact that *Summer's Last Will and Testament* is about a king who must relinquish his power, however reluctantly, made it an ideal source for images and phrases for Shakespeare in the writing of plays rather largely concerned with kings and the surrendering of power (*Richard II, Julius Caesar, King Lear*), or about men seeking to become king (*Richard III*). We know that Shakespeare had, in the words of Park Honan, a 'preoccupation with problems of succession,' but this career-long concern with inheritance may be as much 'subscription to literary convention'[7] as to private interest.

Overall, one appreciates the functional presence of source material, in this instance works of Thomas Nashe, by considering especially *collocation, concatenation* and *context*.[8]

To begin with *King Lear*, we know that Shakespeare reread or recalled a number of Nashe's works during the composition of this particular tragedy. Among these texts are *Pierce Penilesse* (1592), *Summer's Last Will and Testament* (performed 1592, published 1600), *Have With You to Saffron Walden* (1596), and *Nashe's Lenten Stuffe* (1599). *Pierce Penilesse* must have been among the most heavily underlined, bracketed, and asterisked of Nashe's works on Shakespeare's desk (if desk he had). This ironic supplication to the devil begins with the traditional lament that learning is unrecognized and poverty the lot of those with wit. In the body of the text Nashe attacks not only the injustice of having talent go unrewarded, but a number of other abuses, including several of the traditional Seven Deadly Sins. He takes time out to defend the value of stage plays, to attack Richard Harvey, Gabriel's brother, a divine who had written on astrological prophecy, and to discuss the nature of hell and devils, all before providing a beast fable on the theme of hypocrisy, this last item proving especially useful in *As You Like It*, a play Juliet Dusinberre demonstrates (see pp. 239–51) as evoking elements from the Lyly, Nashe and Marprelate writings. In *Pierce Penilesse* there is much ado about bastards, compulsive planetary influence, adultery, corrupt justice, hell, blindness, Fortune's wheel and Dover cliff. Perhaps the most interesting collocation of items absorbed into the fabric of *King Lear* occurs on three consecutive pages (218–20)[9] where in the midst of a discussion of '*Hell*' as '... a place of horror, *stench*, and *darknesse*,' where 'Lust' and 'fornication' are particularly punished, we find its location as distant from heaven as Calais from Dover: 'for, as a man standing on Callis sands may see men walking on Dover Clyffes, so easily may you discerne heaven from the farthest part of Hell' (218). Then follows a reference to the blind goddess Fortune and the phrase, 'As *Fortune turnes* her *wheele*' (219). And between the '*stench and darknesse*' and '*Dover Clyffes*' occurs the fertile expression regarding our knowledge of the pains of the damned, '*We, that* to our terror and grief do know their dotage by our sufferings, rejoyce to thinke how these sillie *flyes plaie* with the fire that must burn them.' These two and a fraction pages have given Shakespeare some of the diction for Gloucester's 'As *flies* to wanton boys are we to the gods,/They kill us for their *sport*' (4.1.38–9), as well as the stocked Kent's '*Fortune*, good night; smile once more; *turn* thy *wheel*' (2.2.171), Lear's misogynistic explosion, 'there's *hell*, there's *darkness*, there is the sulphurous pit, burning, scalding, *stench*, consumption' (4.6.123–5), and even Edgar's concluding, 'The oldest hath borne most; *we that* are young ...' (5.3.324–5).

In the same year that *Pierce Penilesse* was published, Nashe had performed at the Archbishop's palace in Croydon his *Summer's Last Will and Testament*, a text well known as a source for at least Sonnet 12, as noted by Katherine Duncan-Jones, and for earlier plays of Shakespeare, including *1 Henry IV*, according to J. Dover Wilson and C.L. Barber in his influential *Shakespeare's Festive*

*Comedy*, where the derivative relationship of Falstaff to the Bacchus of Nashe's play is featured prominently. *Summer's Last Will and Testament* is concerned with the inevitable change of the seasons in which Summer must relinquish his crown but only after interrogating his possible successors as to the degree of fitness they have as heirs.

It has been argued that elements in the responses of Ver (the youngest of the family of Summer) and Solstitium and Summer's replies, with their respective brevity of statement and consequent anger, including the words '*meads*', '*Scythians*', and '*Nothing*', have contributed to the situation of 1.1, particularly the exchange between Lear and Cordelia.[10] But there is a good deal more that is clearly parallel and causally connected, including Summer (the Lear figure)'s '*mard*' (238) and '*mend*' (243), his frustrated response to the limited reply given by the youngest called to account, '*How now*' (239), his questioning of the Sun who is to justify himself verbally as have the other members of Summer's court, '*What* hast thou done deserving such hie grace? / *What* industrie, or meritorious toyle, / *Canst* thou produce, *to* prove my gift well plac'de? / Some service or some profit I expect: / None is promoted but for some respect' (248). The Sun replies with an independent response to this forced question: 'My Lord, what needs these termes betwixt us two? / Upbraiding ill beseemes your bounteous mind: / *I* do *you honour* for advancing me.' The Sun, who is earlier described as '*Majestie* in Pompe' (247), continues to defend himself by referring to his innocence (249) and arguing that 'What I have done, you gave *me* leave to doe. / The excrements *you bred*, whereon I feede...' (249). Elements of the Sun's defence appear in Cordelia's reply to Lear's insistence, 'I love your *majesty*' (1.1.92) ... '*you* have begot me, bred me ...' (1.1.96) ... '*I* ... honour you' (1.1.96, 98). Summer's words have become Lear's in '*Mend* your speech a little, / Lest you may *mar* your fortunes' (1.1.94–5); his response to Cordelia's '*Nothing*,' '*How*' (1.1.90) and as in the Folio '*How, how*, Cordelia' (1.1.94); and '*What can* you say *to* draw / a third more opulent than your sisters? Speak' (1.1.85–6). In the interest of preserving space for illustrations from two later works of Nashe, we may pass over such additional parallels as the presence in *Summer's Last Will and Testament* and *Lear* of a court fool who is a constant commentator on the action, one who remarks on the frustrations of the retiring monarch, as well as other parallel expressions, such as that of Summer as he banishes the recalcitrant member of his court, Orion: 'Ill-governed starre, that never boad'st good lucke, / I *banish* thee a twelve month and a day, / For of my presence; *come not* in *my sight*' (257). Some of these terms appear in Lear's response to Kent, '*Come not* ... out of *my sight* ... thy *banish*ed trunk' (1.1.123, 158, 178).

*Have With You to Saffron Walden*, Nashe's most brilliant lampooning riposte to Gabriel Harvey, provided Shakespeare with a number of phrases, some in obvious thematically connected clusters. Dover Wilson noted that Edgar's '*Fie, foh, and fum,* / *I smell the blood of a* British *man*' (3.4.179–80) derives from Nashe's indictment of Gabriel Harvey as one delighted '... to dilate a whole daye of the first invention of *Fy,* fa, *fum, I smell the bloud of an* English-*man*' (37). His point could be strengthened by adding that this lengthy sentence continues with reference to Harvey's poor reputation 'throughout *Kent* and Christendome' such that he would willingly change his name '& metamorphosize it from Doctour Harvey to Doctour Ty ...' (37). It is *Kent* who, like Edgar is metamorphosized, invites 'Tom' to join the group leaving the hovel just before 'Tom' speaks Childe Rowland's line. Two obvious clusters occur on pages 81–3 and 112–13. Inasmuch as I have elsewhere argued for their significance in *Lear*, it will suffice to quote the passages with the key expression italicized. The clarity of the relationship is obvious:

> Gabriell was always in love, Dick still in hate, either with Aristotle, or with the *great Beare* in the *firmament*, which he continually bayted; or with Religion, against which in the publique Schooles he set up Atheistical Questions, ... & a little while after I heard there were Attachements out for him: whether he hath *compounded* since or no, I leave to the lurie to enquire ... I have not yet seald and shakt hands with him for making two such false Prophets of Saturne & Iupiter, out of whose iumbling in the darke and conjunction copulative he

denounced such Oracles and alterations to ensure, ... but as he (for all his labour) could not attaine to it, no more could Dick (with his *predictions*) compass anie thing but derision, ... and out of all Authors perspicuously demonstrating what a lying Ribaden and Chincklen Kraga it was, to constellate and *plannet* it so *portentously* ... and then, if it bee a Warrior or Conqueror they would flatter, who is luckie and successful in his enterprises, they say he *is borne under* the auspicious Signe of Capricorne, as Cardan saith Cosmo de Medices, Selimus, Charles the fifth, and Charles Duke of Burbon were: albeit, I dare be sworne, no wizardly Astronomer of them all ever dreamd of anie such Calculations, till they had shewd themselves so victorious, and their propserous raignes were quite expired. On the other side, if he be *disastrous* or retrograde in hys courses, the malevolent Starres of Medusa and Andromeda, inferring suddaine death or banishment, *predominated his nativitie.* But (I thank heaven) I am none of their credulous disciples, nor can they cousen or seduce me with anie of their iugling coniecturalls, or winking or tooing throgh a six penny.

*(Iacobs Staffe*; 81, 82, 83)

Nashe goes on to indulge in some bawdy commentary at the expense of Harvey and his mysterious 'gentlewoman' in terms which seems to have affected Lear's indictment of hypocritical lust in 4.6.156–8:

It would doo you good to heare how he gallops on in commending her; hee sayes shee envies none but are in person and vertue incorporate, and that she is a Sappho, a Penelope, a Minerva, an Arachne, a Juno, yielding to all that *use her* and hers well, that she stands upon masculine and feminine terms & her *hoatest* fury may bee resembled to the passing of a brave Careere by a Pegasus, and wisheth hartily that he could dispose of her recreations. Call for a *Beadle* and have him away to Bridewell, for in every sillable he commits *letchery* ... If she *strip thee* of thy shirt, if I were as thee, I would *strip her* to thy smocke ... As Ovid writes to a *Leno.*... (112–13).

Nashe's *Lenten Stuffe* (1599), the mock-encomium which influenced the composition of a number of plays before *Lear*, including *Julius Caesar*, *As You Like It* and *Twelfth Night* among the non-Bradleian plays, provided a number of terms either unique or rare in the canon and present in *King Lear*, including '*placards*', '*finical*', '*sarum plain*', '*pell-mell*', '*Halycons*', '*Persian*',

'*Pelican*', '*white herring*', '*bratche*', '*bedlam*', and '*pigmey*'. The presence of these terms leads to our noticing that Nashe in describing the Yarmouth fishermen has them find '*a trundle-taile tike*' (182), a parallel to Q's '*tyke* or *trundle-tail*' (3.6.67). This support is so clear that even if Q here were not manifestly superior to F's nonsensical '*tight* or *troudle-taile*,' we would be drawn to choose it as also one among a large number of other influential terms from *Lenten Stuffe*, that large number belonging to the even larger number of Nashean terms pervasively present in the tragedy.

*Hamlet*, as Shakespeare's longest play, has the strongest presence of Nashean material woven into the dramatic text. Arden 2 offers two full pages describing the role of *Pierce Penilesse* in the tragedy, drawing upon the work of Arnold Davenport and G. Blakemore Evans, among others, on the '*dram of evil*' crux (1.4.36) and states succinctly that 'the characterization of the Danish court and especially of its drinking owes something to Nashe's pamphlet' (104). In addition, *Summer's Last Will and Testament* provided not only a number of terms unique in the canon, including '*by gis*', '*excrements*', '*goosequil*', '*dog ... hath his day*' and the rare but not unique '*hobby-horse*', but also an ironic commentator who gives advice to the actors (in this pageant-play actors who are young boys), threatens revenge, and announces that he will 'sit *as a chorus*' (236), even as the prince is described by Ophelia as being 'as good *as a chorus*' (3.2.240). As for Ophelia herself and her would-be mother-in-law Gertrude (see 5.1.237), it is *Christ's Tears Over Jerusalem* (1593, 2nd ed. 1594) that provides so much of the misogynistic vocabulary regarding cosmetics and female duplicity, as well as such expressions as, '*splenitive*', '*rash*', '*an inch thick*', '*nunnery*', '*stewes*', '*corrupted*', '*cheeks*', and '*playstring*' (unique in the canon). We could go on to point out Shakespeare's use of several other works of Nashe including those works we have seen that he would use in *King Lear, Have With You to Saffron Walden* and *Lenten Stuffe*. Note not only the former's '*scholler*', '*cape a pee*', '*portentously*', '*schoole*', and '*retrograde*', all on the same page (83), and the unique phrase '*sextens spades*' (88) and the reference to '*posset curd*' (106) echoed in the Ghost's '*Posset / And curd*' (1.5.69–70), as the Folio has it in contradistinction to Q2's '*possesse*'. It is customary to match the expression with the '*posset curd*' of Bright's *Treatise of Melancholie*, but in Nashe the expression is preceded by '*cut off*' (206) and followed by '*accounts*' (107) and '*in comparison of the incomparable gifts*' (107), terms which are repeated in 1.5.51, 76 and 78. As for *Lenten Stuffe*, perhaps the most influential of Nashean works upon *Hamlet*, it can be represented by the following extract:

> In Act IV, scene iii, the joking over the location of the body of Polonius owes both its humor and some of its diction to the comical anecdote of the oderiferous herring brought into the Pope's palace, and to the page immediately preceding the beginning of the anecdote. Apart from the image of the fish itself (ll. 27–31), one notes the '*politic*' (l. 20) and '*diet*' (l. 21), and the 'interchange of *diet*' and the '*politique* delegatory' on the same page on which appears the already cited '*made* wry *mouthes*' (*LS* 203). Further, the Prince's statement about the location of the body, 'you shall nose him as you go up the stairs in the *lobby*' (*LS* 204). The idea of odor and the kind of place are clear links between the two passages. When the *herring* is smoked again it results in the response 'that not a *scullion*' (not 'stallion') 'but cryed *foh*' (*LS* 208). When Claudius is told by the Prince to '*seek him* in the other place yourself' (l. 34), he is hearing words which Nashe gave to the independent herring who would not be captured by authority, 'let them *seek him*, and neither in Hull, Hell or Halifax' (*LS 210*), where '*Hell*' has provided Hamlet's '*the other place.*'[11]

'*Dram of evil*', '*posset curd*', and '*scullion*' are all supported by appeals to Nashe. It would be useful it we could find another instance of support for a resolution of a crux as important as '*scullion*' or as important and difficult as '*dram of evil*', something on the order of the '*sledded Polacks*' (1.1.6),[12] but we have to satisfy ourselves at the moment with a return to *Christ's Tears* to find confirmation for F's '*hire and salary*' at 3.3.79. Dover Wilson added an emendation of '*bait*' for '*hire*', but as the following passage indicates '*hire*' is easily explained as a near doublet for '*salary*', itself already present:

> London, what are thy Suburbes but licensed Stewes? Can it be so many brothel houses of *salary*, sensuality & sixepenny whoredome (the next doore to the Magistrates) should be sette up and maintained, if brybes

dyd not bestirre them? I accuse none, but certainly *justice* somewhere is *corrupted* (148). ... the devill *buyes* them [i.e., women's bodies] at your handes from Christ. ... (149) ... The soules they bring forth, at the latter day, shall stand up and *give evidence* against them (150).

Claudius speaks of the wicked prize itself which '*Buys* out the law' (3.3.60), for 'In the *corrupted* current of this world / Offense's gilded hand may shove by *justice*' (3.3.57–8). Yet he observes that in heaven above we all must testify honestly as we '*give* in *evidence*' (3.3.64).

When we come to *Othello*, we reach one of the most notorious of cruces, the 'Indian'/'Iudean.' Like the other plays, *Othello* shows elements of several of Nashe's works. In *Pierce Penilesse*, items have caught the eye of scholars in the matter of the unrewarded drudges who '*filche* themselves into some nobleman's service', who are motivated by '*Envie*' and whose plots make Nashe warn courtiers, 'But *beware* you that be great men's favorites ...' (175). He subsequently describes 'Envie [as] a crocodile that weepes when he kils, and fights with none but he *feedes on*. This is the nature of this quick-sighted *monster*' (184). These passages seem rather clearly to have affected the envious Iago's tormenting of Othello in his talk of reputation – 'he that *filches* from me my good name' (3.3.162) – and his warning – 'O *beware* my Lord of Jealousy! / It is the green-eyed *monster*, which doth mock / The meat it *feeds on*' (3.3.167–9). In *Christ's Tears*, Nashe returns to the issue of lack of advancement, this time a lack unfairly created. One notes as well that in *Christ's Tears* J.C. Maxwell and F.P. Wilson found, respectively, parallels between 'one *halfe* of my *soule*' (22) and Iago's comment to Brabantio that he has lost '*Half* your *Soul*' (2.4.86), and '*In a town of warre*' (44) and Othello's identical '*in a town of war*' (2.3.209) (see McKerrow, vol. V, 27, 28).

The frustrated and deserving promotion-seeker speaks of a promise that is '*cashiered* & *non suted*' (102). Iago it is who says that Othello '*nonsuits* my mediators' (1.1.15) where '*nonsuits*' is unique in the canon, and speaks of servants who are '*cashiered*' (1.1.47). *Christ's Tears* itself begins with Christ's lamenting the *adultery* of his bride Jerusalem. Further, the next year's *The*

*Terrors of the Night* provided a description of spirits who derive their strength from 'foggie-braind melancholy, [and] *engender* thereof many uncouth terrible *monsters*' (353).

> And even as slime and durt in a standing *puddle engender toads* and frogs and many other unsightly creatures, so this slimie melancholy humor still still *thickning* as it stands still, engendreth many misshapen objects in our imaginations. ... Our reason yields up our intellective apprehension to be *mocked* and trodden under foote by everie false object or counterfet noyse that comes neere it ... our *senses* defect. ... faile in their report, and deliver up nothing by lyes and fables. Such is our braine oppressed with melancholy ... *monstrously* distracted ... (354).

Compare: '*puddled* his clear spirit' (3.4.142), '*monstrous, monstrous*' (3.3.427), '*thicken* other proofs' (Iago at 3.3.430), '*monster* which doth *mock*' (3.3.166), '*toads* / To knot and *gender* in' (4.2.61–2), and the '*sense* aches' (4.2.68).[13]

With this track record on the part of Shakespeare of borrowing several works from Nashe in the composition of *Othello*, an editor should value especially highly any passage from this proven ground of source material which would help in choosing between two readings, each of which has a claim upon the critic's attention. Professor Honigmann's long note on '*Indian*' (Q) versus '*Iudean*' (F) at 5.2.345 is exemplary, and especially so is its conclusion with reference to Richard Levin's argument that while 'it is appropriate for Othello to compare himself with the Indian, whose action results from ignorance, it is 'very inappropriate for him to compare himself to Judas, whose action was regarded as a conscious choice of evil' (342–3) (see Honigmann, 342). Nashe's description of just such ignorance on the part of Indians in *Pierce Penilesse* appears to be conclusively influential upon the passage at issue – and I pass over the possibility that '*Iudean*' is actually a red herring, with the 'u' an inverted 'n': '... and not cast *away* so many months labour ... all Artists for the most part are *base* minded and *like the Indians*, that have store of gold & pretious stones at command, yet are ignorant of their value ... So they, enjoying and possessing the puritie of knowledge (a treasure farre *richer than* the *Indian* Mines). ...' (241–2).

These words and grammatical constructions find parallels in Othello's concluding speech: 'of one whose hand, / *Like the base Indian,* threw a pearl *away* / *Richer than* all his tribe' (5.2.344–6). It is of supporting interest that Nashe refers on the page immediately preceding those just cited to '*Turks*' and the limited power of devils: 'the *divels* have no power to lie to a just manne, even if they adjure them by the majestie of the high God, they will not onlie *confesse* themselves to be *Divels*, but also tell their names as they are' (24). Othello, of course, mentions his triumph over the 'turbanned *Turk*' (5.2.351) and thinks of Iago as devil: 'If that thou be'st a *devil*' (5.2.284) and 'that demi-*devil*' (5.2.298). In the event only Othello has '*confess'd*' (5.2.293), while Iago refuses to speak further.[14]

In the matter of *Macbeth*, we know of the passages in *Pierce Penilesse* cited by Arnold Davenport regarding spirits, ambiguous gender, rain and vanishing, on pages 230–1, and of those from *The Terrors of the Night*, pointed out by Ann Pasternak Slater, which contain references to '*faire* or *fowle*' (353), witches who 'kill kyne' (352), '*bubbels* in streames' (349), from the 'digression on dreams and the psychological sources of supernatural phenomena.... similarities [which] are multiple and pervasive.'[15] When we come to *Christ's Tears Over Jerusalem* we can find strong support for Theobald's brilliant emendation of '*shoal*' for F's '*schoole*.' *Christ's Tears* provided an infanticidal matron Miriam who is a tender-hearted version of Lady Macbeth, suggestive diction as in '*base*,' '*pluckt*', '*bone*', '*gums*' ... '*birdes doe*,' '*the Pyt-fal, the nette, the ginne*,'[16] as well as the unique plural '*cut-throates*' (63) and such parallel syntactical constructions as '*now* is the tyme ... *one halfe* of your dayes' (63) – compare Macbeth's '*Now* o'er the *one half* world' (2.1.49), and '*There is no* learning or *arte* leading *to* true felicity, but the *arte* of beggary' (89) – compare Duncan's '*There's no art / To* find the mind's construction in the face' (1.4.11–12). Passing over such pre- and post-1.7 parallels like '*blast*' and '*trumpet*' (60) and '*trammels*' (95) and '*surcease*' (101), let me quote the apposite passage which helps to give added probability to Theobald's '*shoal*':

The channell of Jordan was so over-burdened and charged with dead carcasses, that the waters contended to wash theyr hands of them, and

> lightly leapt over theyr *bankes* as shunning to mixe themselves with so
> many millions of murders; but after many dayes abstinence from theyr
> propper entercourse ... they recollected theyr liquid forces and putting
> all theyr wavy shoulders together, bare the whole *shole* of them before
> them, as farre as the Sea of Sodom (68).

We know that '*schoole*' is, as Muir has pointed out, 'A possible
seventeenth-century spelling of "*shoal*" (and Nashe's own spelling
"*shole*" is more than half-way to "*schoole*"). We know also that
"*bank and shoal*" forms a doublet, a device quite as characteristic
of Shakespeare's rhetoric as hendiadys, the trope recently
suggested by Horst Breuer as operative here in his emendation
of "*schoole*" to "*shore*".'[17] We can add other words and phrases
near this passage, including '*most sacrilegiously ... temple*' (66) as
in '*most sacrilegious ... Temple*'[18] (2.3.66–7), in the discovery of
the dead King Duncan, '*my intent ... onely*' (67) as in '*my intent,
but only*' (1.7.26). And from within the passage itself '*leapt over*'
finds a parallel in '*o'erleaps*' (1.7.27), with the '*vaulting*' of the
same line having a stimulus in the '*vault*' of the previous page
(67). And the phrase, 'the *waters* ... to *wash* theyr *handes* of
them' is reflected in the motive and words of Lady Macbeth, 'get
some *water*, / And *wash* this filthy *witness* from your *hand*'
(2.2.45–6). Note that seven lines above the quoted passage on the
same page Nashe writes of 'false *witnesses*' (68).

   The drawing of causal connections in each of these instances
has perhaps just a touch of Dr. Johnson's rebounding from the
large stone after dramatically (and a little self-satisfiedly) striking
it in 'refutation' of Berkeley's doctrine of the subjective nature of
reality.[19] Of course, Johnson did not engage Berkeley on the level
of epistemological theory. But who among us conducts his life as
Berkelian rather than as a Johnsonian? In the matter of finding
resolution to textual cruces there are ever so many tempting
stones to be kicked. I believe that it is not wrong to take advantage
of these candidates whose very multiplicity and similarity of kind
increase the probability of solution in each case. How comes it
then that I have noted them? As Falstaff, himself basically
constructed of Nashean[20] material, in paraphrase put it, solution

lay in his way (and in the way of a good many others), and he found it.

The use of sources to resolve cruces seems persuasive on a scale held up by William of Occam and Dr. Johnson – the strategy 'accounts for the major facts, is contradicted by none of them, and is not unnecessarily complex.'

## NOTES

1 Richard Proudfoot, *Shakespeare: Text, Stage & Canon* (Arden Shakespeare, 2001), 29.

2 For more information about this negative cultural icon, see the FBI webpage, http//www.fbi.gov/fbinbrief/historic/famcases/sutton/sutton.htm

3 Geoffrey Bullough, *Narrative and Dramatic Sources of Shakespeare*, 8 vols (London and New York, 1957–75), vol. 7, 448, quoted to good effect in Ann Pasternak Slater's '*Macbeth* and *The Terrors of the Night*', *Essays in Criticism*, 28 (1978), 112.

4 Line references are to the Arden editions of these plays: E.A.J. Honigmann's *Othello* (1996), R.A. Foakes's *King Lear* (1997), Harold Jenkins's *Hamlet* (1982), and Kenneth Muir's *Macbeth* (1951, 1984 reprint).

5 Park Honan, *Shakespeare: A Life* (Oxford University Press, 1998), 292.

6 Honan, *Shakespeare: A Life*, 332–3.

7 Honan, in a paper for the Biography Seminar, International Congress, Valencia, 2001.

8 These three factors are perhaps obvious, but the importance of their interrelationship is best exemplified in the work and teaching of John W. Velz, the author of *Shakespeare and the Classical Tradition*.

9 Page references are to *The Works of Thomas Nashe*, ed. R.B. McKerrow, 5 vols. (Oxford, 1904–10, 1958 repr.), vol. 1. Volume 1 contains among the works referred to in this essay not only *Pierce Penilesse*, but also *The Terrors of the Night*, vol. 2 has both *Christ's Tears Over Jerusalem* and *The Unfortunate Traveller*, and vol. 3 includes *Have With You to Saffron Walden*, *Nashe's Lenten Stuffe*, and *Summer's Last Will and Testament*.

10 See 'More on "Nothing"', *N&Q* 230 (December, 1985), 479–80, and 'Nashe and the Texture of King Lear', *AJES*, 8 (1983), 114–23.

11 '*Hamlet* and Nashe's *Lenten Stuffe*', *Archiv für Das Studium der Neueren Sprachen und Literaturen*, 219 (1982), 392.

12 Too brief, but suggestive, is the near juxtaposition of '*wedge*', (220), alas not '*sledge*' and '*pol-axe*' (221) in *The Unfortunate Traveller*, a work otherwise marked by diction and theme present in *Hamlet*.

13  For more on Shakespeare's use of Nashe in *Othello*, see 'Nashe and *Othello*', *N&Q*, 229 (1984), 202–3.

14  'Nashe and Othello', 203.

15  Arnold Davenport, 'Shakespeare and Nashe's *Pierce Penilesse*', *N&Q*, CXCVIII (1953), 371–4; Slater, 125.

16  Quoted in *Macbeth*, ed. Muir, p. xiii as from my 'Nashe and *Christ's Tears Over Jerusalem*', *AJES*, 7 (1982), 72–8.

17  Horst Breuer, 'Macbeth's "bank and school o time" once more', *Shakespeare Jahrbuch*, 135 (1999), 93–9.

18  See 'Nashe and Shakespeare: Some Further Borrowings', *N&Q*, 237 (1992), esp. 319–20.

19  *Boswell's Life of Johnson*, ed. G.B. Hill, rev. L.F. Powell (Oxford, 1934), vol. I, 471.

20  See, for example, the work of Dover Wilson in his edition of 1 Henry IV, C.C. Barber in his *Shakespeare's Festive Comedy*, and note 'Texture as Well as Structure: More Sources for *The Riverside Shakespeare*', in *In the Company of Shakespeare: Renaissance Essays in honor of G. Blakemore Evans*, ed. T. Moisan and D. Bruster (Madison, N.J., 2001), 97–110.

# 17

# TOPICAL FOREST: KEMP AND MAR-TEXT IN ARDEN

## *Juliet Dusinberre*

The tedious brief scene of topicality is usually several words too long for the attention-span of anyone except its author. Nothing is sooner dead than the 'in' joke, decorated by a note in which the poor editor tries to explain why on earth this was ever thought to be amusing, while secretly believing that it couldn't possibly have been even in 1600. Even Tarlton, who had the Elizabethans laughing till their faces were creased like the map of India, is within a decade only a memory: 'Alas, poor Yorick'.

One of the characters who seems uncomfortably chained to the corpse of Elizabethan topicality, and who was routinely cut in eighteenth- and nineteenth-century productions of *As You Like It*, is Sir Oliver Mar-text, who appears in 3.3. to marry Touchstone and Audrey, with Jaques at hand to give away the bride. The name Mar-text for a priest (whose qualifications for office Jaques doubts) drags into the play the Marprelate controversy of the last twenty years of the sixteenth century. Why Shakespeare chose to do so, and why his audience found it either funny or relevant even in 1599, when the debate was largely played out, is not at all clear. It remains for an editor to make a learned note, and a director to make a guy of Sir Oliver as best he can. Fascinating. Hilarious. Hmm. Yes. Well.

Three first-rate editions of the play, Arden 2 (1975), the Oxford single volume (1993) and the New Cambridge (2000), demonstrate different ways of dealing with Sir Oliver. Latham (Arden 2) suggests that Sir Oliver demonstrates Catholic scorn for the ignorant Puritan, interesting in the light of recent investigations of Shakespeare's relation to Catholicism (III.iii.37n). Brissenden's interest (Oxford) is theatrical: 'Stage Martexts often carry a large book which they eventually snap shut with rage, producing a cloud of dust' (3.3.37–8n). Hattaway's (New Cambridge) note is linguistic/historical: '**Martext** Presumably an ignorant "priest that lacks Latin"', (3.3.370); the name recalls nonce-words from the Marprelate tracts of the 1580s like "Mar-priest", "Mar-church", and "Mar-religion" (see *OED* Mar-*stem*)'.[1] The modern editor wanders into the topical forest hoping neither to encounter nor be transformed into a monster called Error, spewing up raw gobbets of books and papers. It was once different. People laughed.

They laughed because the jester, Touchstone, had found a straight man, Sir Oliver Mar-text, and sent him up, dispatching him from the stage with a volley of singing, although, wonderfully, Sir Oliver has the last word: ''Tis no matter. Ne'er a fantastical knave of them all shall flout me out of my calling'.[2] Why was the hedge-priest such a good straight man? I believe that it was because Touchstone was played, not as is usually thought, by Robert Armin, but by Will Kemp, and that Kemp's reputation as an anti-Martinist who had many times brought the house down at the Curtain jesting against the Marprelate Puritans would have created instant recognition and mirth in his audience. Here is its favourite comedian with one of his best gags.

This theory obviously has some far-reaching implications, not least for the date of the play, but I shall confine myself to establishing connections between Kemp and the Marprelate controversy. These connections were made both by William Pierce in *An Historical Introduction to the Marprelate Tracts*, and by Baskervill in *The Elizabethan Jig* (1929),[3] but neither they, nor anyone else to my knowledge, has suggested connections with Touchstone's jokes against Sir Oliver Mar-text in *As You Like It*.

The Martinists, who attacked bishops from a Puritan standpoint, were ideologically a part of the anti-theatrical movement of the last quarter of the sixteenth-century, associated with Gosson, Stubbes, Rainolds and many others. The players and their dramatists responded with skits, satires, jigs and interludes making fun of the Martinists, which were staged at a number of venues, but particularly at the Curtain in Shoreditch, where the clown John Laneham was famous, and where Kemp also played. In the mockery of Martinists the Robin Hood myth was prominent. Baskervill notes that in '*Hay any Worke for Cooper* ... one Glibbery of Halstead, a priest, is represented as having been a vice in a play, leaving the pulpit to join "a Summer Lord with his May-game, or Robin Hood with his Morris Dance".' The anti-Martinists fell on this suggestion. 'In *The Returne of Pasquill*, a proposed work called the "May-game of Martinisme" is described, in which Martin is to play Maid Marian, and other well-known Puritans other rôles' (pp. 51–2). If Duke Senior and his followers are playing Robin Hood and his merry men in the Forest of Arden, what more natural than that their court jester should encounter a Martinist in the Forest? Robin Hood, Maid Marian (sometime a farcical drag figure) and jokes against hedge-priests, all go together. In his *Nine Days Wonder* Kemp partners 'a merry Maydemarian',[4] an artless country girl like Audrey. In Lodge's novella Rosalynde wears a 'gown of green' (sig. O3) on her wedding day, the traditional dress of the Maid Marian in the Robin Hood plays of the 1590s. Kemp must have known that talking about dancing with a Maid Marian, even if only a girl willing to partner a Morris dancer on the way to Norwich, was a powerful reminder of anti-Martinist merriments.

One of the writers involved in anti-Martinist theatre was John Lyly, dramatist for the Children of Paul's. The suppression of the Children of Paul's company at some point in the early 1590s may have been due to royal displeasure at its involvement in religious controversy under Lyly's auspices.[5] Gabriel Harvey in *Pierces Supererogation* (1593) attacks Lyly as 'the Vicemaster of Poules, and the Fool master of the Theater for naughtes' (p. 133). His complaints focus on anti-Martinist japes: 'I am threatened with a Bable, and Martin menaced with a Comedie. ... All you, that tender the preseruation of your good names, were best to please Pap-hatchet, and see Euphues betimes: for feare lesse he be mooued, or some One of his Apes hired, to make a Playe of you;

and then is your credit quite-vndone for euer, and euer: Such is the publique reputation of their Playes' (p. 134). Lyly's anti-Martinist pamphlets were called *Papp with a Hatchet* (1589), *A Whip for an Ape* (1589) and *Mar-Martine* (date uncertain). This leads to another tract, which used to be ascribed to Nashe, but is almost certainly by Lyly.

In *An Almond for a Parrat* (1589), a particular stage performance is recalled in which Martin 'was attired like an Ape on yᵉ stage'. This tract is dedicated to Will Kemp (in preference to a knight or courtier who will only pour scorn on the writer as soon as his back is turned): 'Which if your sublimitie accept in good part, or vouchsafe to shadow the curtaine of your countenance, I am yours. ...'.[6] The reference to the 'curtain' (the theatre) and to 'shadow' (the word for an actor) makes the unmistakable connection between Kemp and the theatrical performances against the Martinists. It seems extremely likely that the comedian dressed as an ape was in fact Kemp, performing on the public stage of the Curtain theatre in Shoreditch, where the clown John Laneham had also made his reputation and had been a leading protagonist in anti-Martinist performances.

The dedication to *An Almond for a Parrat* is addressed 'To that most Comicall and conceited Caualeire *Monsieur du Kempe, Iestmonger and* Vice-gerent [*sic*] generall to the Ghost of Dicke Tarlton': 'I haue made choise of thy amorous selfe to be the pleasant patron of my paper' (A2r, A2v). The writer invokes 'that merry man Rablays' as well as Tarlton. The author continues (it's a very long dedication) by describing an encounter in Italy[7] with

> that famous Francatrip' Harlicken, who perceiuing me to bee an English man by my habit and speech, asked me many particulars, of the order and maner of our playes, which he termed by the name of representations: amongst other talke he enquired of me if I knew any such Parabolano here in London, as Signior Chiarlatano Kempino. Very well (quoth I,) and haue been oft in his company (A3v).

'In his company' may mean that they were friends and drinking companions, but it may also mean that they were in the same theatre company, which is the more likely if the writer is Lyly.

Kemp may have acted as a guest performer in some of the interludes against the Martinists which got the Children of Paul's and their dramatist into trouble at court.

If the comedian who satirized the Martinists attired as an ape was in fact Kemp, not only does the encounter with Sir Oliver Mar-text in the Forest of Arden access previous laughter at earlier performances, it haunts the language of Ganymede's impersonation of the fictional Rosalind for Orlando: 'I will be ... more clamorous than a parrot against rain, more new-fangled than an ape, more giddy in my desires, than a monkey' (4.1.144–5). Parrots, apes and amorousness: we are in the world of 'that most Comicall and conceited Caualeire *Monsieur du Kempe*'. Had he in fact danced into the Forest of Arden under the guise of Mr. Touchstone,[8] an 'amorous' jester who remembers doting on Jane Smiles, and who plans to marry plain Audrey with the help of the hedge-priest scorned by Jaques? The epithet 'amorous' itself points away from Robert Armin as the actor for whom Touchstone was written. Armin was not 'amorous'. Feste, Lear's Fool, Autolycus in *The Winter's Tale*, are isolated figures, watchers of other people's amours. Touchstone, wooing Audrey, is nearer to Costard wooing Jaquenetta in *Love's Labour's Lost* than he is to Feste, the Lady Olivia's corrupter of words.

Another moment in *As You Like It* echoes *An Almond for a Parrat*. The author declares to his imaginary adversary: 'Trust me therein thou hast spoke wiser then thou art aware of, for if a man should imagine of fruite by the rottennesse. ...' (sig. C3). On arrival in the Forest of Arden the 'amorous' Touchstone remembers his passionate youth: 'As all is mortal in nature, so is all nature in love mortal in folly', and Rosalind retorts: 'Thou speakest wiser than thou art ware of' (2.4.52–3). In 3.2 they jest about the ripe and the rotten (a Touchstone theme):

TOUCHSTONE
Truly the tree yields bad fruit.
ROSALIND
I'll graff it with you, and then I shall graff it with a medlar. Then it will be the earliest fruit i'th' country; for you'll be

rotten ere you be half ripe, and that's the right virtue of the medlar.

TOUCHSTONE

You have said; but whether wisely or no, let the forest judge.

(3.2.112–19)

Shakespeare's clown apes *An Almond* as if he were in dialogue with the writer. But he is also, as Kemp always was, in dialogue with the audience, at whom he glances conspiratorially while telling the heroine that her jokes are not as funny as his.

Kemp's participation in the Marprelate controversy is demonstrated incontrovertibly by the short *Theses Martinianae* (1589) assigned to 'Martin Junior', which viciously attacks the stage (implying, as many detractors did, its Catholicism): 'Feare none of these beastes, these pursuvants, these Mar-Martins, these stage-players, these prelates, these popes, these diuels, and al that they can do'. The reason for the warning is soon made clear: 'There bee that affirme, the rimers and stage-players, to haue cleane putte you out of countenaunce, that you dare not againe shew your face'. The players are condemned as 'poore seelie hunger-starued wretches ... poor varlets ... so base minded, as at the pleasure of the veryest rogue in England, for one poore pennie, they will be glad on open stage to play the ignominious fooles, for an hour or two together'. But the abuse does not hide the message, which is that the stage has put its victims out of countenance. The piece ends with a warning, to cease pamphleteering, for the tract-writers are on a losing wicket:

> Otherwise thou shalt but commend thy follie and ignorance vnto the world to be notorious. Mar-martin, Leonard Wright, Fregneuile, Dicke Bancroft, Tom Blan.o[f] Bedford, Kemp, Vnderhil, serue thee for no other vse, but to worke thy ruine, and to bewray their owne shame, & miserable ignorance.[9]

Here is Kemp, a Mar-martin, feared by Martinists, in a tract which attacks the theatre. The Martinists were afraid of the theatre and in particular, of Will Kemp.

What sort of a comic act did Kemp perform against the Martinists? He may have had a role as an Ape, or as a Maid

Marian. But his forte as a performer was the singing and dancing of the jig, which became one of commonest forms of satirical assault on the Martinists.[10] Kemp was a phenomenal dancer, and his *Nine Daies Wonder* (1600) describes his dance to Norwich in Lent 1600 when the theatres were closed. He was also a well-known composer of jigs. The song 'O sweet Oliver' with which he sings Sir Oliver Mar-text off the stage in 3.3 was a jig (probably in dialogue form) in fashion in London in 1584, about a year after the first pamphlets in the Marprelate controversy. It was registered in the *SR* in 1584, as 'A Ballat of. *O swete Olyuer Leaue me not behind the[e]*,' and a reply entered within two weeks, which a couple of years later acquired a religious gloss: 'the answeare of "O sweete Olyuer" altered to ye scriptures'.[11] The religious slant is interesting in view of the Marprelate controversy, suggesting an early connection between the jig and tract-writers. The following year, in 1585, Kemp left for the Low Countries with the Earl of Leicester, Sidney, Essex and the Earl of Leicester's players.

Kemp's fame as a comedian, dancer, 'tumbler' and 'instru-mentalist'[12] stems from his time in the Low Countries with Leicester, when he seems to have held a position as guest performer, rather than being fully integrated into the company of Leicester's players (a situation which may throw light on his later relationship with the Chamberlain's Men in 1599–1600). He danced, sang and played on the lute and virginals.[13] Wiles notes that there are four surviving texts of the *Rowland* jigs from the period 1599–1603 probably connected with a tour of the Low Countries in late 1601, pieces thought to have been composed and made famous by Kemp.[14]

The old Sir Rowland of *As You Like It*, father to Orlando, thus acquires a new pedigree. He is not just the inheritor of the chivalric world of the *Chanson de Roland* but the partner of 'Will, my Lord of Leicester's jesting player',[15] a conjunction which allows Leicester's ghost to haunt Shakespeare's comedy in multiple guises. Kemp's continental renown began with Leicester's expedition against the Spaniards in the Low Countries (Ardennes) in the mid-1580s. This enterprise saw the military debut of Leicester's stepson,

Robert Devereux, Earl of Essex, just twenty in 1585. When Shakespeare plundered Lodge's *Rosalynde* for his play of *As You Like It* he found a fiction set in Ardennes, although Lodge's Ardennes is nearer Bordeaux than Flanders. Who fitter to play the jester in the Forest of Arden than a man who had made his reputation in Ardennes with his own Sir Rowland jigs, frolics which drew on an earlier favourite, the jig of 'O sweet Oliver', which Kemp probably took with him to the Low Countries in 1585?[16] Like the Rowland jigs, 'O sweet Oliver' remained current in the Low Countries in the early seventeenth century, where its tune is included in a Leyden anthology by Thysius.[17] If Kemp played Touchstone, then the singing and dancing of 'O sweet Oliver' would have recalled the chivalric and heroic moment of the Flanders campaign, when the twenty-year-old Earl of Essex made his military debut under his stepfather, the Earl of Leicester, and when Sidney, the shepherd of *Arcadia*, lost his life at the battle of Zutphen. The young Earl of Essex carried Sidney's sword at his funeral, in a symbolic act of allegiance.

The tune of 'O sweet Oliver' links Kemp's jigs with the world of Morley and Byrd, for it is the same as that of 'The Hunt is up' and 'Peascod Time', both old songs set for the virginals by William Byrd, and featured in the manuscript Fitzwilliam Virginal Book (1600), alongside Byrd's arrangement of the 'Rowland' jig.[18] For Kemp, far from being a knock-about clown, was an accomplished musician well-known in the circles in which Byrd and Morley, Gentlemen of the Chapel Royal, moved. His jigs regularly feature side by side with the works of well-known virginal and lutanist composers in manuscript collections of the period.[19] It's not true that Robert Armin was Shakespeare's musical clown, and Kemp his slap-stick buffoon. Kemp was known as a composer and instrumentalist in musical circles outside the theatre in a way that Armin was not. Kemp's skills explain Peter's relation to the musicians in 4.5 of *Romeo and Juliet* (a scene often balked at by editors) and 5.3 of *As You Like It* where Touchstone criticizes the Pages' singing almost as Morley criticizes his two young scholars in *A Plain and Easy Introduction to Practical Music* (1597).[20] Marston's cry in *The Scourge of Villanie* (1599): 'Roome for the

Spheres, the Orbes celestiall / Will daunce *Kemps Iigge*',[21] is not altogether satire. Kemp's reputation as a musician went far beyond that of knockabout clown. Indeed, once he is associated with Touchstone, jig titles can be seen to litter the text of *As You Like It* ('The Beggar's Bush', 'A Fool's Bolt is soon shot')[22] which no doubt provided the actor with cues for singing and dancing (like fragments of modern popular song which spark off singing in a rowdy classroom).

Sir Oliver Mar-text is introduced into the Forest of Arden so that Kemp can do one of his favourite comic turns: anti-Martinist satire, through the medium of a renowned jig with multiple associations for the Elizabethans. Song and dance were the two central features of the jig, and were considered a vital element in rustic and pastoral entertainment.[23] For the Elizabethans Arden without jigs (and probably Morris-dancing, at which Kemp excelled) would have been a contradiction in terms.[24] Dancing was a commonplace on the Elizabethan stage and has been lost partly because stage directions were not considered necessary for such a regular activity, and arguably ought to be incorporated into modern editions of Shakespeare's plays. Protests against the lewdness of theatre in this period certainly included music and dancing. Kemp's virtuosity in both would have formed a part of the high jinks of 3.3 against the Marprelates.

The idea that a clown brings on to the stage his past history of clowning would have been a taken for granted in the Elizabethan theatre.[25] When Kemp posed as Tarlton's heir, a significant aspect of his inheritance may have been the independent performance which he took with him into the theatre and for which he was known. Launce's comic act with his dog in *The Two Gentlemen of Verona* imitates a well-known comic routine of Tarlton's. The extant drawing of Tarlton from this period shows him with pipe and tabor, like the boy who accompanies Kemp's dancing on the Frontispiece to *Nine Daies Wonder*. Theatrical tradition at least from the eighteenth century has Touchstone playing a pipe. Like Tarlton, Kemp was well-known for improvising and Hamlet's irritation at extempore clowning may have been directed at Kemp. In *As You Like It* 3.3 Touchstone's disquisition on 'horns' was probably a Kemp insertion in imitation of Tarlton's famous horn routine with an audience member.[26] Kemp's sally against high-born horn-bearers seems aimed at Essex's mother Lettice, well-known to have cuckolded his father Walter Devereux: the Devereux crest is a stag trippant.[27] Elizabeth, infuriated by her subsequent marriage to Leicester, thought her a notorious whore. The routine with Sir Oliver Mar-text tapped Kemp's history of anti-Martinist jigs and (j)apes, but even in this satirical mode he looks back to Tarlton, whom Baskervill believes to have satirized Puritans on-stage.[28]

If Arden in this discussion looks increasingly like Ardennes, where 'O sweet Oliver' helped to make Kemp's name, Mar-text would have drawn the play irresistibly back into its English orbit, and specifically to Shakespeare's Warwickshire. The defiance of authority in the printing of unlicensed Marprelate tracts[29] centred on Warwickshire, where Job Throckmorton was convicted at the Warwickshire Assizes in 1590 for his taking part in illegal printing. His father was a connection of Catherine Parr's and cousin of the Queen; Raleigh's wife, Elizabeth Throckmorton, was also his cousin.[30] The Forest of Arden had its own makers and marrers of text, and there is an inspired congruity in Touchstone's encounter with one of their representatives in a Warwickshire Arden.

Kemp is not, however, the only actor in the list at the beginning of the First Folio to have a connection with the Marprelate controversy. Nathan Field, whom Malone believed to have played Shakespeare's women as a boy actor around 1600, was the son of one of the founder writers of Martinist tracts: John Field, ('preacher', 'minister', 'clerk' according to the register of St Giles Cripplegate) and an ardent opponent of theatres and 'these Heathenishe Enterludes and Players'. If his son played Audrey in *As You Like It*, what better joke than to have a representative of his father's persuasion roped in to marry her off?[31] Nathan Field not only flouted in his career his father's religious beliefs, he also in 1617 wrote an impassioned letter to Mr. Sutton, the minister at his own parish of St Saviour's, Southwark Cathedral, protesting against Sutton's attempt to prevent him, as a player, from taking the sacrament because of his profession.[32] *As You Like It* is based on a story (*Rosalynde*) by Thomas Lodge, one of the very first to defend the theatre against its detractors in a piece printed and instantly suppressed in 1581, some two years before the printing of John Field's unlicensed *A Godly Exhortation by Occasion of the Late Iudgement of God* (1583), one of the first Martinist tracts, which used an accident at the Paris Garden to prove God's judgement against the theatre.[33] Shakespeare might have felt some impulse to mar Field senior's text, especially if his son, a Paul's grammar school pupil and probably a chorister, was there, 'between the acres of the rye' (5.2.21), to help. (The puns on Field's name in this period are innumerable).

Sir Oliver Mar-text is a tiny part. Someone must have doubled it, probably Oliver, the far-from-sweet elder brother of Orlando, whose talk in the first scene of the play is all of making and marring. The Elizabethans found the musty little hedge-priest who struts on to the stage to marry the jester to his maid Marian (Kemp's name for a country girl) funny because he prompted their favourite clown to a reprise of one of his best numbers. The mockery of the Martinists with the jig of 'O sweet Oliver' evokes the golden world of old Sir Rowland as clearly as Shakespeare's play does. The party was almost over, for everyone, but in the topical Forest Kemp had one last laugh at Sir Oliver Mar-text. Little did Touchstone or his creator imagine that within fifty years another Oliver would silence them all.

## NOTES

1 *As You Like It*, ed. Agnes Latham (1975); *As You Like It*, ed. Alan Brissenden (Oxford, 1993); *As You Like It*, ed. Michael Hattaway (Cambridge, 2000). References to these three editions are to Arden 2, Oxford, and New Cambridge, and are contained within the text.

2 *As You Like It*, 3.3.98–9. All quotations from Shakespeare's plays, unless otherwise stated, are from *The Arden Shakespeare Complete Works*, ed. Richard Proudfoot, Ann Thompson and David Scott Kastan (Walton-on-Thames, 1998).

3 William Pierce, *An Historical Introduction to the Marprelate Tracts* (London, 1908), p. 237; Charles Read Baskervill, *The Elizabethan Jig* (New York, 1965 (1929)).

4 William Kemp, *Nine Daies Wonder* (1600), Bodley Head Quartos (Edinburgh, 1966), p. 14.

5  Richard Dutton, *Mastering the Revels* (London, 1991), pp. 75–7.

6  *An Almond for a Parrat, Or* Cutbert Curry-knaues *Almes* (London, 1590), sigs. C3, A2.

7  An encounter dramatized by Day, Rowley and Wilkins in *The Travels of Three English Brothers* (1606–7) in which Kemp plays himself (David Mann, *The Elizabethan Player*, London, 1991, pp. 68–73).

8  At 3.2.11, in the Folio Corin addresses Touchstone as 'M$^r$'; editors traditionally print 'Master'; the New Cambridge conjectures 'Monsieur', which Kemp himself adopts in *Mounsers almaine* (n.19). The question of address may have prompted stage business; the shepherd denies the jester his French gentleman's title, which he then denies to Jaques at 3.3.68: 'Master what d'you call it?' (Oxford *Complete* (*William Shakespeare: The Complete Works*, ed. Stanley Wells and Gary Taylor, Oxford, 1986), and New Cambridge read 'Monsieur'). If Touchstone's name is only invoked in Arden (Folio SD for 2.4 '*alias* Touchstone') this may signal to the audience a move from France to England. Kemp, unlike Armin, always has an English name. But he is also aggressively egalitarian: if he is to be plain 'Master' in the Forest, so is the Frenchified Jaques, whom everyone else calls 'Monsieur'.

9  [Martin Junior], *Theses Martinianae* ([Wolston, 1589]), sigs. Di$^v$, Dij, Dij$^v$, Diij$^v$.

10  Baskervill, p. 52.

11  *As You Like It*, ed. by Richard Knowles, *New Variorum* (MLA, 1977), p. 198.

12  Danish court records, Baskervill, p. 129.

13  See, for example, 'Kempes Jigge' (lute music), in Cambridge MS Dd. II.11, fol. 99$v$, a volume which includes the originals of some Shakespeare songs, among them 'Hearts Ease' (f.44) which Peter begs the musicians to play in *Romeo and Juliet* (4.5.100–1).

14  David Wiles, *Shakespeare's Clown* (Cambridge, 1987), p. 38; Diana Poulton, *John Dowland* (1972), p. 168.

15  Letter from Sidney to Walsingham from Utrecht, 24 March 1586, quoted in S. Schoenbaum, *William Shakespeare* (Oxford, 1975), p. 116.

16  Baskervill, pp. 181, 224, 226n1.

17  *New Variorum*, p. 198.

18  Baskervill, pp. 182–3.

19  *Mounsers almaine*, one of the songs in Morley's *Consort Lessons* (1599), is composed by Kemp (Thurston Dart, 'Morley's *Consort Lessons* of 1599', *Proceedings of the Royal Music Association*, lxxiv (1947–8): 2–9, pp. 6, 8). The Kemp/Morley connection is particularly appropriate for 5.3, where Touchstone hears the pages sing Morley's song: 'It was a lover and his lass'.

20  In the Low Countries Kemp had his own 'boy' with him who presumably helped with singing and dancing (Wiles, p. 40).

21  John Marston, *The Scourge of Villanie* (1599), Bodley Head Quartos (Edinburgh, 1966), p. 106.

22  i) 'The Beggar's Bush', Day, *Parliament of Bees*, quoted in Baskervill, p. 149, cf. *AYL* 3.3.76. ii) 'A Fool's Bolt is soon shot', Baskervill, p. 104, cf. *AYL* 5.4.63.

23  Baskervill, pp. 16–17.

24  The early seventeenth-century Flemish painting: 'View of the Thames with the old Palace at Richmond' shows Morris dancers on the tow-path (Ian Dunlop, *Palaces & Progresses of Elizabeth I*, London, 1962, p. 128), to identify the movement from city to country.

25  Mann, pp. 58–9.

26  *Tarlton's Jests*, 1638, quoted in Mann, pp. 59–60.

27  Reproduced in Peter Beal, *Elizabeth and Essex: The Hulton papers* (Sotheby's catalogue, 1992), p. 3.

28  Baskervill, p. 102.

29  Dutton, p. 74.

30  Pierce, pp. 215, 218.

31  Field was in 1596 a pupil of Richard Mulcaster's at St. Paul's. He may, like Salomon Pavey, have been a chorister at the Cathedral and conceivably played for the Children of Paul's before he first enters theatrical records, as one of the children impressed sometime around or before 1600 for service in the Chapel Royal (Children of Blackfriars). It's not very likely that he played in *As You Like It*, but it is conceivable that he and other boys were 'hired' by the Chamberlain's Men (Ben Jonson, *Poetaster*, ed. Tom Cain, Manchester, 1995, III.iv.208–10). For further discussion, see my forthcoming edition of *As You Like It* for Arden 3.

32  Elaine Verhasselt, 'A Biography of Nathan Field', *Revue Belge de Philologie*, 252 (1946–7): 485–508, pp. 490–1, 507.

33  'By a queer twist of circumstance, it was John Field's son that drew the crowd back to this very spot some thirty years later, when the new Hope Theatre occupied the old Paris Garden site' (Roberta Florence Brinkley, *Nathan Field, actor-playwright*, New Haven, 1928, p. 6).

# 18

## SOME CALL HIM AUTOLYCUS

*John Pitcher*

At this point in the history of studying Shakespeare, to venture a connection between the dramatist, man and writer, and one of his characters is to risk being labelled a crank or witless or (at best) a harmless species of biographer. The academy has become pretty successful over the years at defining and policing what is and what isn't reliable, normal, and (most sacred of phrases) of use to students of Shakespeare. So I am conscious, like anyone whose credibility as a scholar depends on some measure of approval and assent, that I had better be careful when advancing the proposition that we can see Shakespeare in Autolycus or even, with just a little more nerve, that we can see Autolycus in Shakespeare. I'm happy to add that I do have some new evidence to consider, however, and a good amount of old evidence too; but my appeal in the first instance is to something I regard as indisputably obvious.

For this we need to return to the scene of the crime – no, not to the scene where Autolycus steals from the Clown in Act 4 of *The Winter's Tale*, but to the London literary scene of autumn 1592 where Robert Greene, on his death bed, committed the crime of accusing Shakespeare of stealing from contemporary writers. The accusation almost certainly didn't come from Greene himself (he died a short time before), but from another writer using his persona. We are not sure who this writer was (probably Henry Chettle, but possibly Thomas Nashe), but we do know that the Greene persona wasn't his; appropriately he had stolen it from the real Robert Greene. The persona was that of the gentleman writer of talent who ruins himself through gambling, drink and women but who then repents – in essence the story of the Prodigal Son. The real Greene got a fair amount of mileage out of being the Prodigal Son in person for two or three years until poverty, ill-health and perhaps the plague finally finished him off. The pamphlet in which Shakespeare was accused of thieving was, true to the theme of the Prodigal, called *Greene's Groatsworth of wit, bought with a million of repentance.*[1]

Whether Shakespeare ever found out that it wasn't the real Greene who had attacked him we can't say, although there are signs he suspected it.[2] What is clear is that after 1592 no-one else tried (or cared or perhaps dared) to attack him like this again. He received an apology of sorts in print from Chettle, one of Greene's former chums, and the matter looks as though it ended there, at least to public eyes. As for the crime scene itself – what was actually said against Shakespeare – even though it has been well-trodden over, the tell-tale marks are still visible. 'There is an upstart crow,' Greene is made to say, to fellow graduates who write for the stage,

> beautified with our feathers, that with his *Tygers hart wrapt in a Players hyde*, supposes he is as well able to bombast out a blanke verse as the best of you: and beeing an absolute *Johannes fac totum*, is in his owne conceit the onely Shake-scene in a countrey.[3]

The allusions in this have been construed in several different ways, most of which are plausible because the passage is obviously overfull with what it can mean. *Johannes Factotum*, for instance, can mean Mr. Know-it-all, or Mr. I-can-do-everything, or Jack of all trades (and master of none). The phrase 'beautified with our feathers' is equally overdetermined, referring either to the feather hats and head-dresses that were the mark of Elizabethan actors[4] (thus 'beautified' or adorned by the parts the gentlemen writers have created for them) or to the quills for writing made out of feathers (that is, the crow has tricked himself out with styles of writing he has plucked from them: even more richly suggestive if they were swan's feathers, since the swans on the Thames were already symbols of many things, including poets and poetry; and of course the Greene persona speaks of *Groatsworth* being his swan song).[5]

The exact charge against Shakespeare is not something that scholars are likely to agree on, but fortunately, for present purposes, the fine distinctions in interpretation don't matter too much. The accusation may be that he's a plagiarist, or that he's a hack imitator aspiring to be a rival, or that he's an uneducated common player with a cruel heart and an ambition to outdo even the best of the university poets. But whichever of these explanations we take to be the most plausible, all of them have one thing in common: in each case Shakespeare is accused of being a thief. The theft is either of lines and scenes from other writers, or their ways of writing, or their livelihoods, reputation and social status (since he challenges their claim that only they, as university men, have the competence and learning to write plays). He's not merely a thief, though; he's a deceiver too. The line '*Tygers hart wrapt in a Players hyde*' is a deliberate misquotation from 3 *Henry VI* 1.4.137, addressed by the Duke of York to the Queen of France, with her 'tiger's heart wrapped in a woman's hide.' York has earlier called the Queen the 'she-wolf of France, but worse than the wolves of France' (1.4.101), which confirms the impression that the original line ('a woman's hide') and in turn the misquotation alludes to or is drawn from the familiar image in Matthew, 7.15, of the wolf in sheep's clothing. It's noticeable moreover that the real Greene substituted the tiger for the wolf in some of his pamphlets,[6] both animals being synonymous at this date with greed and merciless savagery. The outcome in short is that Shakespeare, like one of his own characters, is referred to, at one remove, as a sheep in wolf's clothing.

The next part of the story is equally familiar. Almost two decades after *Groatsworth*, Shakespeare returned to Greene – the real one, that is – for a new play about jealousy and reconciliation called *The Winter's Tale*. By this stage, around 1610, the Greene persona, added to by yet more writers, had merged with stories of

Greene's life as a prodigal and with his own works from the 1580s and early 1590s. It was from one of the authentic pieces, a short romance novel entitled *Pandosto, the Triumph of Time*, that Shakespeare took the plot for *The Winter's Tale*. Given how popular and well-known the story of *Pandosto* was, it looks as though Shakespeare wanted to make sure (or at least was wholly content) that the debt to Greene would be apparent to everyone in the know, from his fellow-writers to members of his theatre audiences at the Globe, and at the court too. Shakespeare altered the story line in *Pandosto* in several places, particularly at the end, and he introduced a number of new incidents and characters: much of the rural feast in Bohemia is his, as are the characters Paulina, Antigonus and the Clown. His most notable additions, however, were the Bear, the personification of Time as the Chorus, the Statue that comes to life and the role of (as the 1623 Folio list of characters puts it) 'Autolycus, a rogue'. For some of the things Autolycus gets up to (stealing from the Clown in 4.3 and the description of how he worked the crowd and stole from it in 4.4), Shakespeare turned to Greene again, this time to two of his pamphlets published in 1592 about con men, pickpockets and cutpurses called *The Second Part* and *The Third Part of Cony-Catching* (the conies or rabbits in question were country bumpkins who could be duped, or householders from whom linen could be filched, and so forth).[7] One current view, which may be true, is that Shakespeare wanted his contemporaries to know what he had acquired from Greene, in stories and detail, to show just how startling and magical he could make such simple originals.

This is to get ahead of ourselves, though, into the area of Shakespeare's own persona and motive. The proposition I want to steer us towards for now – I said it was indisputably obvious above – is that the character Autolycus, whatever else he represents or amounts to in the play, is an objectification of the thief that Shakespeare was accused of being in *Groatsworth*. Even without the evidence that is to come later, this is not an unreasonable conclusion. Recall, for instance, the allegation (made by turning one of his own lines against him) that Shakespeare was a wolf in sheep's clothing. It is hard to imagine a better way of responding to this than to have Mr. Wolf himself come on stage in person – that is, to introduce into Greene's story the most cunning thief of all, Autolycus, whose name, as the Renaissance commentaries explained, was a Greek compound meaning (among other things) *ipse lupus*,[8] the very wolf himself, or the quintessential wolf. At the end of 4.3 this thieving wolf – a loner, as 'auto' also suggests – proceeds to a sheep-shearing feast where, as promised, he makes the 'shearers prove sheep': in disguise as a low entertainer, in other words, he treats his audience like stupid animals, mercilessly fleecing them as they stand senseless, charmed by nothing but the Clown's innocent singing.[9]

There are other instances in Act 4 which may allude even more specifically to *Groatsworth*. One of them is the speech in 4.3, in which Autolycus describes himself to the Clown in the third person (thus assuming a persona, we notice). 'I know this man well' says Autolycus, he was once a servant of the prince, but after being whipped and driven out of court, he became

> an ape-bearer, then a process-server (a bailiff), then he compassed a motion of the Prodigal Son, and married a tinker's wife within a mile where my land and living lies, and, having flown over many knavish professions, he settled only in rogue. Some call him Autolycus.[10]

The remark that Autolycus 'compassed a motion of the Prodigal Son' is usually taken to mean that he acquired a puppet-show ('motion' *OED* 13a) and took it about the country (to all compass points), making the puppets act out the parable of the Prodigal Son in Luke 15.11–32. As we saw earlier, though, the subject of the Prodigal was one that Greene had identified himself with personally – he had gone out of his way to make it his own – and even as late as 1610 a reference to it may have called Greene to mind at once. Of course this doesn't mean that every mention of the Prodigal Son in Shakespeare (four or five times at least) is an invocation of Greene; it is the context, the way the allusions knit together, that matters. Seen this way, 'compassed a motion of the Prodigal Son' could also mean 'thought up a show for actors taken from Greene, the prodigal talent' ('motion' was another word for puppet, and *Groatsworth* called actors puppets), or even 'stole the life [i.e., warm movement, 'motion' *OED* 2] out of Greene the Prodigal' (a recollection of the charge that Greene was destitute because of the upstart crow). As for the sequence of jobs Autolycus tries, and (one must assume) fails in or is sacked from, it's worth noting that this makes him, in all senses, a *Johannes Factotum*, a botcher who masters nothing, but who thinks he can do everything. Perhaps the most intriguing detail in this respect, of allusions to Greene, is the claim that Autolycus 'married a tinker's wife', which is a euphemism (from rogues' cant) for 'he started living out of wedlock with a whore.' Although Shakespeare is accused of quite a number of things in *Groatsworth*, this isn't one of them. It is in fact one of the features of the story of the Prodigal – who abandons his wife for a lower-class mistress – which Greene confessed to several times over. This is a useful reminder, before we move on, that in Shakespeare's hands the Autolycus persona was almost sure to be a compound of contradictory things.

Finding out where Autolycus came from is of course a much bigger task than simply tracking him back to *Groatsworth*. I am fully aware that his appeal to Shakespeare's first audiences was not limited to rebuttals or to counter satire against some long dead writer. Autolycus is a character who lives on the margins of rural society, literally so in his filching linen off hedges (boundaries planted to mark and to protect ownership), in his keeping to the back roads, away from highways, and in his associations, as a country pedlar, with the unreformed old faith, popish relics and superstitions.[11] He combines in himself all the features of low life and feckless freedoms that Jacobean men – sound citizens and good husbands no doubt – could ever have fantasized about. He might be wearing rags,[12] but he could have sex with women without marrying them and without any delay or fuss, he didn't have to work or to worry about the seasons, and (perhaps most exciting of all) he was able to give his word lightly, not bothering about whether something was true or not. His apparent indifference to whether there was any reward or punishment in the afterlife must have seemed scary, but wonderfully unburdened.[13] In *The Alchemist*, acted a year before *The Winter's Tale*,

Jonson had shown audiences the comedy of a serving man, together with a rogue and a prostitute, taking over his master's house in the city and gulling various people. Autolycus by contrast (perhaps one that Shakespeare intended deliberately) is a rogue out of doors and a man cast off by his master, but the thrills and shocks of seeing members of the underclass unashamedly lying and stealing, and dressing up and impersonating people, were not dissimilar.

That Autolycus is indeed from the lower orders – never more than a serving man and certainly not someone of rank – shouldn't be in doubt, but on occasions he has managed to take in even the most subtle of Shakespeare's critics. Coleridge, for instance, had this to say about Autolycus's line 'for the life to come, I sleep out the thought of it' (4.3.30):

> Fine as this is, and delicately characteristic of one who had lived and been reared in the best society, and had been precipitated from it by dice and drabbing; yet still it strikes against my feelings as a note out of tune, and as not coalescing with that pastoral tint which gives such a charm to this act. It is too Macbeth-like in the 'snapper up of unconsidered trifles'.[14]

Whether the line is truly incongruous, because too close to tragedy, may be open to question, but it is certainly *not* the case that Autolycus has 'lived and been reared in the best society'. Coleridge evidently thought he was dealing with something like a regency rake who had fallen from the heights of the *beau monde*, or one of the middle class prodigals in Hogarth, desperate for cash and beyond all shame. Autolycus had certainly been at court as a servant of Prince Florizel's, snapping up things even then (the way fashionable courtiers picked their teeth, for instance),[15] but all the signs are that the job he had was a very humble one, and that he wasn't at all close to the Prince. He tries to suggest the contrary to the audience – that he is a gentleman prodigal who has known grand days – but this is a barefaced lie. He says he once wore three-pile, the plush velvet livery of superior royal servants, but when he's dressed in the Prince's countryman clothes towards the end of Act 4 he can't even convince the

Shepherd that he knows how to wear them properly.[16] He is in fact surely nothing more than a footman, as he lets slip, or lets us know on purpose, in one of his exchanges with the Clown (4.3.61–7). 'I am robbed, sir, and beaten', he tells the Clown, 'my money and apparel ta'en from me, and these detestable things put upon me.' Who did it, asks the Clown, was it 'a horseman, or a footman?', by which he means a robber on horseback, or a thief on foot. Autolycus replies – already speaking of himself in the third person we recall – that his assailant was a footman, a footpad that is, but also the word, as the Clown's response confirms, for a very lowly servant, 'indeed, he should be a footman by the garments he has left with thee.' So Autolycus had been the Prince's footman, which at this date (before the coach and new table etiquette arrived in polite society) meant no more than the attendant who had to run and keep up alongside his master's horse. His preposterous suggestion that he had been forced down the social ladder must have been greeted by laughter and catcalls from the audience in the Globe, and one can easily imagine how audiences at court performances would have relished this cheeky menial, a lackey who ought to be blacking their boots, trying to pass himself off as a superior royal servant[17] (perhaps Florizel never recognizes him, not because of any convention in drama, but because top people often look straight through the lower beings around them).

But if Autolycus hasn't fallen from any high position *within* the play, he certainly has, in terms of literary genealogy, when we look outside it. Critics and editors haven't paid much attention to this aspect of him because, I suspect, they don't think that Shakespeare would have known anything substantial about Autolycus's classical ancestors and namesakes, other than what he found in Ovid, in the *Metamorphoses*. This is a mistaken view, based on the unproven notion that Shakespeare's knowledge of Greek was so limited that he couldn't have known what was in Homer, unless it was in an English translation. It is true that there was no complete *Iliad* or *Odyssey* in print in English at the date of *The Winter's Tale* (Chapman's version was published in 1614) but there were Latin and Italian translations,[18] and, just as important, there were the commentaries and dictionaries of mythology that set out, in rudimentary Latin, the basic things about people and places in classical literature, Autolycus among them. From the entry in the Stephanus dictionary, for example, it was possible to learn that Autolycus lived on Parnassus, that he was the son of Hermes and grandfather of the cunning men, Sinon and Odysseus, that he was the founder of the city of Sinope and a friend of Jason, and that the authorities to consult were Homer, Plato in the *Republic*, Ovid, and Strabo's *Geography*.[19] The profile of Autolycus from classical sources, much of it noted in the dictionaries, was varied and contradictory, including thief, plunderer, embezzler, swindler, rival and friend of Sisyphus, bawd, wrestler, the maternal grandfather who gave Odysseus his name, equivocator and cattle thief.[20] In his *Mythologiae* Comes also reported that were other, more popular post-classical accounts of Autolycus that emphasized his roguishness (in one of which, for instance, he is said to have stolen a friend's lovely wife and replaced her with a toothless hag).[21]

Autolycus in the *Odyssey* is a superior man – the head of a clan of elite warrior hunters – but he is not the son of Hermes. He sacrifices to the god, who shows his favour by making him the greatest of men in thieving and in deceiving everyone, friends as well as enemies, with cunning (that is, breakable) oaths. In this culture of the hunt, the mountain and the forest, it's the man who can steal best from his neighbour who thrives, so lies and theft, far from being improper, are the mark of leadership and care for one's family. When his daughter asks him to think of a name for his new-born grandson, he tells her that because he himself has been at odds with so many people, all over the place, the boy's name should be Odysseus – the angry one – because he in time would have to suffer from these enmities.[22] One reason his own name is Autolycus is that he is the wolf by himself, the greedy one looking after himself and his own – the embodiment of an ancient code of resourcefulness and self-sufficiency. But for Autolycus after Homer, it's all downhill. The warrior chief in his lair, whose sons had hunted the great boar with Odysseus, is reduced, bit by bit, by later writers. They do make Hermes his father, and include him among the Argonauts, but neither honour is exactly rare.[23] Plato has his doubts about him (how can this thief be a just man, even if he steals to help his friends and to harm his enemies?),[24] but this isn't as bad as making him, as some authorities do, a pander who gives his daughter to Sisyphus on the night before her wedding to Laertes (making Sisyphus the true father of Odysseus). Well before Autolycus reached imperial Rome and was metamorphosed by Ovid, his sexual character had grown murkier, his thefts had become more banal, and he had turned into little more than a trickster, a magician, a shape-changer. He had become, and Shakespeare may well have noted it, another kind of *Johannes Factotum*, a showman who was once a lord.

Ovid does perhaps the worst thing of all to Autolycus: he makes him a bit player and a bit bizarre. In the *Metamorphoses*, 11.301–17, Mercury, and then a few hours later, Apollo have sex with the same woman, Chione, but they impregnate her together, miraculously, with male twins, one boy to each god. Mercury (Hermes), the god of thieves and cheats, is the father of Autolycus, while Apollo, the god of music and poetry, is the father of Philammon, the man who will excel all others in singing and playing the zither. Twin fathers, as it were, beget twin sons; impossible of course, but a subject, as scholars have pointed out, germane to the fantasy of twinship between Leontes and Polixenes that is the starting-point for *The Winter's Tale*.[25] In Ovid, the complex cross-currents of meaning in this passage are evident, but there's not much left of the old Autolycus, shrinking now into a couple of verses. Autolycus, a worthy heir of his father's art (*patriae non degener artis*), was

> Cunning in theft, and wily in all sleights:
> Who could with subtilitie deceave the sight;
> Converting white to black, and black to white.

I quote this from the translation by George Sandys, which wasn't done until fifteen years or so after Shakespeare's death, because Sandys, in his accompanying notes, finally empties Autolycus of any grandeur he had. He was not, Sandys insists, Mercury's son, but rather 'a notable Impostor' who 'feigned to be his son, as borne vnder his Plannet, or participating those conditions: who by his thefts & cousonage attained to great riches.'[26] The miraculous conception in Ovid bothered him more. 'Can we believe' he asked his readers, 'that Divells, for these Gods were no better, can carnally lust and ingender with mortals?' Trying to answer this led him into the taboo territories of incubi, fallen angels, heavenly and earthly devils and even the possession of a woman's corpse by the devil himself. No doubt it was moral and theological concerns such as these that prompted the Jesuit Pontanus to expurgate the whole passage from his edition of the *Metamorphoses*, at last removing Autolycus from the picture altogether.[27]

When Autolycus arrived on the London stage in May 1611, we can see that he was carrying a good deal of baggage from the past (perhaps literally as well, if he had his tinker's bag and begging box with him).[28] The two lines that flow into him, I suggest, are from the ancient world (by way of contrast sometimes), and from the quarrel that Greene had begun with Shakespeare. Other past influences are visible – patently he is in the tradition of the stage Vice[29] – but these don't connect themselves to him with the same specificity of allusion. Autolycus in Ovid is said to be able to convert 'white to black, and black to white', so Autolycus in Shakespeare offers for sale (4.4.220–1)

Lawn as white as driven snow,
Cypress black as e're was crow,

which brings with it a reminder too of that other crow, the upstart one in *Groatsworth*. As for the other twin in Ovid, the musical one Philammon, he isn't forgotten either: Shakespeare simply metamorphoses him into his brother, so that Autolycus in Bohemia is both thief *and* singer. But, we may ask, did these two lines of influence, which are the key literary ones, ever come together in any way outside or before *The Winter's Tale*? Is there a missing link between them, or did Shakespeare himself do all the work of joining them? This is another way, I suppose, of returning to the bigger question, *why* Autolycus, why not some other infamous thief, ancient or modern.

I can't pretend, whatever my interest in him, to have searched out every reference to Autolycus in England before 1600, but I'm fairly sure that he was of peripheral interest to the Tudor dramatists and poets (there is no Autolycus character in the printed drama before Shakespeare,[30] and nothing important about him in Spenser). In fact when he does reappear, in 1607, it's not in a work of fiction, but in a short study of the four humours by a Cambridge don. This, I believe, is the missing link, a passage in a book called *The Optic Glass of Humours* by Thomas Walkington, a Fellow of St John's College, Cambridge.[31] Why Shakespeare read this book can be answered in a moment, but first we must go to the passage. The subject of *The Optic Glass*, although it's written on a much smaller scale, overlaps with Burton's *Anatomy of Melancholy*.[32] Walkington doesn't have much to add to the established theories of the humours, but he is interesting in several smaller areas. One of these is his description of different kinds of wit, determined by what he calls the 'temperature of the body'. There are nine of these, to which he gives names. There is

> a *Simian* or apish wit, an *Arcadian* wit, a *Roscian* wit; a *Scurril* wit: an *AEnigmatical* wit, an *Obscene* wit, an *Autolican* or embezel'd wit: a *Chance medlay* wit, and lastly there is a smirke, quicke & *dextericall* wit.[33]

The seventh – the *Autolican* wit – is the one we're interested in, and of this he writes, inventing much that might catch Shakespeare's eye,

> An *Autolican* wit is in our thread-bare humorous cavialeroes, who like chap-fallen hackneies feed at others rack and manger: never once glutting their mindes with the heavenlie Ambrosia of speculation whose braines are the very broakers shoppes of al ragged inventions: or rather their heads bee the block houses of all cast and outcast peeces of poetrie: these be your pick-hatch courtesan wits, that merit (as one jeasts upon them) after their decease to be carted in *Charles* waine: they bee tearmed not laureat but poets loreat that are worthy to bee jirkt at with the lashes of the wittiest Epigrammatists.[34]

Walkington, as others before him, has made Autolycus (here by implication) much less than he was in Homer, or even in Ovid.

Autolican wits are associated with the bottom layer of the city: impoverished swaggerers ('cavialeroes'), broken-down horses, tatty second-hand clothes shops, and whores who are to be carted and whipped. Everything they have is stolen from someone else, especially what others have said, thought or written. These are wits, Walkington continues,

> that like roving dunkirkes or robbing pyrats sally vp and downe i'the printers ocean, wafted too and fro with the inconstant winde of an idle light braine: who, (if any new work that is lately come out of presse, as a barke under saile fraughted with any rich marchandise appeare unto them) doe play upon it eft with their silver peeces, board it incontinently, ransacke it of every rich sentence, cull out all the witty speeches they can finde appropriating them to their own use: to whom for their wit we will give such an applause as once Homer did unto *Autolycus* who praised him hilie …[35] for cunning theevery, and for setting a jolly acute accent upon an oath.

This isn't the place to attempt a detailed exposition of the passage, but one can see at once the decisive change that Walkington has made to Autolycus. His name has been lent, as it was in Comes, to the dregs of society – outcasts fearful of the whip, pretenders in cast-off clothes, and pirates. The analogy Walkington intends is with people with superficial ('idle light') minds who steal from books of poetry, paying a few coins ('their silver peeces') for the latest thing from the press. The satire and vein of writing draws on the new generation of writers – Jonson and the younger university men like Marston and Hall – but inevitably we recall the bitter gibes in *Groatsworth*, and ask whether this is a renewal, again from a Cambridge Master of Arts, of the old attack on Shakespeare (who throughout the years had carried on taking from every writer in sight, Plutarch, Holinshed, Boccaccio, *et al.*).

The answer to this is not in the slightest, indeed quite the contrary. In his argument that 'a fat belly has a leane ingenie' (overeating makes you stupid), Walkington says that 'this is set downe by a moderne english poet of good note pithyly in two verses' and he then quotes the familiar fat paunches and lean pates couplet from *Love's Labour's Lost*.[36] It is inconceivable that Walkington was unaware of *Groatsworth* (he became a Fellow of

St John's when the *Parnassus* plays were in vogue, and his own writing is shot through with the language of poetry and drama).[37] My guess is that he calls Shakespeare a 'poet of good note' – meaning a good poet of good social standing – as a sort of belated half-apology for the earlier attack from Greene, a writer educated at St John's at the end of the 1570s. It's impossible to know whether Shakespeare read all the contemporary notices about himself and his work, but if he read any, surely it would be this one, and it would be here that the opportunity of Autolycus (newly associated with beggars and the social fringe) presented itself. The materials Shakespeare would find in the dictionaries, the *Metamorphoses* and the *Odyssey*, and he would of course give the character particular functions within the new play – as a parody of the control freaks Leontes and Polixenes for one thing[38] – but there would also be the intricate pleasure (and possibly pain) of putting on stage his persona from *Groatsworth* as an upstart thief. Some traces of Walkington have survived into the play, I think (when Autolycus first sees the Clown, at 4.3.31, for instance, he calls out 'A prize! a prize!', the shout of pirates as they spotted a ship they could take), but the deliberate allusions had *Groatsworth* as their target.

We can only guess why Shakespeare did all this. I myself am not convinced that he returned to Greene two decades on simply for payback or to show that his plays were a hundred times better than anything Greene ever wrote.[39] It is possible that he felt that at least part of him *was* a thief – the Autolycus in Shakespeare – and maybe this was a way of owning up.[40] The world of writers and the stage had changed a lot since the early 1590s (no-one complained about him borrowing from an earlier play for *King Lear*, for instance), but the upstart persona may have continued to serve him well, as a stimulus in private. He was an actor too, though (how good a one we don't know), so perhaps the slippery thief – one who could cringe and beg where he needed to[41] – was just another of the roles, surfaces on the prism as it were, that made up his personality.

## NOTES

1 The most recent edition, *Greene's Groatsworth of Wit bought with a Million of Repentence (1592)*, ed. D. Allen Carroll (Binghamton, New York, 1994), contains reliable reviews of the evidence and arguments about the pamphlet and who wrote it.

2 Allen Carroll, p. 5.

3 Allen Carroll, pp. 84–5.

4 The interpretation offered by Katherine Duncan-Jones, *Ungentle Shakespeare: Scenes from his Life* (London, 2001), p. 47.

5 Allen Carroll, p. 42.

6 See Allen Carroll, p. 84 n.5 for the tiger substituted for the wolf.

7 Extracts from these are printed in *Narrative and Dramatic Sources of Shakespeare*, ed. Geoffrey Bullough, 8 vols (1957–75), 8: 214–19.

8 Natalis Comes, *Mythologiae* (Venice 1551), p. 331 (quoted here from the 1976 Renaissance and the Gods Garland facsimile; the same series of facsimiles is used for the Estienne, Sandys and Pontanus references in notes 19, 26 and 27 below).

9 Described at 4.4.604–20: quotations and citations throughout are from the Arden edition, *The Winter's Tale*, ed. J.H. Pafford (London, 1963).

10 4.3.92–7.

11 4.3.5–7 and 28–30; 4.4.597–603. The social contexts are examined in David Kaula, 'Autolycus' Trumpery', *SEL* 16 (1976), 287–303, and Simon Palfrey, *Late Shakespeare: A New World of Words* (Oxford, 1997), pp. 115–25.

12 4.4.52–5. Simon Forman, who saw a performance (perhaps the premiere) of *The Winter's Tale* at the Globe on 15 May 1611, says that Autolycus came on stage 'all tottered', that is, in tatters (Pafford, xxii).

13 4.3.10–12; 4.4.263ff; 4.3.30.

14 Quoted from *The Romantics on Shakespeare*, ed. Jonathan Bate (Harmondsworth, 1992), p. 509.

15 4.4.753–4: see Robert G. Collmer, 'A Collection of Toothpicks from *The Winter's Tale* to *Leviathan*', *Connotations* 3 (1993), 13–25.

16 4.3.13–14 and 4.4.750–1. Since pimps and whores also wore velvet at this date, *three-pile* was often associated with sexual disease (compare *Measure for Measure*, 1.2.30–3).

17 William T. Hastings, 'The Ancestry of Autolycus', *Shakespeare Association Bulletin* 15 (1940), 253. The concept of preposterousness (inversion of rank as one form of it) is fundamental to *The Winter's Tale*, as Patricia Parker has convincingly demonstrated in *Shakespeare from the Margins* (Chicago and London, 1996), pp. 20–55, especially pp. 20ff.

18 See R.R. Bolgar *The Classical Heritage and its Beneficiaries* (Cambridge, 1958), pp. 516–17: the whole of the *Odyssey*, the primary source for Autolycus, was in print in Italian by 1581. The narrower view of Homer's influence is summarized in Stuart Gillespie, *Shakespeare's Books* (London and New Brunswick, NJ, 2001), pp. 251–4 (see also p. 27 for Shakespeare's Italian).

19 Charles Estienne, *Dictionarium Historicum, Geographicum, Poeticum* (Geneva, 1596), p. 88b.

20 For a list of Greek and Romance sources in which Autolycus appears, see the entry for him in the index to Robert Graves, *The Greek Myths*, 2 vols. (Harmondworth), 2: 383.

21 Merritt Y. Hughes, 'A Classical *vs.* A Social Approach to Shakespere's Autolycus', *Shakespeare Association Bulletin* 15 (1940), 219–26 (224).

22 See *Odyssey*, 19.399–466.

23 There were at least fifty Argonauts, excluding Autolycus, and Hermes was said to have fathered numerous sons (see Graves, *The Greek Myths*, 2: 217–18 and 1: 65–6).

24 *The Republic*, 1.334a–b, trans. Paul Shorey, in *The Collected Dialogues of Plato*, ed. Edith Hamilton and Huntington Cairns (Princeton, 1961), pp. 583–4.

25 See Joan Hartwig, 'The Tragicomic Perspective of the *Winter's Tale*', *ELH* 38 (1970), 12–36; Jonathan Bate, *Shakespeare and Ovid* (Oxford, 1993), pp. 228–9; *The Winter's Tale* ed. Stephen Orgel (Oxford, 1996), pp. 50–2.

26 George Sandys, *Ovid's Metamorphoses Englished* (Oxford, 1632), p. 393.

27 For the omission of 11: 303–19, see *Metamorphoseon*, ed. Jacobus Pontanus (Antwerp, 1618), p. 428; Pontanus as editor is considered by Ann Moss, *Latin Commentaries on Ovid from the Renaissance* (Signal Mountain, Tennessee, 1998), pp. 159ff. Much later, Autolycus was extruded from *The Winter's Tale* too, in Charles Lamb's *Tales from Shakespeare*.

28 The tinker's bag is referred to in his first song, at 4.3.20; the begging box is suggested by the word 'tirra-lirra' a few lines earlier, 4.3.9. In Cotgrave's dictionary of 1611, the definition of the French verb 'tirelirer' is to warble or to sing like a lark, and the noun 'tirelire' is the birdsong itself ('tirra-lirra' is meant to represent the sound of the skylark); but Cotgrave also says that 'tirelire' can be a box for collecting money (in France used by mendicant friars and in England by butlers and apprentices, for collections on saints' feasts presumably), so Autolycus may well have had a box with him which he rattled at this point in the song.

29 See Hastings, p. 253, countering the claims in Christine White, 'A Biography of Autolycus', *Shakespeare Association Bulletin* 14 (1939), 158–68 (166).

30 See the entries under Autolycus in Thomas Berger, William C. Bradford and Sidney L. Sondergard, *An Index of Characters in Early Modern English Drama* (Cambridge, 1998), p. 21. Autolycus is a character in two other seventeenth-century plays (both influenced by Shakespeare), Shakerly Marmion's *Holland's*

*Leaguer* of 1631, and the manuscript play, *Salisbury Plain* (a.k.a. *Stonehenge* and *The Converted Robber*), written for performance in St John's College, Oxford in 1635: see Gerald Eades Bentley, *The Jacobean and Caroline Stage*, 7 vols (Oxford, 1941–68), 5: 1181–4

31  STC 24967; for Walkington (d.1621), see *DNB* and Charles F. Mullet, 'Thomas Walkington and his "Optick Glass"', *Isis* 36 (1945–6), 96–105. I am indebted to Henry Woudhuysen for the Mullet reference, which led me to examine *The Optic Glass*.

32  For Walkington's contribution to seventeenth-century discussions of melancholy, see the index in Lawrence Babb, *The Elizabethan Malady* (East Lansing, 1951), p. 205.

33  *The Optic Glass*, G2r.

34  *Ibid.*, G5r.

35  Walkington quotes in Greek from the *Odyssey*, 19:396 at this point.

36  *Love's Labour's Lost*, 1.1.26–7, ed. H.R. Woudhuysen (London, 1998), p. 114 (see note to l.26).

37  Walkington could have read *Groatsworth* in either the 1592 edition or the reprint of 1596 (see Allen Carroll, p. 33). Much of *The Optic Glass* is concerned with resisting the temptations of intemperate drinking and sex, and the consequences of not doing so, as reported by the poets in particular: subjects obviously relevant to the theme of the Prodigal Son. The Parnassus plays, the important link between Cambridge and the London theatres, were performed at St John's between 1598 and 1603 (see *The Three Parnassus Plays (1598–1601)*, ed. J.B. Leishman (London, 1949), p. 26); Walkington was elected to his Fellowship in 1602.

38  Joan Hartwig, 'Cloten, Autolycus, and Caliban: Bearers of Parodic Burdens', in Carol McGinnis Kay and Henry E. Jacobs (eds), *Shakespeare's Romances Reconsidered* (Lincoln, Nebraska, and London, 1978), pp. 91–103 (98–101); see also Lee S. Cox, 'The Role of Autolycus in *The Winter's Tale*', *SEL* 9 (1969), 283–301. Students of the play owe a considerable and continuing debt to Richard Proudfoot for his detailed scrutiny of the connections and contrasts between the worlds of Sicily and Bohemia, and the characters in them, in 'Verbal Reminiscence and the Two-Part Structure of "The Winter's Tale"', *SS 29* (1976), 67–78.

39  See Duncan-Jones, pp. 229–30.

40  The possibility is explored in a different way by Louis MacNiece in his poem 'Autolycus' in *Collected Poems* (London, 1979), where the 'master pedlar' is able to slit 'purse-strings as quickly as his maker's pen.'

41  See 5.2.129ff, and compare Sonnet 89.

# APPENDIX

## BIOGRAPHICAL NOTE

Richard Proudfoot was born in Edinburgh in 1934 and educated at Fettes College, Edinburgh, where he took Advanced level examinations in Latin, Greek, Ancient History and Music. He won an Open Exhibition to study Classics at Worcester College, Oxford, in 1952. Having taken nearly three years out for National Service in 1953–5, he decided not to continue with Classics but switched to English, taking a B.A. in 1958 and a B.Litt. in 1961; he reflects now that this probably meant that he read more of English Literature than if he had 'already had a vaccination at A-level.' While at Oxford he developed his interest in bibliography on the one hand and theatrical performance and production on the other, including participation in a number of student productions. He first taught at the University of Toronto (1961–3), then at the University of Durham (1963–6), and finally at King's College London (1966–99), where he became a Professor in 1985. At King's he both produced and acted in many plays, mainly from the Elizabethan and Jacobean period. He has maintained his interest in music as an active member of the Oxford and Cambridge Musical Club, contributing both as a clarinettist and as a singer, and he has sung with various university choirs. He has held appointments as a Visiting Professor at the University of Virginia, Charlottesville and at the University of California, Los Angeles.

Richard Proudfoot as the King of France with Derek Hutchinson as Parolles in Richard's 1979 production of *All's Well that Ends Well* at King's College London.

Richard's first publication was an edition of *A Knack to Know a Knave* for the Malone Society in 1963; he subsequently became General Editor of the publications of the Malone Society (1971–83) and made a substantial contribution to many volumes during that period. He established his formidable reputation as an editor and textual critic with numerous essays in periodicals and chapters in books, including the annual review articles on textual studies in *Shakespeare Survey* from 1969 to 1977. He also published important reviews of Peter Blayney's book on *King Lear* and Donald Foster's edition of the 'Funeral Elegy' (at that point attributed to Shakespeare) in the *Times Literary Supplement*. He became General Editor of the Arden Shakespeare in 1982 and launched the third series which began publication in 1995. His British Academy lecture in 1985 was on '*The Reign of Edward III* and Shakespeare', and he is currently co-editing *Edward III* for Arden 3 with Nicola Bennett.

# PUBLICATIONS BY
# GEORGE RICHARD PROUDFOOT

## BOOKS

*Shakespeare: Text, Stage & Canon*, The Arden Shakespeare, Thomson Learning (2001)

## EDITIONS

In the case of Malone Society editions, the first date is the year to which the publication is assigned, the second is the actual date of publication.

*A Knack to Know a Knave* (1594), The Malone Society, (1963 (1964))

J. Fletcher and W. Shakespeare, *The Two Noble Kinsmen*, Edward Arnold and University of Nebraska Press 1970 (Regents Renaissance Drama Series)

J. Heywood, *Johan Johan The Husband* (1533), The Malone Society, (1967 (1972))

'Five Dramatic Fragments from manuscripts in the Folger Library', Malone Society *Collections IX*, (1971 (1977)), 52–75

*Tom a Lincoln*, an edition of BL MS Add. 61745, The Malone Society (1992)

R. Brome, *The Antipodes*, with D.S. Kastan, Globe Quartos (2000).

with G.M. Pinciss: *The Faithful Friends*, edited from Dyce MS 110, The Malone Society, (1970 (1975))

with S.D. Feldman: *A Yorkshire Tragedy* (1608), The Malone Society, (1969 (1973))

with J. Pitcher: J. Heywood, *The Pardoner and the Friar* (1533), The Malone Society, 1984

## *Forthcoming*

*The Reign of King Edward III*, Arden 3, with Nicola Bennett

## Articles, Chapters etc.

'Shakespeare and the New Dramatists of the King's Men', in J.R. Brown and B. Harris (eds), *Later Shakespeare* (Stratford-upon-Avon Studies, 8), (1966), 235–61

'Shakespeare: His Career and Development', in *Sphere History of Literature,* vol. 3, *English Drama to 1710* (1971), 131–47

'Dramatic Manuscripts and the Editor', in A.B. Lancashire (ed.), *Editing Renaissance Dramatic Texts English, Italian, and Spanish,* (New York and London, 1976), 9–38

'Verbal Reminiscence and the Two-Part Structure of *The Winter's Tale*', *Shakespeare Survey 29,* 1976, 67–78

'Peter Brook and Shakespeare', *Themes in Drama 2* (1980), 157–89

'The Virtue of Perseverance', in P. Neuss (ed.), *Aspects of Early English Drama,* (Cambridge, 1983), 92–109

'*Love's Labour's Lost*', *Essays and Studies* 34, (1984), 16–30

'*The Reign of King Edward III* and Shakespeare', British Academy Annual Shakespeare Lecture for 1985, in *Proceedings of the British Academy,* 1986; reprinted in E.A.J. Honigmann (ed.), *British Academy Shakespeare Lectures, 1980–89* (Oxford, 1993), 137–63

'"The play's the thing": Hamlet and the conscience of the Queen', in J.W. Mahon and T.W. Pendleton (eds), '*Fanned and Winnowed Opinions*': *Shakespearean Essays presented to Harold Jenkins* (1987), 160–5

'"It is an accident that heaven provides": Shakespeare's Providence in *Measure for Measure*', in S. Rossi and D. Savoia (eds), *Italy and the English Renaissance,* (Milan, 1989), 155–65

'*Henry VIII (All Is True), The Two Noble Kinsmen,* and the Apocryphal Plays', in S. Wells (ed.), *Shakespeare: a Bibliographical Guide,* (Oxford 1990), 381–403 (revised from earlier version in *Shakespeare: Select Bibliographical Guides,* (Oxford, 1973))

'Richard Johnson's *Tom a' Lincoln* Dramatized: A Jacobean Play in British Library MS. Add. 61745', Renaissance English Text Society of America, First Annual Lecture, delivered at the Newberry Library, Chicago, January 1986, in W. Speed Hill (ed.), *New Ways of Looking at Old Texts: Papers of the Renaissance English Text Society, 1985–1991* (New York, 1993), 75–101

'Shakespeare's Coinage', paper for Société Française Shakespeare, Congrés 1992, in M.T. Jones-Davies (ed.), *Shakespeare et l'argent,* (Paris 1993), 101–15

'Marlowe the Playwright', lecture for Marlowe Quatercentenary celebrations at King's School, Canterbury, privately published by King's School, Canterbury, 1994, as King's School Monographs, No. 4, 1–12

'Speech Prefixes, Compositors and Copy: Illustrated from Speech Prefixes Plays of the Shakespeare *Apocrypha*', in G.W. Williams (ed.), *Shakespeare's Speech-Headings* (Newark, Delaware, 1997), 121–30

'Shakespeare's most neglected play', in Laurie E. Maguire and Thomas L. Berger, (ed.), *Textual Formations and Reformations* (Cambridge, 1998), 149–57

'The Globe Season 1998', in *Shakespeare Survey 52*, 215–28

'Marlowe and the Editors', J.A. Downie and J.T. Parnell (eds), *Constructing Christopher Marlowe* (Cambridge, 2000), 41–54

'Unfolding and Cutting: *Measure for Measure* at the Old Vic, 1957–8', in Grace Ioppolo (ed.), *Shakespeare Performed: Essays in Honour of R.A. Foakes*, (Newark, Delaware, 2000), 164–79

'Shakespeare and the Sea', Portsmouth Grammar School (2002)

## *Forthcoming*

'Modernizing the printed play-text in Jacobean London: some early reprints of *Mucedorus*', in J. Lull and L. Anderson (eds), festschrift for Tom Clayton (2002)

'Editing and the New Conservatism', *International Yearbook of Shakespearean Studies* 2 (2002)

'Some Lears', *Shakespeare Survey* 55 (2002)

'Richard Johnson (*floruit* 1592–1622)', *New Dictionary of National Biography* (2004)

## Notes

'A Note on Titus and Vespasian', *N&Q* n.s 15 [213], (1968), 131

'Othello's History: I.iii.139', *N&Q* n.s. 21 [219], (1974), 130–1

'Francis Beaumont and the Hidden Princess', *The Library*, 6th ser. 4 (1982), 47–9

'Two Notes on Shakespeare's Text', in P. Edwards, *et al.* (ed.), *K.M. at 80*, privately printed by Liverpool University Press (1987), 119–20

## Reviews

'The Year's Contributions to Shakespearian Study: Textual Studies', annual review articles in *Shakespeare Survey 22*, (1969), 176–83; *23*, (1970), 176–86; *24*, (1971), 170–9; *25*, (1972), 193–200; *26*, (1973), 17–84; *27*, (1974), 179–92; *28*, (1975), 173–81; *29*, (1976), 177–85; *30*, (1977), 203–210

Occasional reviews in other journals, including *Durham University Journal, Notes & Queries, TLS, Critical Quarterly, Cahiers Elisabéthains, Review of English Studies, Theatre Notebook, Slavonic and East European Review, Around the Globe*

## General Editorships

The Malone Society, general editor, 1971–83; editorial committee, 1998–present. Volumes (other than collaborations) to which substantial editorial contribution was made include:

*Collections VIII*, (1969 (1974)), 'Dramatic Records of Lincolnshire', ed. S.J. Kahrl, Jr.

*Collections XI*, (1980–1), 'Dramatic Records of Norfolk and Suffolk', ed. D. Galloway and J. Wasson

*Captain Thomas Stukeley*, ed. J.C. Levenson, (1970)

*The Wasp*, ed. J.W. Lever, (1975)

*Timon*, ed. J.M. Nosworthy and J.C. Bulman, (1978)

*The Wisest Have their Fools about Them*, ed. Elizabeth Baldwin, (2001)

W. Shakespeare, quarto facsimiles, ed. T.L. Berger:
   *The Second Part of King Henry IV (1600)*, (1990)
   *A Midsummer Night's Dream (1600)*, (1995)
   *Romeo and Juliet (1597)*, (2000)

J. Lyly, quarto facsimiles, ed. Leah Scragg:
   *Gallathea (1584)*, (1998)
   *Sapho and Phao (1584)*, (2002)

The Arden Shakespeare. (1982–present)

Initial commissioning of volume editors for third series of The Arden Shakespeare and establishment of new editorial guidelines.

## PUBLICATION OF ARDEN 3 VOLUMES

1995  *Antony and Cleopatra*, ed. John Wilders
      *King Henry V*, ed. T.W. Craik
      *Titus Andronicus*, ed. Jonathan Bate

1996  *Othello*, ed. E.A.J. Honigmann

1997  *King Lear*, ed. R.A. Foakes
      *Shakespeare's Sonnets*, ed. Katherine Duncan-Jones
      *The Two Noble Kinsmen*, by W. Shakespeare and J. Fletcher, ed. Lois
      Potter

1998  *Julius Caesar*, ed. David Daniell
      *Love's Labour's Lost*, ed. H.R. Woudhuysen
      *Troilus and Cressida*, ed. David Bevington

1999  *King Henry VI, Part 2*, ed. Ronald Knowles
      *The Tempest*, ed. Virginia Mason Vaughan and Alden T. Vaughan

2000  *King Henry VI, Part 1*, ed. Edward Burns
      *King Henry VIII*, by W. Shakespeare and J. Fletcher, ed. Gordon
      McMullan
      *The Merry Wives of Windsor*, ed. Giorgio Melchiori

2001  *King Henry VI, Part 3*, ed. John D. Cox and Eric Rasmussen

2002  *King Richard II*, ed. Charles R. Forker

## FORTHCOMING 2003

*King Henry IV, Part 1*, ed. David Scott Kastan

*The Winter's Tale*, ed. John Pitcher

# INDEX

Shirley, James
*The Ball* 57
Shoenbaum, S. 250n
Shorey, Paul 267n
Sidney, Sir Philip 245, 246, 250n
*Arcadia* 246
Singer, S.W. 14n
Sisson, C.J. 66
Slater, Ann Pasternak 235, 237n,
238n
Smith, M.A.W. 78n
Snyder, Susan 208n
Sondergard, Sidney L. 267n
Spenser, Edmund 9, 59n, 222, 263
*Complaints* 59n
*Daphnaida* 59n
*The Shepheardes Calendar* 9
Stallybrass, Peter 42, 45, 46n, 47n
Staunton, Howard 8, 14n, 69, 79n
Steele, Sir Richard 181
Steevens, George xxii, 5, 10, 13n,
16n, 68, 71, 77, 80n, 93n,
182, 185, 186, 192, 192n, 212,
213
Stephanus 14n, 260
Stoddard, Roger 47n
Strabo 260
Stubbes, Philip 240
Suckling, Sir John
*Aglaura* 49
Sutton, Mr. 248
Sutton, Willie 222
Swift, Jonathan 10, 16n

Taccone, Tony 89
Tanselle, Thomas G. xviii, 41, 46,
46n, 47n, 150, 155n
Tarlton, Richard 239, 242, 247,
248
Tate, Nahum 181
Taylor, Gary 23, 34, 35, 45, 66, 67,
74, 75, 78n, 80n, 93n, 94n,
96, 97, 106n, 107n, 155n, 164,
208n, 250n
Terence 6, 7, 13n, 52
*Eunuchus* (Webbe's version), 52

Thacker, David 74
Theobald, Lewis xx, xxii, 8, 9, 10,
11, 13n, 15n, 16n, 103, 117,
182, 205, 208n, 211, 217, 223,
235
Thompson, Ann viii, 100, 101, 102,
103, 249n
Thomson, Leslie 80n, 123n, 125,
137n
Throckmorton, Elizabeth 248
Throckmorton, Job 248
Thysius 246
Tibullus 5
Tillotson, Geoffrey 94n
Tillyard, E.M.W. 3, 10, 12n
Tilney, Edmund 20, 75, 202, 208n
*The Flower of Friendshippe* 202,
208n
Tobin, John J.M. viii
Tomarkin, S.A. 155n
Tonson, Jacob 4, 9, 14n, 15n
Took, John 61n
Turner, Robert Kean 60n, 80n.,
215, 217
Twine, Laurence 71, 72
Twycross, M. 155n

Vander Meulen, David L. 16n
Vaughan, Alden T. 275
Vaughan, H.H. 65, 66
Vaughan, Virginia Mason 275
Velz, John W. 237n
Verhasselt, Elaine 251n
Vessey, Mark 46, 47n
Virgil 6, 14n, 191

Walker, Alice 82, 83, 85, 86, 92,
93n
Walkington, Thomas
*The Optic Glass of Humours*
263–5, 268n
Wall, Cynthia 2
Walsh, Marcus 13n
Walsingham, Sir Francis 250n
Warburton, William xxii, 12n, 15n,
83, 182, 185